$1.99

CAPITALISM AND UNFREE LABOUR

Anomaly or necessity?

Robert Miles

Tavistock Publications

London and New York

First published in 1987 by
Tavistock Publications Ltd
11 New Fetter Lane, London EC4P 4EE

Published in the USA by
Tavistock Publications
in association with Methuen, Inc.
29 West 35th Street, New York NY
10001

Typeset by Hope Services, Abingdon
Printed in Great Britain at Richard
Clay Ltd, Bungay, Suffolk

British Library Cataloguing in
Publication Data

Miles, Robert
Capitalism and unfree labour:
anomaly or necessity?
1. Labour economics   2. Capitalism
I. Title
331   HD4901

ISBN 0–422–61730–X
ISBN 0–422–79250–0 Pbk

Library of Congress Cataloging in
Publication Data

Miles, Robert, 1950–
Capitalism and unfree labour.
Bibliography: p.
Includes index.
1. Capitalism.   2. Wages.   3. Labor
policy.   4. Slave labor—Cross-cultural
studies.   5. Labor and laboring classes.
I. Title.   II. Title: Capitalism and
unfree labor.
HB501.M654   1987   331.11'734
87–3599

ISBN 0–422–61730–X
ISBN 0–422–79250–0 (pbk.)

Contents

Acknowledgements	iv
Introduction	1
Part 1 Capital and wage labour	15
1 Capitalism as a mode of production	17
2 Accumulation and articulation	35
3 Capitalism and unfree labour	50
Part 2 Historical studies of unfree labour	71
4 The Caribbean	73
5 Australia	94
6 South Africa	118
7 Western Europe	143
Part 3 Anomaly or necessity?	169
8 On relations of production	171
9 Unfree labour: an anomalous necessity	196
Conclusion	223
Bibliography	226
Index	248

Acknowledgements

Many people have assisted me in the writing of this book by discussing and criticizing my ideas and preliminary drafts, and by providing me with references. I am particularly grateful to David Frisby, Vic Satzewich, and Anne Dunlop for reading the text in full and commenting in detail. Other people have contributed in smaller, but no less essential ways, notably Michael Banton, Rohit Barot, Huw Benyon, Frank Bovenkerk, John Eldridge, Janie Ferguson, Adrian Graves, Kees Groenendijk, Peter Gutkuid, Marie de Lepervanche, Claude Meillassoux, David Pearson, Annie Phizacklea, Derek Sayer, John Solomos, and Daiva Stasiulis. I also learnt a great deal from participants in seminars at the Department of Sociology and Anthropology at Macquarie University in Sydney, the Department of Sociology at the University of Wollongong, and at the Centre for Research in Ethnic Relations at the University of Warwick.

Some material was collected while I was teaching and presenting papers to seminars in New Zealand, Australia, and Canada, and hence I am grateful for financial assistance from the Carnegie Trust for the Universities of Scotland, the British Council, the British Academy, the University of Glasgow, and the University of Sydney which made it possible for me to accept the various invitations. I must also acknowledge the untiring services of the Inter-Library Loans Department of the University Library at the University of Glasgow. I hope none of these people or organizations is embarrassed by being publicly associated with this book. They do not need to be because the responsibility for its final form lies with myself alone.

A final word of thanks must go to all those who have had to bear the personal consequences of my obsession with this project over the last three years.

Robert Miles,
Glasgow,
October 1986

'The fact is, therefore, that definite individuals who are productively active in a definite way enter into these definite social and political relations. Empirical observations must in each separate instance bring out empirically, and without any mystification and speculation, the connection of the social and political structure with production. The social structure and the State are continually evolving out of the life-process of definite individuals, but of individuals, not as they may appear in their own or other people's imagination, but as they really are; i.e., as they operate, produce materially, and hence as they work under definite material limits, presuppositions and conditions independent of their will.'

(Marx and Engels 1968b: 36–7)

'Thus events strikingly analogous but taking place in different historical surroundings led to totally different results. By studying each of these forms of evolution separately and then comparing them one can easily find the clue to this phenomenon, but one will never arrive there by using as one's master key a general historico-philosophical theory, the supreme virtue of which consists in being super-historical.'

(Marx, in Marx and Engels 1965: 313)

Introduction

'The mechanical utilisation of the product led to entirely opposite effects in Europe and America. In the former, cotton gave the impulse to the organisation of a free labour force, the first factories developing in Lancashire in England, while in America the result was slavery.'

(Weber 1981:82)

'In fact the veiled slavery of the wage-labourers in Europe needed the unqualified slavery of the New World as its pedestal.'

(Marx 1976:925)

These remarkably similar quotations from Marx and Weber serve to locate the central theme of this book which analyses and explains why the development of capitalism has not immediately or systematically swept away forms of non-wage or unfree labour. The retention and expanded reproduction of forms of unfree labour in parallel with the growth of capitalism is a long-established historical fact. Thus, in both the Weberian and the Marxist traditions, there is an awareness of the historical interdependence of wage labour and slave labour but, until recently, only a few attempts at systematic explanation. I shall evaluate the Marxist tradition in some detail in Part 1, but here I want to explore briefly the Weberian tradition in order to demonstrate the nature of the problem and how deep-rooted it is.

Weber, capitalism, and unfree labour

Weber distinguishes between free and unfree labour in the context of a discussion about the division of labour and methods for the disposal of 'human labour'. He defines free labour as occurring when 'the services of labour are the subject of a contractual relationship which is formally free on both sides' (1978:127–28), a situation which contrasts with unfree labour where an individual procures the right to utilize a labourer's labour services by gaining property rights in the latter (1978:126). Weber refers to slavery and serfdom as examples of unfree labour. Although this distinction is not a major theme, there are theoretical assertions about, and historical references to, it scattered in Weber's writing.

His most significant theoretical claim is that unfree labour is incompatible with formal rationality (as opposed to substantive (see Brubaker 1984: 10–16, 36–43)). In the case of slavery, he argues that this was so because too much capital is involved in the purchase and maintenance of slaves, because of difficulties in recruitment, and because slave labour is incompatible with the use of tools and machinery (1978: 129, 162–63). Weber maintains that no such incompatibilities are present in the case of free labour. He states that only in the modern Western world 'rational capitalistic enterprises with fixed capital, free labour, the rational specialisation and combination of functions, and the allocation of productive functions on the basis of capitalistic enterprises, bound together in a market economy, are to be found' (1978: 165). His analysis of the emergence of agricultural commodity production in eastern Germany in the late nineteenth century is consistent with this view in so far as he traces the parallel gradual displacement of 'patriarchal labour relations' by 'capitalist labour relations' (i.e. wage labour) (Weber 1979: 199; 1980: 432–33; Winson 1982: 391–400; Tribe 1983: 203).

This seems to suggest that Weber considered capitalism and free labour to be synonymous. However, although Weber does argue that free wage labour has advantages of efficiency and profitability (1978: 163), he also notes, as one mode of 'capitalistic orientation of profit-making', those colonial plantations using slave labour where business activity originates in, and is sustained by, force (particularly in the arena of labour appropriation) (1978: 164–65; see also 1981: 298–300). Thus although Weber regards the use of slave labour as being *generally* unprofitable (1981: 132), he also identifies specific *historical* conditions under which its use could be profitable (1981: 83, 132, 300).

These were evident, Weber argues, in the Cathargo-Roman plantations of 'ancient society' and in the nineteenth-century plantations in the United States (1978: 133–63; 1981: 80). Of the former, he claims that 'these are cases of the capitalist utilisation of unfree labour' (1978: 382). He argues that this utilization depended upon the existence of a particular set of historical conditions (including a regular supply of slaves from military conflict and high prices for plantation products (1976: 54, 59, 393)); that there were historically specific barriers to the full development of capitalism within 'ancient civilization' (1976: 65–6) which included difficulties in ensuring a fully rational exploitation of slave labour (1976: 324, 356) and which eventually led to the 'throttling' of capitalism (1976: 363); and that the capitalist character was historically specific and therefore different in important respects from subsequent capitalist development in Western Europe (1976: 352–65). In the eighteenth and nineteenth centuries the capitalistic exploitation of colonies was achieved, in Weber's view, by means of plantation production under conditions of strict discipline and a guaranteed and regular supply of new slaves, conditions which ensured the realization of large profits (1981:298–301).

Similarly, in his analysis of changing relations of agriculture in north-eastern Germany in the latter half of the nineteenth century, Weber identifies 'the principle of economic rationality' behind the emergence of relations of production that he referred to as the *Deputant* system. Under this system, the labourer was bound to work for an estate owner for a year, was provided with a house (sometimes in return for a small rent) and with some food in kind. Additionally, a small cash wage was paid but land was made available, from which the family unit produced the remainder of its material needs. Weber's explanation is that 'a substantial part of the process of producing the *Deputant*'s needs is shifted from his master's to his own shoulders, using his own free time . . . and that of his family. . . . [This] permits the reduction of the costs of maintenance and reproduction of the labour force to a minimum' (1979: 185–86). These were a transitional set of relations of production (Weber 1979: 188; Hussain and Tribe 1981: 20–71; Winson 1982: 399–400) which emerged in a context shaped by increasing commodity production. We should note the similarity of Weber's argument here with arguments offered by Marxist writers concerning the economic advantages to capital of a migrant labour system (e.g. Meillassoux 1981: 110–26).

Of greatest significance here is the issue raised by assertions about the 'compatibility' of capitalism and unfree labour. Weber's view appears to have been that free wage labour is the most appropriate form for the disposal and organization of labour for rational capitalism. Indeed, Weber identifies free wage labour as one of the distinguishing features of capitalism (1981:277; see also Andreski 1983:110). In this context, to argue that the plantation, where the social relations of production are grounded in unfreedom, can be described as capitalistic under certain historical conditions is to suggest that such conditions, and their consequences, are anomalous. In other words, the use of unfree (slave) labour in a rational and calculable way to realize a profit is exceptional, an exception which is historically contingent.

I have three critical comments. First, conceptual problems remain and, indeed, are highlighted. For example, Weber's characterization of the use of slave labour in 'ancient civilizations' as capitalistic derives from a definition of capitalism which refers to 'wealth used to gain profit in commerce' (1976:48), a definition which makes no reference to the rational use of free labour. Second, Weber does not offer a thorough explanation for this contingency, only a list of the conditions under which it has arisen. Third, the scope of his analysis is limited and the historical content is perfunctory. As we shall see, different forms of unfree labour have been used more extensively than Weber acknowledges, and this further confirms that historical contingency, by itself, is not an adequate explanation.

So, within the Weberian problematic, we locate a theoretical and historical problem. If capitalism, conceived as an expression of formal rationality, is defined by the presence of wage labour, why can its existence be equally compatible in certain circumstances with forms of labour appropriation which are apparently inimical with formal rationality but which can nevertheless realize a surplus? Or should we withold the designation of such conditions as capitalism? A similar problem arises within the Marxist tradition, as we shall see in Part 1. This interrelationship between capitalism and unfree labour is the predominant theme of this book.

Capitalism and migration

A second theme is the interrelation between capitalism and migration. The large-scale movements of people into Western Europe after 1945 to fill vacant positions in the labour force has awakened Marxist interest in migration (e.g. Castles and Kosack 1973; Nikolinakos 1975; Sassen-Koob 1978, 1981, 1985) and it is now commonplace for the mainstream Marxist tradition to include reference to the significance of this development when analysing 'late capitalism' (e.g. Mandel 1975). But the conjunctural context of this new interest tends to shape a particular conception of migration, one where the term becomes synonymous with twentieth-century movements of (unskilled) people (of rural origin) from the *periphery* of the capitalist world economy to its *centre* where they are proletarianized. Such a process has been occurring, but it is misleading to limit our conception of the interrelation between capitalism and migration to this instance for the following reasons.

First, not all twentieth-century migration flows are of people induced to seek paid labour by 'underdevelopment'. Many migrants are political refugees; their spatial mobility is induced by various sorts of political pressures (Zolberg 1981a; Bach and Schraml 1982:327). Additionally, a smaller proportion of those involved in migratory movements do so as petit bourgeois (or even bourgeois) merchants or producers or as professional or skilled non-manual workers (e.g. Birks and Sinclair 1980; Salt 1981:154–56). Skilled non-manual migration to the Middle East has become particularly significant since the 1970s (Halliday 1977; Alessa 1981:39–43; Serageldin *et al.* 1983:31–6; Sirageldin *et al.* 1984:76–8; Al-Moosa and MacLachlan 1985:17–20).

Second, migration is not solely a twentieth-century phenomenon and therefore is not a phenomenon of 'late capitalism' alone (e.g. Zolberg 1978; Sassen-Koob 1980; Stuckey and Fay 1981; Hoerder 1985). During the eighteenth century, there was a large movement of population from Africa to the Americas and the Caribbean to provide a labour force for other migrants of European origin who had settled (temporarily or permanently) in these regions with the aim of developing commodity production. During the nineteenth century, there were large-scale movements of people from Europe to the United States and various settler colonies where capitalist development was, in certain circumstances, dependent upon additional migrations from elsewhere in the world (e.g. India, China, South Pacific). It is with these migrations that this book is largely, but not exclusively, concerned.

But widening the historical scope leads to difficult theoretical questions. The post 1945 migration to Western Europe is often explained as a consequence of the capital accumulation process, a process which leads to the incorporation of people as wage labourers who were previously outside those relations of production (History Task Force 1979; Miles 1986). The explanation draws directly upon Marx's analysis of capital accumulation (1976:762–870) and so migration is theoretically located by reference to a central feature of the capitalist mode of production (see Standing 1981:192; for a general critique, see Wood 1982).

This explanation applies to a significant part of the nineteenth-century European migration to the United States and to British settler colonies because, whether by design or default, a large proportion of those who constituted those migrations became sellers of labour power. However, one must not ignore those who, following migration, successfully established themselves as independent land (and other forms of property) owners and who were capable of independent subsistence production and, later, of commodity production (e.g. Friedmann 1978). Moreover, other nineteenth- and early twentieth-century migrations involved people from India, China and the South Pacific who were recruited under contract and who were bound to an employer by legal relations in a form of servitude. During the eighteenth century, the largest migration was from Africa to the Americas and the Caribbean under conditions of physical and political/legal compulsion and the migrants were incorporated into production as slaves. Empirically, these latter migrations do not have the same character as the former. Thus Sassen-Koob has distinguished between forced-labour mobilization and colonizing migrations on the one hand, and international labour migrations on the other (1981:68; 1980).

It is true that these instances demonstrate that migration and labour recruitment have been on an international scale for at least four centuries. What is controversial is the conceptual and theoretical framework within which this historical fact is analysed and explained. Moreover, one can criticize the adequacy of Sassen-Koob's descriptive distinction because both forced labour mobilization and colonizing migrations were international in the sense that they involved the movement of people from one social formation to another and in the sense that migration was, in part, determined by economic consider-ations, namely a shortage of labour. What is equally problematic is how these migrations are understood in relation to the development of the capitalist mode of production. A common resolution is to adopt the *world system* approach of Wallerstein (1974, 1980). Given that this theory claims that the world capitalist system was formed by 1650, all these migrations may be conceived as phases in the expansion of that system and as therefore synonymous with capitalism (e.g. Sassen-Koob 1981; Petras 1981).

Thus Sassen-Koob analyses forced-labour mobilization, colonizing migrations, and international labour migrations as reflections of different phases of development of the world capitalist system: 'Characteristics of the labour supply systems in a given area . . . can be accounted for by that area's role in the world economy' (1981:66, 1980:3). This claim is not only economistic, functionalist, and teleological (all of which are features of world system analysis (Skocpol 1977)), but it also raises the issue of the analytical significance of the relations of production to the characterization of modes of production. If relations of production are considered to be an essentially defining feature of a mode of production, then the fact that the forced migration from Africa to the Americas and the Caribbean during the eighteenth century placed those people in slave relations of production means that there can be no direct relationship between capitalism (conceived as a mode of production characterized by, *inter alia*, wage labour) and migration in that historical instance. This is similarly the case with respect to the nineteenth-century migrations of people under relations of indenture.

Thus because not all migrations are determined by the demand for *wage labour*, and because not all migrations result from individual choice under structural constraint, the connection between capitalism and migration should not be conceived to be a necessarily direct one but may be, at the very least, a mediated connection. Moreover, the positions to which migrants are recruited, characterized as they are by various forms of physical and legal compulsion, suggest again that we need to establish the nature of the relationship between capitalism and unfree labour.

In order to facilitate this, the category of *migration* requires some comment. Implicit in much of the use of the concept is the assumption that it refers simply to the spatial mobility of people, an assumption which is largely geographical and which sustains the interest of certain schools of geographers in migration studies (e.g. Salt and Clout 1976). This conception abstracts people from their material context because the significance of migration does not lie in spatial mobility *per se*, but in the position in the relations of production occupied before and after such movement. The conception of migration employed in this book is therefore one which refers to spatial mobility which relocates people in the relations of production.

Relocation may be in different relations of production, or in a different position in the same relations of production, or in a similar position in the same relations of production (those same relations of production being in a different social formation). Migratory processes are therefore spatial movements of people to different sites of class relations, difference being understood in the dual sense of either a different position in the relations of production, or in the sense of a historically distinct set of the same relations of production. Migrants are always class agents, and migration refers to the movement of people from one class site to another, both within and between social formations and, therefore, potentially (but not necessarily) from one mode of production to another.

Beyond the 'race relations' problematic

My concern with the interrelationship between the history of capitalist development and both unfree labour and migration has its origin in my critique of 'race relations' sociology (Miles 1982; see also Miles 1984a,b; Miles and Spoonley 1985). This writing had a negative character in so far as it was concerned largely with the deconstruction of 'race relations' sociology. Its constructive content was limited specifically to the United Kingdom in the nineteenth and twentieth centuries and, more generally, to Western Europe in the same time-period. An awareness of these historical and geographical limits necessitated work on a broader theoretical and historical canvas. Thus I want to show that many of the issues appropriated by the sociology of 'race relations', once liberated, take us to the heart of long-established debates about the nature of capitalism and the manner of its historical development.

Earlier I labelled my alternative theoretical framework the 'political economy of labour migration'. Although I now have certain reservations about this label, it does retain a core element to which I remain committed. That core element is the view that there are no special or distinctive social relations in the form of 'race relations' and that there is no need for a distinct theory of 'race (or ethnic) relations'. Those which are offered are therefore ideological. The historical conjunctures that are selected for attention and theorization by this problematic are, in my view, better understood within a framework which takes as its objective the historical analysis of the capitalist mode of production and, in particular, the analysis of the different forms in which labour power is appropriated.

Although there is a historical specificity to those circumstances and conjunctures where the appropriation of labour power is accompanied by a process of racialization, it is a specificity within the context of the development and reproduction of the capitalist mode of production. I use the concept of *racialization* to refer to a process of signification in which human beings are categorized into 'races' by reference to real or imagined phenotypical or genetic differences (see Banton 1977: 18–19; Miles 1982: 20–1, 120). Processes of racialization, in which racism is a dominant ideological element, are not, in themselves, explained by the fact of capitalist development for that is to revert to functionalism. But the process of racialization cannot be adequately understood without a conception of, and explanation, for the complex interplay of different modes of production and, in particular, of the social relations necessarily established in the course of material reproduction.

In *Racism and Migrant Labour* (Miles 1982), that analysis was primarily limited to a conception of the role of migrant labour in recent capitalist development in Western Europe, and it assumed that the category of *migrant labour* referred to spatially mobile persons who occupied primarily proletarian positions in capitalist relations of production. There was only a brief mention of slave labour in the context of discussion about the origin and reproduction of racism (1982:104–09). But historically the process of racialization is also connected with other forms of labour exploitation where labour power is not commodified (or only partially commodified) and is recruited and exploited primarily by means of political/legal compulsion. Consequently, a political economy of labour migration which restricts its scope to nineteenth- and twentieth-century capitalist development will ignore a large part of the history of racialization. It is in order to expose that wider history that the emphasis of this book is upon the interrelation between capitalism and different forms of unfree (non-wage) labour.

The distinctiveness of the argument that follows from these observations is highlighted by critical comment on two books (Greenberg 1980; Baker 1983) which deal with similar historical subject matter but which remain grounded in the 'race relations' problematic (Miles 1982:22–43). Baker's chosen object is the analysis of 'race relations' in six English settler colonies. He employs the idea of 'race' as an independent variable (1983:3–4), using 'race' to refer to groups with different somatic characteristics (p. 63). He describes 'race/ethnic' relations as 'power contests' (p. 29) and conceives of history as being to a large extent the consequence of conflict between 'races' (p. 69). Baker's analysis of 'race relations' leads him to the conclusion that:

> 'No single factor fully explains or accounts for the enduring hostile white response to nonwhites, but the three noted – identity (color and cultural norm images), power and psychological factors – together were and are amongst the most important.'
>
> (1983:179)

Baker ranks 'development factors' (his synonym for economic factors) as secondary (p. 138).

Baker, like all who write within the 'race relations' problematic, reifies 'race', transforming what is an influential idea into an active subject with an undefined and unexplained power to determine historical processes. There is no biological phenomenon with such power. There is only a wide range of phenotypical and genetic variation and a historically contingent belief in the existence of such a phenomenon. What matters, therefore, is not biological different *per se* but people's belief in its potential as a determining factor and their consequent patterns of behaviour. This process of racialization is certainly a matter for explanation, but 'race relations' sociology cannot undertake this task because of its assumption about the 'naturalness' of 'races' and 'race relations'.

This book differs in two further ways from Baker's analysis. First it seeks to identify the specific determination of the relations of production within any social formation, and the manner of the articulation of those relations with political an ideological relations. Baker abstracts and isolates economic relations, to the point that they become one more variable in what amounts to a 'multivariate' analysis. Below I shall show how production relations are inseparable from political and ideological relations and, specifically, from the process of racialization. In particular I shall argue that the social relations which are abstracted and highlighted by the ideological category of 'race relations' are social relations which have an origin in the expanding activities of merchant and, later, industrial capital. For reasons to be explained, these expanding activities involved the establishment and development of commodity production utilizing various forms of unfree labour.

Second, and consequently, it asserts that the concept of *class* is central to the explanatory task. Baker utilized phenotypical categories such as 'whites' which obscure class differentiation and which treat as unproblematic the extent to which such categories serve as a focus for political mobilization. Categories such as 'whites' and 'blacks' are of little analytical value because the populations to which they refer are invariably distributed across a number of different sites in class relations. Thus it is never 'whites' who dominate, but a ruling class, itself composed of various fractions, which may or may not signify a phenotypical characteristic in the process of creating and/or maintaining hegemony. 'Whiteness' may become a measure of the assumed ability to rule, and such a belief may sustain practices of exclusion, but all those who share that phenotypical characteristic cannot also occupy those few positions in economic and political relations which allow them to make, for example, investment and legislative decisions which determine the economic and political circumstances of the majority.

The work of Greenberg (1980) also highlights the distinctiveness of this book, although his analysis is closer to its themes. Greenberg's focus is upon the development of the capitalist mode of production in particular historical circumstances, specifically those characterized by slave relations of production and those where property-owning European settlers have attempted to incorporate the labour power of sections of the indigenous population into new relations of production. Unlike Baker, Greenberg identifies a number of key features of the capitalist mode of production which shape the pattern of political and ideological relations in South Africa, Alabama, Northern Ireland, and Israel (e.g. 1980: 278–80). Greenberg is also aware of the significance of the distinction between free (wage) labour and unfree labour, although this is given only fleeting mention (1980: 31, 53, 134, 387, 399) and is not theorized.

Nevertheless, Greenberg's analytical objective places his text within the framework of the 'race relations' problematic. He poses the question 'What impact does capitalist development have on patterns of racial and ethnic domination?' (p. 22). The centrality of this question is revealed when, elsewhere, he refers to the failure of analyses of core/periphery relations to formulate a 'theory of race or ethnic relations' (p. 20). His conclusion is that capitalist development 'both preserves and remakes the racial order, extending and reinforcing racial barriers' (p. 26).

It is not clear what Greenberg means when he employs the idea of 'race', but he implies that there are biological differences between populations when he defines a 'racial order' as a society where 'racial differences are formalized and socially pervasive' (p. 29). He also claims that 'race' has its own ontological status (p. 406), suggesting that he conceives 'race' as an objective phenomenon with the capacity to have determinant effects. The uncertainty is compounded by his additional concern with capitalist development in 'ethnically divided societies', of which he cites as examples, Northern Ireland and Israel (pp. 23, 43). Greenberg does not explain the criteria by which one distinguishes between a social formation divided by 'race' and one divided by 'ethnicity' (p. 41).

There are further problems. In asserting that 'race' and 'ethnicity' have their own ontological status, Greenberg theorizes them as equivalents to class, in the sense that all three concepts refer to realities of the same order and type (cf. Miles 1980). Yet he wants to attribute class to superordinate determinacy, as illustrated in his claims that 'Racial domination . . . is essentially a class phenomenon' and that 'Racial domination is . . . a series of specific class relations' (p. 406). Consequently, he is then forced into *ad hoc* qualifications which allow him to assert the existence of 'race and ethnic groups' which are independent of classes (p. 406).

I argue, alternatively, that all classes exhibit a particular cultural profile (which is not necessarily homogeneous) and that the history of class domination and struggle necessarily includes the manipulation of cultural criteria and symbols (for example language, dress, religion, beliefs about biological superiority and inferiority). Every historically specific bourgeoisie and proletariat (here I am limiting the discussion to the capitalist mode of production) therefore exhibits a pattern of cultural differentiation in which specific characteristics are signified as criteria of inclusion/exclusion. The reference to historical specificity signals the fact that class formation and reproduction are structured by political relations in so far as the nation-state constitutes the framework for working-class political organization and representation. The dominant class within each nation-state therefore lays claim to a particular cultural profile which supposedly differentiates all those who live within its boundaries (Miles 1987).

One particular process of signification is that which refers to real or alleged genetic or phenotypical variation (i.e. the process of racialization) and which can employ the ideology of racism. This process does not create, or constitute the measure of the existence of, a 'race' (i.e. a group with a distinct ontological status grounded in biological difference) but it does frame class relations and class struggles in a particular cultural form and create the ideological foundation for the organization of political alliances between and within greater or smaller sections of different classes.

Consequently, the object of my analysis is not the effect of capitalist development upon 'race relations' but, in part, the cultural and ideological content and profile of certain instances of capitalist development (or, in other words, why it is that in certain circumstances the ideology of 'race' and 'race relations' is an integral component of class formation and capitalist development). Thus a focus of this book is the interrelationship between such processes and the utilization of forms of unfree labour.

On historical sociology

Because this book is concerned with aspects of the history of the development of the capitalist mode of production, it may be typified as a work of *historical sociology*. What is described as *historical sociology* may be seen as a return to the thematic preoccupations not only of Marx (whose historical materialism ensured that any matter of contemporary significance was analysed as the consequence of historical process), but also of Weber and Durkheim (Abrams 1982: 1–5; Skocpol 1984a: 1–7). The use of this descriptor is predicated on the more specific features of the following study which is concerned, first, with a number of distinct social formations situated differentially in space and time; second, with historical process in those different social formations, focusing in particular upon the changing character of relations of production; third, with the determinate influence on historical process of specific structures and relations (cf. Skocpol 1984a: 1).

The analytical work that is subsumed under this descriptor follows various research strategies and this book demonstrates that they are not 'hermetically sealed from one another' (Skocpol 1984b: 362). I do not attempt in any thorough way to apply a general model to history, although I do attempt to demonstrate the significance of certain concepts, derived from Marx, some of which have a universal application and some of which apply to all instances of the development of the capitalist mode of production. I also attempt to delineate the detail of historical process in a number of distinct social formations and I therefore attempt to provide a meaningful understanding of events and process. In this sense, the book has an interpretive component. Although it assumes that certain regularities can be found, the analytical generalizations that are offered highlight the significance of historical context and political struggles in the determination of outcomes. In other words, the generalizations that are offered acknowledge the significance of historical contingency and so emphasize that there is no single 'law' of historical development (cf. Skocpol 1984b: 362–86).

If the book is a work of historical sociology, it is also a work of *historical materialism*. By this I mean that I identify an historical problem which I attempt to resolve analytically using concepts and a method derived critically from Marx. Marx's work is not treated here as 'holy script' because part of my purpose is to identify certain 'silences and limits' in it. But I also attempt to resolve the problem of unfree labour using an analytical framework which remains firmly grounded in certain of Marx's concepts which he derived from his critique of political economy. But the analytical task is not one of mechanical application of received concepts. First, the concepts themselves require critical reworking. Second, as Sayer has argued from more general premises about Marx's *Capital*,

> 'Marx's critique threatens, in practice as well as in theory, to blow that world apart. It is, in one sense, only a starting point. It is not of itself a historical analysis. . . . It *opens the way* to a recovery of history. It shows capital's apparently natural and eternal forms to rest on relations that are social and historical; relations, in other words, which have been constructed by human beings and are thus capable of being changed by other human beings.'
>
> (1979:149)

The book is offered, therefore, as a contribution to the recovery of the history of the articulation of free and unfree labour.

Matters of method

In Part 1, I set out the theoretical problem, arguing that, within the Marxist framework, it is necessary to explain why it is that unfree, non-wage relations of production have been reproduced and extended in parallel with the emergence and extension of free, wage labour. I seek an answer to that problem by historical analysis which is offered in Part 2, from which analytical conclusions are drawn in Part 3. The social formations and historical periods chosen for analysis in Part 2 were selected according to the following criteria.

First, I included instances that would allow an analysis of the full period of the history of capitalist development. The periodization of that history is problematic, but I have followed Marx in identifying the emergence of the capitalist mode of production in the seventeenth century in Europe (specifically England). Consequently, I begin with the case of the Caribbean where commodity production was initiated in that century and continued through to the present period (although I terminate my analysis with the ending of the use of indentured labour) and I conclude with the example of Western Europe in the post 1945 period. The case of South Africa covers a similar time-period, but allows a more detailed analysis of the nineteenth century, as does the Australian case.

Second, I wished to highlight the fact that the use of unfree relations of production has characterized the expansion of commodity production by means of the development of what Marx called the *colonial system*. Hence I have chosen three examples (the Caribbean, Australia, and South Africa) which exhibit different paths of colonial development but which share a common colonial heritage as a result of their economic and political connection with the development of the capitalist mode of production in Britain.

Third, I wished to demonstrate that the conservation and reproduction of unfree relations of production is not only confined to the colonial period and to the 'original' transition from feudalism to capitalism but is also a contemporary feature of capitalist development. Put another way, I wanted to show that the theoretical *issues* and *concepts* thrown up in the course of the debate about the transition to capitalism have a relevance to the analysis of contemporary capitalist development. Consequently, I have included analyses of the reproduction of unfree relations of production into the twentieth century in South Africa and in Western Europe over the past three decades.

Fourth, I selected examples which the sociology of 'race relations' has traditionally analyzed. The latter problematic has consistently focused on the examples of the Caribbean and, in particular, South Africa (e.g. Banton 1967:164–92, 1983:209–38; Rex 1973:243–83) and has more recently been used to interpret the Australian case (e.g. Evans *et al.* 1975). All three cases have varying degrees of association with Britain, and it is in British ideological relations that one can identify some of the main intellectual roots of 'race relations' sociology, although the latter is more systematically developed and deep-rooted in the United States (e.g. George 1984). By choosing these examples, I can challenge the adequacy of the sociology of 'race relations' on its own intellectual terrain.

Fifth, I selected cases which highlight not only the articulation of free and unfree relations of production, but also the interrelation of this articulation with the history of international migration. I did so in order to emphasize that the history of the expansion of the capitalist mode of production is inseparable from the history of the spatial mobility of human agents who 'circulate' to fill different class positions. The four cases selected allow the analysis of a wide range of distinct international migrations and highlight the circumstances under which migrants are differentially inserted into economic, political, and ideological relations.

A comment on the sources of evidence is also required. The scale of the historical and spatial canvas is ambitious and necessitated the use of secondary sources. But this method is not predicated on practical necessity alone:

'If a topic is too big for purely primary research – *and* if excellent studies by specialists are already available in some profusion – secondary sources are appropriate as the basic source of evidence for a given study. Using them is not different from survey analysts reworking the results of previous surveys rather than asking all the questions anew, or students of comparative ethnography synthesising results from many different published field studies.'

(Skocpol 1984b: 382)

Secondary historical analyses relevant to the subject matter of this book are available in great profusion and so the problem was to identify criteria by which to include and exclude (cf. Skocpol 1984b: 382–83). The chosen strategy was to read as widely as possible, particularly amongst non-Marxist analysts, seeking for significant points of convergence relevant to the articulation of free and unfree labour. Consequently, the theoretical argument that I offer is grounded in historical evidence.

Conclusion

In sum, this book is conceived and offered as a contribution at three different but interrelated levels. First, it is concerned with the theoretical and historical problem of the interrelationship between capitalism and unfree labour. Second, it is concerned with the political economy of migration. Third, it is concerned with the process of racialization and its articulation with production relations. I emphasize that these three themes are interrelated in order to highlight my view that any account of the historical development of capitalism is necessarily incomplete if it is divorced from an understanding of either migration or processes of racialization. In other words, the terrain partially occupied by the sociology of 'race relations' must and can be contested, reoccupied, and restructured by a historical and materialist analysis of migration and racialization, processes which are integral to capitalist development.

Part 1

Capital and wage labour

'The real science of modern economy only begins when the theoretical analysis passes from the process of circulation to the process of production.'

(*Marx 1972:337*)

1

Capitalism as a
mode of production

Introduction

I begin with Marx, not as a eulogy to some unquestioned truth in what
he wrote, but rather to identify an analytical and historical problem.
The objective of this chapter is to outline Marx's conception of the
defining, or essential, features of the capitalist mode of production. I
argue that, for Marx, one of the essential features was the particular
form taken by the relations of production, specifically the dialectical
interdependence of wage labour and capital. I then expand on Marx's
conception of wage labour as free labour, from which I shall derive a
distinction between free and unfree labour.

Mode of production

For Marx, the concept of *mode of production* refers to the way in which
people produce their means of subsistence, subsistence being biologically
determined and culturally/historically defined. In *The German Ideology*,
Marx and Engels argue that

> 'Men . . . begin to distinguish themselves from animals as soon as they begin
> to *produce* their means of subsistence, a step which is conditioned by their
> physical organisation. By producing their means of subsistence men are
> indirectly producing their actual material life. . . . This mode of production
> must not be considered simply as being the reproduction of the physical
> existence of the individuals. Rather it is a definite form of activity of these
> individuals, a definite *mode of life* on their part. As individuals express their
> life, so they are. What they are, therefore, coincides with their production,
> both with *what* they produce and with *how* they produce. The nature of
> individuals thus depends on the material conditions determining their
> production.'
>
> (Marx and Engels 1968b: 31–2)

A mode of production is socially produced by human beings, and therefore, potentially, can be transformed by human beings. Thus 'the economic forms in which men produce, consume, and exchange, are *transitory and historical*' (Marx, in Marx and Engels 1965:36).

In order that production can occur, certain sorts of relations have to be established and maintained. These relations are of two kinds, between people and nature, and between people and people. The former category refers to the process by which labour power is combined with instruments (flint-axe, plough, loom, blast furnace) in order to make objects from raw materials in order to satisfy human needs. These instruments, along with the raw materials, are defined by Marx as the *means of production*, while the whole process which results in the production of objects is defined as the *labour process*. The second category of relations, between people and people, are understood by Marx as the *social relations of production*, a concept which refers to the social relations between people that are necessarily established in the course of material production.

The social relations of production, and therefore the mode of production, are not purely economic in character. The assumption that economic relations can be divorced from political and ideological relations must be questioned. Marx, himself, did not work from this assumption. First, he attributed to the relations of production a constitutive role in shaping the political and ideological relations in any mode of production:

> 'The specific economic form, in which unpaid surplus-labour is pumped out of direct producers, determines the relationship of rulers and ruled, as it grows directly out of production itself and, in turn, reacts upon it as a determining element. Upon this, however, is founded the entire formation of the economic community which grows up out of the production relations themselves, thereby simultaneously its specific political form. It is always the direct relationship of the owners of the conditions of production to the direct producers – a relation always naturally corresponding to a definite stage in the development of the methods of labour and thereby its social productivity – which reveals the innermost secret, the hidden basis of the entire social structure, and with it the political form of the relation of sovereignty and dependence, in short, the corresponding specific form of the state.'
>
> (Marx 1972:791)

It is clear from Marx's reference to political relations reacting back upon production that this interrelation between economic and political relations is not to be viewed as being one-way. Second, although there are many places where Marx writes as if economic, political, and ideological relations are distinct and separate (e.g. 1971:20–1), there are other places where he offers a more dialectical view, such that, for example, economic relations have also a political content. Elsewhere, and earlier, Marx had written with Engels (Marx and Engels 1968b: 79–80; see also Marx:

'Since the State is the form in which the individuals of a ruling class assert their common interests, and in which the whole civil society of an epoch is epitomised, it follows that the State mediates in the formation of all common institutions and that the institutions receive a political form.'

(1976: 915–16))

Analysis of the interrelationship between these different relations presumes materialist assumptions (that human consciousness is determined by material relations), but Marx argues that there is a multitude of circumstances and conditions 'which can be ascertained only by analysis of the empirically given circumstances' (1972: 792). This again echoes an earlier claim:

'Empirical observation must in each separate instance bring out empirically, and without any mystification and speculation, the connection of the social and political structure with production. The social structure and the State are continually evolving out of the life-process of definite individuals, but of individuals, not as they may appear in their own or other people's imagination, but as they *really* are.'

(Marx and Engels 1968b: 36–7)

Economistic readings of Marx cannot be sustained in the light of these formulations. More significantly in this context, it follows that analysis of any mode of production must be an analysis of of economic *and* political and ideological relations. Thus

'It is impossible to separate either forces of production (narrowly conceived) or legalistic notions of property control, from the extensive political, cultural and other social relations which make that kind of production possible.'

(Corrigan *et al.* 1980: 3)

In other words, we must understand the concept of *relations of production* to include not only the relations between people involved directly and immediately in producing objects to satisfy human needs, but also the much wider set of relations which are required to exist in order to ensure that production takes place. Thus, it follows: 'The forms of State are facets of a given mode of producing things, as essential to reproduction as particular kinds of property or technology' (Corrigan *et al.* 1980: 5).

Marx identified a number of distinct modes of production (e.g. 1971: 21), although he attempted a systematic analysis of only one, the capitalist mode of production. His brief comments about non-capitalist modes of production are scattered throughout his writings, although a more systematic analysis was outlined in the *Grundrisse* (1973: 471–514; see also Hobsbawm 1964; Wolf 1982: 75–100). This limited attention in Marx's writing has given rise to a debate about the identifying features of these other modes of production and their interrelation (e.g. Hindess and Hirst 1975; Asad and Wolpe 1976; Foster-Carter 1978; Wolpe 1980; Crummey and Stewart 1981), a matter to which I shall return. Here I am concerned with Marx's concept of the *capitalist mode of production*.

Capitalism as a mode of production

For Marx, the capitalist mode of production is a form of commodity production, that is a system whereby goods are produced in order to be exchanged by means of sale on a market. Production for exchange is distinct from a system where people produce goods for their immediate subsistence, and it is only in the former instance that Marx regards the products of labour power as *commodities*. But not all forms of commodity production are capitalist. The capitalist mode of production exists where commodity production is generalized, to the point where it determines the production and distribution of *labour power*. Thus

> 'The historical conditions of its (capital) existence are by no means given with the mere circulation of money and commodities. It arises only when the owner of the means of production and subsistence finds the free worker available, on the market, as the seller of his own labour-power.'
>
> (Marx 1976:274)

The capitalist mode of production therefore depends upon the existence of a particular set of social relations of production which permits an individual to offer labour power for sale as a commodity and allows another to purchase it. What is presumed is, first, that there is a group of people who neither own nor control any means of production which they could otherwise combine with their own labour power to reproduce themselves independently; second, that control over the means of production must be concentrated in the hands of a small minority. This group purchases labour power, which is combined with tools and raw materials to facilitate production. These social relations of production embody a process of exploitation and therefore a particular set of *class relations*.

Exploitation occurs when a minority group is able to appropriate a surplus produced by another, majority group under conditions of compulsion. This surplus takes two interrelated forms. *Surplus labour* is all that labour which is performed over and above that which is necessary to ensure the individual's subsistence and the reproduction of the means of production, this excess taking material form in a *surplus product*. Thus, class relations exist wherever surplus labour is compelled and where surplus product is appropriated by a group of non-producers because these groups of producers and non-producers have distinct interests. The form in which surplus labour is compelled and surplus product appropriated is historically variable.

In order to understand Marx's conception of exploitation in the capitalist mode of production, and therefore class relations, it is necessary to understand the labour theory of value. Within the capitalist mode of production, all commodities have a value which is determined by the labour time which is socially necessary to produce them. Because labour power is a commodity, it too has a value determined in this way. The capitalist purchases labour power with a wage (or variable capital) and combines it with tools and raw materials and so on, (or constant capital) to produce commodities. Surplus labour is all that labour which occurs after the worker has reproduced the value of his or her labour power. Surplus labour is embodied in the value of those commodities produced in excess of the value of the worker's labour power expended in production. But, by working *for* the capitalist, all commodities produced are owned by the capitalist who is able to realize the *surplus value* (i.e. the total value of the commodities produced, less the value of labour power purchased with wages in order to produce them) by selling the commodities on the market. Thus

> 'Capitalist production is not merely the production of commodities, it is, by its very essence, the production of surplus value. The worker produces not for himself, but for capital. It is no longer sufficient, therefore, for him simply to produce. He must produce surplus-value.'
>
> (Marx 1976:644)

In sum, surplus value is created by the worker producing commodities whose value is greater than the value of his or her labour power expended in their production. The worker is exploited because that surplus value is appropriated by the capitalist.

However, surplus value can only be realized if the surplus product is exchanged on the market for money. Thus commodity circulation and exchange is integral to production, although subordinate to it (Marx 1973:83–100, esp. 99). The market is served by a number of different producers, each with commodities for sale. This competitive situation forces producers to compete to persuade buyers to purchase commodities from one unit of production rather than from another. Various means can be used to achieve this, but the most effective is to produce the commodity for a price which is lower than other producers. This requires the producer to reduce the socially necessary labour time embodied in the commodity, something that is best achieved by combining labour power with new means of production in such a way as to increase the number of commodities produced in the same period of time. Thus

> 'the development of capitalist production makes it necessary constantly to increase the amount of capital laid out in a given industrial undertaking, and competition subordinates every individual capitalist to the immanent laws of capitalist production, as external and coercive laws. It compels him to keep extending his capital, so as to preserve it, and he can only extend it by means of progressive accumulation.'
>
> (Marx 1976:739)

Hence capitalist production is characterized by the constant growth in the size of units of production, and by the increase in labour productivity achieved by the increasing use of machinery in production.

The cyclical and expansionary nature of capitalist production is, however, dependent upon the reproduction of capitalist relations of production. By means of the sale of labour power and by means of the transformtion of surplus value into capital, capital constantly reconfronts labour with its own product (transformed into new machinery etc.) and in a way which leaves labour always without access to the means of production. Thus the process of capital accumulation reproduces the requirement that the labourer sells labour power as a commodity:

'Therefore the worker himself constantly produces objective wealth, in the form of capital, an alien power that dominates and exploits him; and the capitalist just as constantly produces labour-power, in the form of a subjective source of wealth which is abstract, exists merely in the physical body of the worker, and is separated from its own means of objectification and realisation; in short, the capitalist produces the worker as wage labourer. This incessant reproduction, this perpetuation of the worker, is the absolutely necessary condition for capitalist production.'

(Marx 1976:716)

Consequently

'The capitalist process of production . . . seen as a total, connected process, i.e. a process of reproduction, produces not only commodities, not only surplus value, but it produces and reproduces the capital-relation itself; on the one hand the capitalist, on the other the wage-labourer.'

(1976:724)

The purpose of this exegesis is to emphasize that for Marx the existence of wage labour is integral to his concept of the capitalist mode of production. That wage labour is no incidental, or secondary, feature is indicated by the centrality of the appropriation of surplus value produced by wage labour to the cycle of capitalist production. Moreover we have seen that for Marx the reproduction of the capitalist mode of production requires and ensures the reproduction of the relationship between capital and wage labour. Hence without wage labour, capital itself (in its specifically capitalist form, and therefore not merchant's or usurer's capital (Marx 1972:593)) has no meaningful existence. This is made explicitly clear where Marx warns that capital should not be reified:

'capital is not a thing, but rather a definite social production relation, belonging to a definite historical formation of society, which is manifested in a thing and lends this thing a specific social character. Capital is not the sum of the material and produced means of production. Capital is rather the means of production transformed into capital. . . . It is the means of production monopolised by a certain section of society, confronting living labour-power as products and working conditions rendered independent of this very labour-power, which are personified through this anti-thesis in capital.'

(1972:814–15)

This is no isolated claim (e.g. Marx 1976:932; 1973:303, 514). The point is made more explicitly in the following passage:

'*the sale and purchase of labour power* . . . *forms the absolute foundation* of capitalist production and is an integral *moment* within it. Material wealth transforms itself into capital simply and solely because the worker sells his labour-power in order to live. The *articles* which are the material conditions of labour, i.e. the *means of production,* and the articles which are the precondition for the survival of the worker himself, i.e. the *means of subsistence,* both become *capital* only because of the phenomenon of *wage-labour.* Capital is not a *thing* . . . Without a *class dependent on wages,* the moment individuals confront each other as free persons, there can be no production of surplus-value, without the production of surplus-value there can be no capitalist production, and hence no capital and no capitalist! Capital and wage labour . . . only express two aspects of the same relationship.'

(1976:1005–6)

Thus within the capitalist mode of production, both capital and wage labour presume the other as part of a social relationship that constitutes the foundation for a particular sort of production process. Even Marx had to contradict those who questioned this:

'There are . . . those who consider that wage-labour, the sale of labour to the capitalist and hence the *wage form,* is something only superficially the characteristic of capitalist production. It is, however, one of the essential mediating forms of capitalist relations of production, and one constantly reproduced by those relations themselves.'

(1976:1064; see also 1973:832)

Within the capitalist mode of production, a variety of political and ideological relations is essential to the formation and reproduction of wage labour. Included amongst these is the *state* which, Marx argued (as we shall see in Chapter 2), played a central role in the creation of a class of wage labourers in the development of capitalism in England (Marx 1976:899–900). And after the successful establishment of capitalist relations of production, the state has a central role in so far as it guarantees the reproduction of those relations of production by intervening in not only political and ideological but also in economic relations (cf. Fine and Harris 1979:95). Within the capitalist mode of production, the state is therefore an essential relation of production, regulating *all* those relations which sustain the commodification and exploitation of labour power (Corrigan and Sayer 1985:184–88, 199).

In sum, Marx's historical materialism leads him to attribute primacy to the mode of production, that is to a 'specific, historically occuring set of social relationships through which labour is deployed to wrest energy from nature by means of tools, skills, organisation and knowledge' (Wolf 1982:75). Thus what distinguishes capitalism from other modes of production is precisely the way in which production is carried out. Marx identifies the particularity in the interdependence of capital and wage labour. He did not ignore other facets of generalized commodity production, such as commodity circulation and exchange, but he did insist that the relations of production, and their reproduction, were historically prior to such features (1973:99). Thus the necessary expansion of the market under the capitalist mode of production has its origin in the increased *production* of commodities which must be exchanged in order to realize surplus value (1976:967). So for Marx, wage labour is a historically constituted form by which surplus labour can be appropriated. It can be understood only in terms of its relationship with capital. Without wage labour, there is no capitalist mode of production, although 'antediluvian' forms of capital may exist within the framework of other production relations, as with usurer's or merchant's capital in feudalism.

Wage labour as free labour

We can now explore further Marx's characterization of wage labour in order to compare it with other methods of surplus appropriation. Of prime significance is Marx's consistent reference to wage labour as *free labour* (e.g. 1968:74). On first sight, this seems to contradict the description of wage labour as one pole in an exploitative relation with capital. Moreover, elsewhere, Marx refers to wage labour as 'economic bondage' (1976:723), or even as 'slavery' (In Marx and Engels 1965:40), and argues that, as with slave labour, wage labour is a form of 'external forced labour' (1973:611).

What is at issue is simultaneously the definition of freedom and the nature of the distinctiveness of wage labour compared with other forms of surplus appropriation. The former issue is evident in Marx's contrast between wage, slave, and serf labour with 'really free working' where labour is the 'individual's self-realisation' (1973:611). Here we find an echo of a distinction made elsewhere by Marx and Engels between materialist and idealist conceptions of freedom (1968b:333n).

The latter refers to individual self-determination in conditions where formal constraint is absent while the former refers to the ability of human beings to determine the circumstances and conditions under which they live. 'Really free labour' can only occur when the conditions that would allow such determination have been realized, conditions that, for Marx and Engels, could only be achieved by transcending the capitalist mode of production and the bourgeois (idealist) conception of freedom (1968b:493–95). But, prior to such a revolutionary transformation, in all forms of class society there is some form of compulsion upon the majority to provide labour power, from which a minority can extract a surplus product. Nevertheless, the form that the compulsion takes and the means used to achieve it differ and give rise to specific relations of production. Hence the specificity of wage labour is found in the contrast with other forms of labour power, a contrast which reveals the emergence of the bourgeois conception of freedom. This is expressed in the fact that the wage labourer possesses labour power as a form of private property.

Marx is precise in his designation of the freedom of wage labour. He writes:

> 'this worker must be free in the double sense that as a free individual he can dispose of his labour-power as his own commodity, and that, on the other hand, he has no other commodity for sale, i.e. he is rid of them, he is free of all the objects needed for the realisation of his labour-power.'
>
> (1976: 272–73; see also 874–75)

Elsewhere, Marx argues that wage labour is

> 'free from the old relations of clientship, bondage and servitude, and secondly free of all belongings and possessions, and of every objective, material form of being, *free of all* property; dependent on the sale of its labour capacity or on begging, vagabondage and robbery as its only source of income.'
>
> (1973: 507)

The freedom of the wage labourer is grounded in an ability to decide whether, and to whom, his or her labour power will be sold. Therefore, the wage labourer possesses his/her labour power as a form of private property. This gives to the wage labourer an area of personal determination within the limits set primarily by market conditions. In principle, there are a number of potential buyers of labour power, requiring different skills and abilities, for which different wages and conditions are offered. The wage labourer is free to determine which of these positions he or she will attempt to fill, if necessary as a consequence of retraining and further education. Moreover, the wage labourer is formally free to move from one employer to another.

The freedom of the wage labourer extends to the arena of consumption. In return for providing labour power, the individual receives a wage, with which he or she can enter the market to buy the commodities necessary to ensure material and cultural reproduction. The individual is, in principle, free to choose how the wage might be spent, a freedom of some significance as commodity production expands and as the boundary of what is deemed to be socially necessary to ensure the reproduction of labour power widens. Thus 'he acts as a free agent; he must pay his own way; he is responsible to himself for the way he spends his wages' (Marx 1976: 1033).

But the freedom of the wage labourer is conditional because, through the operation of the labour market, a range of constraints operate. Most obviously, the ability to sell labour power depends upon the presence of a buyer. The freedom to sell labour power means that the worker is subject to the demands of capital and therefore subject to the cyclical nature of capitalist production, characterized as it is by periods of crisis and recomposition when labourers are expelled from the production process (Marx 1976: 762–802). Where a buyer cannot be found, the wage labourer's freedom is an abstraction. Marx writes: 'According to his economic conditions he is merely a *living labour capacity*. . . . If the capitalist has no use for his surplus labour, then the worker may not perform his necessary labour; nor produce his necessaries' (1973:604). For this reason, Marx refers to the free labourer as always potentially a pauper.

Considered historically, this relative freedom involves an overriding compulsion. In the course of the transition from the feudal mode of production to the capitalist mode of production (Marx 1976:873–940), people were freed from a variety of forms of constraint and legal obligations over the use of labour power. But they were also freed from access to and ownership of the means of production. Consequently, they were freed from the ability to produce their own means of subsistence, leaving them with only their labour power to sell to those who had gained the means of production as their own private property:

'With the "setting free" of a part of the agricultural population . . . their former means of nourishment were also set free. They were now transformed into material elements of variable capital. The peasant, expropriated and cast adrift, had to obtain the value of the means of subsistence from his new lord, the individual capitalist, in the form of wages.'

(Marx 1976:908–09)

Thus although the direct producer gains the freedom to dispose of his or her labour power, the producer is nevertheless compelled to find a buyer as a consequence of having been deprived of access to the means of production. In principle, the individual gains control over the disposal of labour power, but in a set of social relations where there is little option other than to submit it to the discipline of the capitalist labour process. Consequently, what in one sense is a real individual freedom is historically constrained by the new social relations of production. The apologists of the capitalist mode of production ignore these social relations of production in order to highlight the individual's freedom to enter the market for labour power:

'Hence, the historical movement which changes the producers into wage-labourers appears, on the one hand, as their emancipation from serfdom and from the fetters of the guilds, and it is this aspect of the movement which alone exists for our bourgeois historians.'

(Marx 1976:875)

The history of the forced appropriation of the agricultural producer and the reality of the necessity to exchange labour power for a wage, with which to obtain the means of production, define free wage labour as another, historically constituted form of compelled labour.

Therefore Marx's description of wage labour as free labour must be understood relatively and dialectically. Within the capitalist mode of production, labour power is the individual's private property. Labour power is free to circulate within a market but the individual 'owner' of labour power is compelled to make it available in this way to capital. The nature and characteristics of this dialectic of freedom and compulsion are elaborated by Marx in his scattered comparisons between wage labour and slave labour.

Wage labour and slave labour

There is no systematic discussion of slave labour in Marx's writing. Where references occur, they tend to be instrumental to another line of argument. There are a number of references to the use of slave labour in Greece and Rome (e.g. 1970: 483), a larger number to slave labour in the United States (e.g. Marx and Engels 1974: 67–9, 81; Marx 1976: 303–4, 345) and a variety of references to the interrelationship between slave production and merchant capital (e.g. Marx 1972: 177, 325). These scattered comments are an insufficient foundation in themselves for a developed theory, but they advance our understanding of Marx's conception of the nature of wage labour as free labour.

Marx contrasts slave labour and wage labour on a number of criteria. First, he suggests that the individual who produces as a slave is possessed as a thing whereas an individual who produces as a wage labourer possesses labour power as private property which is exchanged as a commodity. For Marx, this is a fundamental distinction:

> 'The slave did not sell his labour power to the slave owner, any more than the ox sells its services to the peasant. The slave, together with his labour power, is sold once and for all to his owner. He is a commodity which can pass from the hand of one owner to that of another. He is himself a commodity, but the labour power is not his commodity.'
>
> (1968a: 74; see also 1976: 1032)

The consequence of the purchase of human beings as things (as property) is that those who become slaves thereby have an exchange value (Marx 1973: 289) and form part of the means of production (Marx 1976: 874). Hence 'In the slave system, the money capital invested in the purchase of labour-power plays the role of the money-form of fixed capital, which is but gradually replaced as the active period of the slave's life expires' (1970: 483). This means that

> 'The price paid for a slave is nothing but the anticipated and capitalised surplus-value or profit to be wrung out of the slave. But the capital paid for the purchase of the slave does not belong to the capital by means of which profit, surplus labour, is extracted from him. On the contrary. It is capital which the slave-holder has parted with, it is a deduction from the capital which he has available for actual production. . . . The fact that he has bought the slave does not enable him to exploit the slave without further ado. He is only able to do so when he invests some additional capital in the slave economy itself.'
>
> (1972: 809; see also 1976: 377)

The human being who becomes a slave therefore plays the same role in production as any other item of fixed capital. Consequently, the human being enmeshed in such a relation of production has little ability to determine how his own labour power is utilized: the individual loses control over labour power by virtue of becoming the private property of another.

Hence, and second, by becoming a slave, the human being loses formal autonomy over that activity which reproduces himself/herself as a living person. Labour power becomes an object of the owner's will and is therefore divorced from the individual as a subject. Marx writes:

> 'In the slave relation, he belongs to the *individual, particular* owner, and is his labouring machine. As a totality of force-expenditure, as labour capacity, he is a thing belonging to another, and hence does not relate as subject to his particular expenditure of force, nor to the act of living labour. . . . The totality of the free worker's labour capacity appears to him as his property, as one of his moments, over which he, as subject, excercises domination, and which he maintains by expending it.'
>
> (1973: 464–65)

Thus by comparison the human being who enters production relations as a wage labourer retains the ability as a free and active subject to dispose of labour power on the market. Although freedom over the disposal of that labour power is lost as soon as a buyer is found, at which point the individual has to submit to the discipline of the capitalist labour process, the individual nevertheless remains formally free to take that labour power back to the market. This relative autonomy is the foundation of a greater sense of individuality and freedom.

This difference in individual autonomy extends beyond the process of production. Without money, and without the product of his/her labour power, there is no basis for the slave to participate in any market. Consequently, slaves do not constitute a market of independent consumers. The slave, as personal property, is either provided directly with the means of subsistence (i.e. like a farm animal or a tractor, the slave is maintained) or the slave is forced to produce his/her means of reproduction. However:

> 'in production based on capital, consumption is mediated at all points by exchange, and labour never has a *direct* use value for those who are working. Its entire basis is labour as exchange value and as the creation of exchange value . . . the wage worker as distinct from the slave is himself an independent centre of circulation, someone who exchanges, posits exchange value, and maintains exchange value through exchange.'
>
> (1973: 419)

The wage labourer, who receives money in exchange for labour power, gains the responsibility for organizing his or her reproduction, a responsibility which requires that the individual participates in exchange as a consumer of commodities. This not only contributes further to the (bourgeois) sense of being an active subject, an autonomous individual with the ability to shape his/her own life (1976: 1032–3), but also constitutes a real autonomy when compared to the situation of slavery. Consequently, in the latter instance, there is a direct and nearly absolute personal dependence of the slave upon the owner whereas, with wage labour, the employer has no direct responsibility or obligation to the worker outside of the workplace.

Third, Marx argues that slave labour is necessarily less efficient, adaptable, and productive than wage labour:

> 'It is one of the civilising aspects of capital that it enforces this surplus-labour in a manner and under conditions which are more advantageous to the development of the productive forces, social relations, and the creation of the elements for a new and higher form than under the preceding forms of slavery, serfdom, etc.'

> (1972:819)

Marx argues (1976:1031–4) that the slave is guaranteed to receive the means of subsistence because, as fixed capital, the slave has to be maintained in order that the value expressed in the purchase price be fully realized in production. There is, therefore, no direct economic compulsion upon the slave to work for the master. The master has to compel the slave to labour, using physical force if necessary. Moreover, the slave does not choose his/her master and has little incentive to provide or develop any special skill or talent. This is because labour power is not the individual's private property and so he or she can gain no direct benefit from the use of such a skill or talent in the labour process.

When this is considered in relation to the fact that the slave is also excluded from direct participation in commodity exchange, it follows that the slave has a very limited incentive not only to work but also to improve the contribution of his or her labour power to the production process. Additionally, as a result of being treated primarily as an instrument of production, the slave has only limited space for resistance. One relatively easy expression of resistance is to sabotage the means of production, an activity which does assert a sense of being a human subject (Marx 1976:303–4). Consequently, the owner provides slaves with only the crudest, simplest, and heaviest tools of production in order to minimize the possibility of destruction. This, too, militates against any revolutionary modification of the labour process.

On the other hand, the wage labourer, by having to offer labour power on the market, is given the responsibility of obtaining the means of subsistence by exchange using the money paid as a wage. Within limits, the wage labourer can choose the exploiter of his/her labour power. By participating within a market, the wage labourer has constantly to review the quantity and quality of labour power made available in order to ensure that he or she remains employed by capital. Competition between sellers of labour power can ensure the introduction of a new labour process, requiring greater productivity, where those without employment are willing to fill 'new' positions which the current labour force may resist filling. But in addition the labour market provides a range of wages for a variety of types of work, providing an incentive for the worker to improve the quantity and quality of labour power.

These are real, material processes and benefits for wage labour and have to be assessed in addition to the purely ideological role of the ideas of individualism, self-determination, and responsibility which are used to obtain the participation of the wage labourer. So

'The effect of all these differences is to make the free workers' work more intensive, more continuous, more flexible and skilled than that of the slave, quite apart from the fact that they fit him for quite a different historical role.'
(Marx 1976: 1032–3)

Hence

'The constant development of *new forms of work*, this continual change . . . and in consequence the progressive division of labour in *society as a whole*: all this is the product of the capitalist mode of production.'   (1976: 1034)

Fourth, the relations of exploitation and domination, and the individual's experience of these relations, differ. With wage labour there is the appearance of equal exchange in so far as the worker is paid for every hour worked or every piece produced. Consequently all labour appears as paid labour. With slave labour, all labour appears as labour for the owner, including that part of the working day which replaces the value of the slaves' own means of subsistence. Hence:

'In the one case, the property-relation conceals the slaves' labour for himself; in the other case the money relation conceals the uncompensated labour of the wage-labourer.'

(Marx 1976: 680)

Moreover, the 'appearances and illusions' which are integral to the relations of production differ. In the case of wage labour

'we have the complete mystification of the capitalist mode of production, the conversion of social relations into things, the direct coalescence of the material production relations with their historical and social determination.'
(1972: 830)

Labour power is confronted with the transformation of its own surplus product into new capital which then reproduces the domination over labour by re-engaging with it in the labour process. And, with the wage, labour is forced to buy back from capital its means of subsistence. Consequently it appears that capital itself dominates labour power, when in reality it is the relations of production themselves, social relations between people, which contain at their heart the production and appropriation of surplus labour. This mystification is a product of the 'inner organisation of the capitalist mode of production' (1972: 831).

But, Marx argues, in the case of slave labour (and serfdom) mystification takes a different form:

'Here, the domination of the producers by the conditions of production is concealed by the relations of domination and servitude and is evident as the direct motive power of the process of production.'   (1972: 831)

In other words there is no process of reification which obscures the relations of exploitation. Because the slave is an item of property, the owner exercises direct compulsion in order to yield a surplus product. The political relations of compulsion and domination function directly and without mediation as relations of production; production occurs only as a consequence of the exercise of 'the relations of domination and servitude'. The social relations of exploitation are therefore immediately visible to both master and slave. Thus 'Wealth confronts direct forced labour not as capital, but rather as a *relation of domination*' (Marx 1973:326).

In sum Marx portrays slave and wage labour as antithetical because in the case of the former, the human being becomes the private property of another while in the case of the latter, it is labour power which is the private property of its 'owner' and which is exchanged. Thus in the case of the former there is an obvious external constraint on the autonomy of the individual who is enslaved, while in the case of the latter, the individual becomes an autonomous subject in so far as he/she is freed from direct physical and politico-legal compulsion. Hence although both permit a process of surplus appropriation by a non-labouring minority, they differ inasmuch as the emergence and generalization of wage labour represents the emergence of a relation of production in which the labourer has a formal political freedom to determine the disposal of labour power. The distinction can be generalized in the antithesis between free and unfree labour.

Free and unfree labour

Marx uses the idea of free labour to refer exclusively to wage labour which, to repeat, refers to the commodification of labour power: the individual relates to labour power as private property which he/she disposes of in a market. In other words, the concept of *free labour* refers to labour which circulates in a labour market (cf. Nichols 1980:74). Formally the individual can freely choose an employer, subject to the economic constraints operating within that market at any given time, and is not subject to direct politico-legal compulsion requiring him/her to make labour available either generally or to a specific employer. The constraint or compulsion is economic because the individual has no means of obtaining the means of subsistence other than by selling labour power in exchange for money with which to purchase in commodity form those items essential to material reproduction.

Marx's antonymous conception is of relations of production where there is a direct, unmediated relation of domination. The reference is to those circumstances where direct physical and/or politico-legal compulsion are used to acquire and exploit labour power. Thus in the case of slave labour the labourer is transformed forcefully into an item of exchange and is required to work for an owner by means of direct force which can be sustained and legitimated by a legal code. Those enslaved have no choice in the matters of whether they provide labour power for another or for whom they provide labour power. In the case of serf labour, the labourer is required by custom or law to provide either a certain quantity of labour power or the proportion of the product of labour power for the use of the non-labouring class. Although Marx does not do so, we can refer to relations of production characterized by direct domination as *unfree labour*.

The free/unfree labour distinction has not been systematically explored by Marxist writers and further analytical clarification is required. The general contrast between free and unfree labour that we can derive from Marx can be extended to consider an additional dimension. We have referred to the circulation and distribution of labour power by a labour market, but not to the possibility of the imposition of politico-legal constraints which limit the circulation of labour power within a labour market. One example of this is contract labour (e.g. Nzula *et al.* 1979: 82) where individuals contract with an employer for a specified period of time, as a result of which they give up the right to return at will to the labour market. Certain forms of indentured labour share this characteristic. Another occurs where legal provisions prevent certain categories of labourer from offering their labour power in particular sectors of the labour market. In both cases, there is a formal appearance of wage labour in so far as the labourer receives a cash payment in exchange for the alienation of his/her labour power, but direct relations of legal domination significantly obstruct the operation of the labour market. In other words, the process of exploitation is effected by the payment of a wage which is less than the total value produced by the labourer, the surplus value being appropriated by the individual owning the means of production and contracting the labourer, but the labourer's ability to dispose of labour power as an item of private property is limited by extra-economic constraints.

In these circumstances, the circulation of labour power as a commodity is subject to politico-legal constraints which restrict the individual's ability to determine the allocation of his/her labour power subject to the conditions of the market. The formal appearance of wage labour can therefore be subordinated to real relations of exploitation which set precise limits to the exchange (and hence commodification) of labour power. I call these relations of production *unfree wage labour* to differentiate them from the earlier example where there was no wage element or commodification of labour power. The latter can be defined as *unfree non-wage labour*. The essential criterion for the category of unfree wage labour is found in the existence of politico-legal restrictions on the operation of the labour market.

The concept of unfree wage labour refers specifically and primarily to the manner in which labour power is retained and exploited. It is therefore a concept which refers to economic relations, locating the characteristic of unfreedom in the means used to expropriate a surplus product. But the relations of production are not 'purely economic'. By definition, unfree wage labour is necessarily dependent upon politico-legal intervention; hence the importance of regarding the state as a relation of production (Corrigan *et al.* 1980). The state implements and regulates the conditions of unfreedom which characterize the exploitation of labour power. It follows that the conception of unfreedom employed here is not defined in relation to forms of political restriction *per se* (e.g. the absence or withdrawal of rights of political participation or trade union activity). Historically, there is no necessary correlation between the existence of wage labour and the availability of bourgeois political freedoms. However, the absence of such freedoms is not synonymous with the existence of unfree labour. We can refer to unfree labour only where politico-legal restrictions are specifically intended to restrict the circulation of certain categories of labour power within the labour market. Such restrictions may be overdetermined by related political constraints (e.g. the absence of the right to vote) but the latter do not by themselves constitute the defining feature of unfree labour.

But this is not the only limit to the commodification of labour power. The capitalist requires that the labour market 'produces' labour power at a price which permits the realization of surplus value. Thus, capital requires not only the commodification of labour power and not only a market, but also the availability of labour power within a particular price range. The conditions of the labour market must 'produce' labour power both in sufficient quantity and at a price which is within the range consistent with the continuation of the realization of a surplus. For Marx, one such condition was the existence of a *reserve army of labour* (1976:790). But in certain circumstances more direct forms of political intervention have been required. Hence we understand the reasons for state intervention to hold down wages, to restrict certain categories of labourer to certain sectors of the labour market, and to compel certain categories of labourer to make labour power available in exchange for a wage, demonstrating that the labour market is important not in itself but only in so far as it meets the needs of capital in particular historical circumstances by delivering labour power at a price which allows accumulation and the reproduction of the mode of production.

Thus the distinction between free and unfree labour derives from Marx's analysis of capitalism as a mode of production, and refers to the form of compulsion employed in the course of reproducing the relations of production. In the case of free (wage) labour, the compulsion is principally economic, although the resulting relations of production are sustained by politico-legal intervention. Thus the state intervenes principally 'only' to guarantee and mediate the distribution of labour power as a commodity by means of the market. In the case of unfree labour (which takes a number of different forms, e.g. slave labour, serfdom), the compulsion is achieved by physical force and/or legal restrictions and the resulting relations of production are also sustained by politico-legal intervention. But in this case political–legal relations directly determine the distribution of labour power, with the consequence that the state plays an unmediated role in securing and maintaining the relations of production. Additionally, I have introduced the concept of unfree wage labour to take account of state intervention in the distribution of labour power by mean of market mechanisms, an intervention which imposes a form of direct domination and partially obviates the commodification of labour power.

Conclusion

Marx conceptualizes capitalism as a distinct mode of production which is distinguishable from other modes of production by, *inter alia*, relations of production between capital and wage labour (cf. Dobb 1963; Brenner 1976, 1977). Given the central role of production relations in Marx's historical materialism, it follows that he contrasts wage labour and slave labour. This contrast is articulated explicitly in his writing, from which one can derive an analytical distinction between free and unfree labour, a distinction which draws attention to the means by which labour power is appropriated and exploited. The role of the state as a relation of production differs in each case.

2

Accumulation and articulation

Introduction

The concern in the preceding chapter was with Marx's *concept* of capitalism. Here the focus is on aspects of Marx's *historical* analysis of the emergence and development of the capitalist mode of production. Two issues will be dealt with, both arising from the conceptual discussion in the preceding chapter. First, and assuming that the capitalist mode of production is not a universal and natural phenomenon, it is necessary to explain how and why the wage labour/capital relation emerged. This is the problem of *primitive* or *primary accumulation*. Second, and assuming that the capitalist mode of production did not immediately become a universal phenomenon, it is necessary to explain how and why this new set of production relations interrelated with other, extant production relations. This is the problem of *articulation of modes of production*. Marx considered both issues, albeit briefly, and his historical analysis of both will be reviewed in this chapter.

Primitive accumulation

Marx traces the emergence of the capitalist mode of production in Europe, more specifically in England, to the sixteenth century (1976: 876). Capitalist production is therefore historically specific, and was preceded by some other mode of production (feudal). Consequently, Marx was required to demonstrate how capitalist relations of production emerged. He refers to the formation of capital and wage labour as the process of *primitive* (1976: 775, 873–76) or *original accumulation* (1973: 319–20, 459–60). Tracing this transition from feudalism to capitalism requires historical analysis and this can be found principally in *Capital* and in the *Grundrisse*. When evaluating Marx's historical analysis, it is necessary to take account of the objective and scope of *Capital* (cf. Tribe

1981: 4; also Brewer 1984: 11–18). In the Introduction to the first volume, Marx notes:

> 'What I have to examine in this work is the capitalist mode of production, and the relations of production and forms of intercourse that correspond to it. Until now, their *locus classicus* has been England. This is the reason why England is used as the main illustration of the theoretical developments I make.'
>
> (1976: 90, see also Marx and Engels 1965: 312–13, 339–40)

The concept of primitive accumulation is one of Marx's theoretical developments (see 1976: 873) and the significance of his discussion of the historical process to which the concept refers lies in the fact that it was a discussion which focused largely on England alone. In this historical analysis of the emergence of the capital/wage labour relation, he identifies two main processes.

Marx devotes most attention to the first, the creation of a class of free workers:

> 'So-called primitive accumulation, therefore, is nothing else than the historical process of divorcing the producer from the means of production. It appears as 'primitive' because it forms the pre-history of capital, and of the mode of production corresponding to capital.'
>
> (1976: 875–76; also 1973: 507)

Marx documents the process by which various categories of agricultural producers were denied access to the land, the latter becoming the private property of a small group of people who became capitalist farmers, hiring labour by means of the payment of wages. A precondition for this was the creation of the notion of ownership in order that the right to utilize the land could be conferred on an individual. By denying the agricultural producer access to land, the labourer was forced to provide labour power as a commodity and to become a consumer of commodities to sustain subsistence and reproduction. Consequently, the process of expropriation created a pool of labour and, simultaneously, a market for the sale of commodities produced with the labour power of those who filled that pool. The historical adequacy of Marx's analysis is not at issue here (e.g. Lazonick 1974; Tribe 1981: 35–100).

This dimension of primitive accumulation may be conceived as a process of *proletarianization* because the process of primitive accumulation creates a worker with only labour power for sale, i.e. a proletarian. It is therefore synonymous with the creation of a labour market and the commodification of labour power. Marx's analysis therefore emphasizes that a labour market, and the exchange of labour power for a wage, are not universal constants but are the result of human interventions in particular historical circumstances (cf. Pentland 1981: 25). The character of those circumstances will be discussed further in Part 3.

The second dimension of primitive accumulation is described by Marx as follows:

'The discovery of gold and silver in America, the extirpation, enslavement and entombment in mines of the indigenous population of that continent, the beginnings of the conquest and plunder of India, and the conversion of Africa into a preserve for the commercial hunting of blackskins, are all things which characterise the dawn of the era of capitalist production. These idyllic proceedings are the chief moments of primitive accumulation.'

(1976:915)

Marx refers collectively to this complex of historical processes with the concept of *colonial system*. He claims that the colonial system contributed to the development of the capitalist mode of production in a number of ways. Most important of all, the colonies provided both a market for manufactured commodities and a source of wealth which could be transformed into capital (1976:918). Thus the colonies furthered the realization of surplus value embodied in generalized commodity production and served as a source of wealth which could be used to confront wage labour and expand production. In addition, Marx mentions the encouragement of trade and of a credit and banking system, as well as the formation of the national debt, as consequences of the colonial system which assisted the development of the capitalist mode of production (1976:918–22).

Marx emphasizes the central role of the state in both processes of primitive accumulation by, for example, holding down wages and organizing the national debt (1976:899, 915–16). The state was the agency for the various forms of force that made possible the formation of capital and wage labour, and the classes to which they correspond, and was subsequently responsible for organizing and regulating those social relations which guaranteed their reproduction, and hence, the reproduction of the capitalist mode of production (see Corrigan and Sayer 1985). Clearly these class relations were formed on a stage which was already wider than the political framework (the boundaries of England as a territorial unit) within which they were constituted. In the process of primitive accumulation, England specifically, and Europe more generally, were linked with other parts of the world, notably the Americas and the Caribbean, during the seventeenth and eighteenth centuries. The state must be viewed, therefore, as a central mediating institution between emergent capitalist relations within the political units of Europe and colonial enterprises elsewhere in the world.

The analysis of the process of primitive accumulation in volume one of *Capital* is little more than a brief historical sketch. Marx was aware of this limitation (1976:928) although elsewhere he makes further reference to this process, notably in his observations on merchant's capital where he considers the influence of trade and the colonial system on the transition from feudalism to capitalism (1972:323–37; 1973:856–61). Marx distinguishes merchant's from industrial capital. He identifies the conditions of existence of merchant's capital as the simple circulation of commodities and money, and its role as being to promote the exchange of commodities. Merchant's capital predates the capitalist mode of production and can be found in other modes of production characterized by simple commodity production (1972: 323–25, 593). Merchant's capital is no more than a sum of money with which to facilitate the transfer of commodities from one place to another. Profit is obtained by buying commodities below their value in order to sell them above their value (1973: 856). Merchant's capital is therefore secondary to production, operating within the sphere of circulation and often linking different parts of the world and different modes of production: 'Money and commodity circulation can mediate between spheres of production of widely different organisation, whose internal structure is still chiefly adjusted to the output of use values' (1972: 328).

Marx draws three conclusions concerning the influence of merchant's capital. The first is that it has never been an independent force, with the power to promote by itself the transition from one mode of production to another. Any transition depends primarily upon the contradictions within the disintegrating mode of production (1972: 327, 332; cf. 1972: 594). However, and second, merchant's capital can facilitate such a transition. In the case of the transition from feudalism to capitalism in England, Marx claims that it helped to dissolve the extant relations of production by, *inter alia*, encouraging the sale of commodities, and by concentrating money in fewer hands. He refers to the disintegrative role of the commercial revolution and the geographical discoveries of the sixteenth and seventeenth centuries, arguing that the feudal fetters of production were destroyed partly by the resulting expansion of the world market, by an increase in commodity circulation and by the development of the colonial system (1972: 332–33; 1973: 858; see also Marx and Engels 1968b: 73–7). Moreover, commerce and trade encouraged the transformation of craft and domestic industry into capitalist production proper (1972: 336). However, these effects were historically specific because once capitalist production was firmly established, the functions of merchant's capital were directly incorporated into the activities of industrial capital (1976: 336; 1973: 859).

Third, Marx argues that where merchant's capital has achieved a certain degree of dominance, it has always had retrogressive effects, obstructing economic development (1972: 327–28). In particular, where merchant's capital has gained control over production, there is a tendency for producers to be organized within the framework of the extant mode of production. Referring to the 'putting out' system organized by merchants, Marx claims:

'This system presents everywhere an obstacle to the real capitalist mode of production and goes under with its development. Without revolutionising the mode of production, it only worsens the conditions of the direct producers.'

(1972: 334–35)

This brief discussion of the history of merchant's capital confirms that for Marx the transition from feudalism to capitalism in England was, in part, dependant upon the colonial system. However, although the various processes connected with merchant's capital are associated by Marx with dissolutionary effects on the feudal mode of production, they cannot be equated with capitalism. Merchant's capital operates in the sphere of circulation, being concerned with the purchase and sale of use values after they had been produced. Circulation presupposes production, and it is in the latter realm that Marx identifies the relationships between people and between people and things which determine the nature of the *mode* of production. Although circulation and production are interdependent, Marx attributes a primacy to the latter:

'The conclusion we reach is not that production, distribution, exchange and consumption are identical, but that they all form the members of a totality, distinctions within a unity. Production dominates not only over itself, in the antithetical definition of production, but over the other moments as well.'

(1973: 99)

Thus Marx warns in the *Resultate* (1976: 949–50; see also 1976: 267–69) that, although trade and the circulation of commodities are necessary conditions for the emergence of capital, their existence is not a sufficient condition. Indeed, trade and commerce are found in a variety of preceding historical periods and modes of production, as is now well documented (e.g. Wolf 1982: 32, 71, 101–25). What is crucial is the transformation of labour power itself into a commodity. Only then is the basis for a constant revolutionizing of the forces of production established and only then can capital and wage labour meet in order that surplus value can be created, to be transformed into, and accumulated as, capital. Commerce and the colonial system did play a role in opening up markets but this effect remained dependent upon the capacity to continually expand production, a capacity that was achieved, argues Marx, only when labour power also became a commodity.

The historical specificity of the transition to capitalism in England must be emphasized. The subsequent expansion of the capitalist mode of production cannot be considered to have proceeded by a series of transitions in precisely the same way as in England because the particular combination of circumstances that *led* to this emergence were transcended *by* it. Because the historical context has been transformed by the emergence of the capitalist mode of production, the latter must be expected to have had effects upon extant, non-capitalist modes of production as a result of the inherently expansionary nature of the accumulation process.

So wherever the capitalist mode of production has emerged, its origin is to be traced in a historically prior process of primitive accumulation. Consequently in each instance it is necessary to trace the emergence of capitalist *relations* of production, i.e. the capital-wage labour relation. The reproduction and spread of the capitalist mode of production therefore presumes a continuing process of primitive accumulation. Hence the process of primitive accumulation, as Meillassoux has observed, should not be regarded as transitory and initiatory but rather as a necessary and permanent companion to the spread of the capitalist mode of production (1981: 105). The same point is made by Frank when he claims that

> 'insofar as primitive accumulation refers to accumulation on the basis of production with noncapitalist relations of production, it need not be prior to, but can be contemporary with capitalist production and accumulation.'
>
> (1978b: 241)

The concept of primitive accumulation refers to a historically continuous process of transformation of relations of production and not to a single, unique event in seventeenth-century England.

It is necessary to distinguish clearly the process of primitive accumulation from the use of direct politico-legal compulsion to reproduce relations of exploitation. In other words, there is an analytical distinction between the formation of a labour market and a class of wage labourers using various forms of direct force on the one hand, and, on the other, the reproduction of unfree relations of production. This distinction is obscured in some discussions of unfree (forced) labour (e.g. Legassick 1975: 233–37). There are therefore two historically distinct objectives of compulsion in relation to the exploitation of labour power.

On the one hand, the very existence of free wage labour and a labour market depends on the prior use of various forms of compulsion: dispossession is not freely chosen by those who are its victim. But it is a temporally specific use of compulsion to create the conditions where the labourer retains his/her labour power as an item of private property. The process of primitive accumulation is, therefore, synonymous with the use of various forms of compulsion. On the other hand, compulsion can be sustained as an integral feature of the relations of production. That is to say, physical force and legal constraint can be used to appropriate and utilize labour power, either in the absence of and as a substitute for a market, or as a means of constraining the operation of the market. It is this second objective of compulsion that can be referred to as a defining feature of the unfree labour, while the use of compulsion in the process of primitive accumulation is analytically distinct.

Articulation of modes of production

In the case of England, the role of the colonial system in the process of primitive accumulation is theoretically comprehensible. Analytically, the connection between capital formation in England and the plunder of wealth from the colonies, alongside the activities of merchant capital, require no additional concepts for the purpose of explanation, although there remains a debate about the validity of the historical evidence (e.g. O'Brien 1982). However, given Marx's concept of the capitalist mode of production, there is no necessary reason why the forms of wealth that were transformed into capital had to originate in colonial activity. *Analytically*, all that it is necessary to demonstrate is that an initial accumulation occurred. It would not contradict Marx's conception of the nature of capitalism if it were shown *historically* that this accumulation took place wholly *within* feudal Europe.

But certain theoretical problems are raised by other aspects of Marx's observations about the colonial system. First, the hypothesized role of the colonial system as a consumer of commodities produced in England/Europe assumes both a demand for them and the availability of a surplus with which to purchase or barter for them. Second, in referring to the mining of silver and to the slave trade, Marx was shifting from discussing the colonial system as a sphere of circulation and accumulation to discussing it as a sphere of *production*.

Both of these dimensions of the colonial system require an analysis of the nature of the mode of production in those regions of the world which were thereby brought into contact with the capitalist mode of production in England/Europe, and of the consequent interrelationship. The first of these dimensions assumes the existence of a mode of production capable of producing a surplus. This, by itself, does not create a theoretical problem because the feudal mode of production realized a surplus product and there were well-established trade routes between feudal Europe and other non-capitalist modes of production elsewhere in the world (e.g. Wolf 1982: 101–4), but it does lead us to ask questions about the implications and effects not only of this inter-relationship of non-capitalist modes of production effected by means of the activity of merchant capital, but also the interrelationship of capitalist and non-capitalist modes of production.

The second of these dimensions (the nature of the relations of production) is particularly important because the colonial system was more than a system of commerce providing the European ruling class with luxury goods produced in precapitalist modes of production in India and beyond (Wolf 1982: 32; Fox-Genovese and Genovese 1983: 4). As Hobsbawm has observed (1965: 43–51), this pattern of commerce gave way in the seventeenth century to a new form of trade in commodities such as tobacco and sugar, and later cotton. These commodities were produced using human labour power, organized in relations of production created by colonial merchants and settlers. We are therefore required to ask, just as we ask of production in England in this same period, what were the social relations of production that governed the production of these and other colonial products. The answer is that they were usually unfree relations of production. Similarly, in so far as the growth of specialization in trade and manufacture in towns in Western

Europe from the fifteenth century depended upon the import of food from Eastern Europe, there developed an interrelationship between the emergent capitalist mode of production and one typified by serfdom (Hobsbawm 1965: 20; cf. Brenner 1976: 47–60; Klima 1985: 192–207).

But the development of cotton and tobacco commodity production outside Europe using forms of unfree labour was not the only form of colonial development connected with the emergence of the capitalist mode of production in Western Europe. During the nineteenth century, there were large-scale migrations of population from Britain (and the rest of Europe) to sparsely inhabited regions of the world which were motivated by the idea of permanent settlement and independent production for subsistence and commodity production. Marx discussed the early stages of this form of colonial activity but seems to have been largely ignorant of the subsequent introduction of unfree relations of production in several of these colonial formations. He briefly took up the question of the nature of the relations of production in colonies where there were large expanses of unoccupied land not held as private property and where politically free individuals were settling (1976: 931–40).

Although Marx refers to some of these settlers as capitalists confronting obstacles to the establishment of the capitalist mode of production (1976: 931), he denies that capitalist relations of production exist where the settler was able to gain access to the land and produce the means of subsistence:

> 'So long, therefore, as the worker can accumulate for himself – and this he can do so long as he remains in possession of his means of production – capitalist accumulation and the capitalist mode of production are impossible. The class of wage-labourers essential to these is lacking.'
>
> (1976: 933)

Indeed, Marx describes the capitalist mode of production and that mode based on the existence of the free producer in the colonies as 'two diametrically opposed economic systems' (1976: 631). Thus the conclusion that Marx draws from his observation on the nature of the relations of production in this type of colonial system is consistent with his conception of the capitalist mode of production being defined by the presence of a class of free, wage labour. We should also note Marx's discussion of the role of political force, which induces a section of the population to work for others rather than on their own behalf, in this type of colonial context because it parallels the role of the state in the emergence of a waged labouring class in England.

In developing this discussion of the relations of production established in the colonial system, I limit it to the example of slave labour in the colonial system. Given that Marx regards the form in which a surplus production was extracted from human labour power (the relations of production) as constitutive, but not exclusively so, of political and other relations, and given the explicit contrast that he drew between wage and slave labour, one would expect Marx to identify a distinct slave mode of production. And he does so in a number of places:

'But then the production of the country . . . must be structured to allow of slave labour, or (as in the southern part of America etc.) a mode of production corresponding to the slave must be created.'

(1973:98)

Elsewhere he writes:

'The capitalist mode of production differs from the mode of production based on slavery, among other things, by the fact that in it the value, and accordingly the price, of labour-power appears as the value, or price, of labour itself, or as wages.'

(1972:30)

In the same text, in the context of a discussion about labour rent, Marx refers to the 'slave or plantation economy' (1972:791). He did not offer a systematic analysis of a slave mode of production, identifying its 'inner dynamic', its conditions of existence and contradictions. These are but a few passing comments which allow only the conclusion that Marx loosely conceptualized a slave mode of production. Moreover, he was not consistent in applying this concept of a slave mode of production because on at least one occasion he referred to plantation owners in the United States as capitalists (1973:513).

Marx acknowledges an interdependence between the slave mode of production and the capitalist mode of production. He argues that the mechanization of the English cotton industry required a large increase in the supply of cotton, a demand that had consequences for the areas supplying the raw cotton:

'Direct slavery is as much the pivot of our industrialism today as machinery, credit, etc. Without slavery no cotton; without cotton no modern industry. Slavery has given value to the colonies; the colonies hve created world trade; world trade is the necessary condition of large-scale machine industry. Thus, before the traffic in Negroes began, the colonies supplied the Old World with only very few products and made no visible change in the face of the earth. Slavery is therefore an economic category of the highest importance.'

(Marx and Engels 1965:40–1; see also Marx 1976:925)

There was, therefore, an interdependence between two distinct modes of production. But interdependence did not signify equal influence or importance.

In the particular historical circumstances of the United States in the nineteenth century, where the slave mode of production had expanded in response to the demand of the capitalist mode of production in England, an economic, political, and ideological conflict developed as a capitalist mode of production emerged within the same social formation. The political conflict led to civil war, about which Marx comments in a newspaper article:

'The present struggle between the South and North is, therefore, nothing but

a struggle between two social systems, between the system of slavery and the
system of free labour. The struggle has broken out because the two systems
can no longer live peacefully side by side on the North American continent. It
can only be ended by the victory of one system over the other.'

(Marx and Engels 1974:81)

Marx regards this as a struggle which could have blocked the
development of capitalism in the United States because elsewhere he
suggests that the existence of slavery obstructs the development of the
capitalist mode of production. Marx, referring to wage labour, argues:

'His valuelessness and devaluation is the presupposition of capital and the
precondition of *free* labour in general. . . . So long as the worker as such has
exchange value, industrial capital as such cannot exist, hence nor can
developed capital in general.'

(1973:289)

Elsewhere, he describes the following point as 'crucial':

'The production of commodities leads inexorably to capitalist production,
once the worker has ceased to be a part of the conditions of production (as in
slavery, serfdom), or once primitive common ownership has ceased to be the
basis of society (India). In short from the moment when labour-power in
general becomes a commodity.'

(1976:951)

These quotations suggest that Marx regards slave labour and wage
labour as the foundations of distinct sets of social relations of
production and, in turn, of distinct modes of production (see also Marx
and Engels 1965:313). But what can we conclude concerning the
interrelation of distinct modes of production from these fragmentary
comments on the capitalist and slave modes of production?

A minimal conclusion is that Marx has some notion of an *articulation
of modes of production* (cf. Hall 1980:320). In suggesting this, I am not
arguing that the recent debate about this concept (e.g. Foster-Carter
1978; Wolpe 1980; Van Binsbergen and Geschiere 1985:4–9) can be
resolved by citing Marx's texts. I only note that there are some passages
in Marx's writing which refer to the interrelation of modes of
production and that these passages set out certain assertions about the
nature of this interrelation. In so far as they deal with the *juncture* of
modes of production, we can refer to an *articulation* of modes of
production which we can understand initially as mutual effectivity.
Indeed, Marx wrote more generally as if there was an inevitability about
such articulation because 'Since bourgeois society is itself only a
contradictory form of development, relations derived from earlier forms
will often be found within in an entirely stunted form, or even
travestied' (1973:105–6). An almost identical claim is made in *Capital*,
although it suggests something more than mutual effectivity:

'In all other spheres, and just like the rest of Continental Western Europe, we
suffer not only from the development of capitalist production, but also from

the incompleteness of that development. Alongside the modern evils, we are oppressed by a whole series of inherited evils, arising from the passive survival of archaic and outmoded modes of production, with their accompanying train of anachronistic social and political relations.'

(1976:9; see also p. 931)

The reference to 'passive survival' suggests that Marx believes that the 'antiquated modes of production' have purely dependent, secondary, or negative consequences (both economic and political). These references are to Western Europe, but the idea of articulation also occurs, as we have seen, in comments on the colonial system and on the United States. Moreover, as we shall see shortly, the evident assumption that the development of the capitalist mode of production has an essentially progressive character has an echo in Marx's writing on India.

There is reason to question further the idea that an articulation of modes of production involves mutual effectivity in the sense of equivalence. Marx's references to, on the one hand, the obstructive effects of slave labour, blocking the development of the capitalist mode of production, and on the other to the slave mode of production being the creation of, and assisting the expansion of, the capitalist mode of production in England, suggest that, at any given time, and depending upon the structural context (within or between social formations), one mode of production will dominate over others. Marx confirms this:

'In all forms of society there is one specific kind of production which predominates over the rest, whose relations thus assign rank and influence to the others. It is a general illumination which bathes all the other colours and modifies their particularity.'

(1973:107)

This introduces a notion of hierarchy into the idea of the articulation of modes of production. This is sustained by Marx's observation that one mode of production can block the development of another, from which develops the idea of necessary contradictions between different modes of production (cf. Post 1978:27). But does it follow from this that there is a single hierarchy of domination and succession in the articulation of modes of production? Some of Marx's texts suggest that he conceived that there was.

Marx defines his aim in the first volume of *Capital* as being to abstract the central categories with which to understand the nature and development of capitalism as a historical reality. Having identified the 'natural laws of capitalist production', Marx believes that he has the conceptual apparatus with which to understand the capitalist mode of production and the manner of its development wherever it appears. In the Preface to *Capital*, after a reference to the implications of the analysis for a reader interested in Germany, he writes:

'It is a question of these laws themselves, of these tendencies winning their way through and working themselves out with iron necessity. The country that is more developed industrially only shows, to the less developed, the image of its own future.'

(1976:91)

This suggests a considerable degree of inevitability about the pre-dominance of the capitalist mode of production over all other modes, an inevitability that, in places, Marx seems to have welcomed in so far as it guaranteed the destruction of 'backwardness' and 'barbarism'. This is clearly evident in his writings on India and Ireland (Marx and Engels 1986a; 1971).

In the case of India, Marx predicts the development of capitalist industrial production as a consequence of the desire of British capital to import cotton as the raw material for its productive activities in Lancashire and elsewhere:

'You cannot maintain a net of railways over an immense country without introducing all those industrial processes necessary to meet the immediate and current wants of railway locomotion, and out of which there must grow the application of machinery to those branches of industry not immediately connected with railways. The railway system will therefore become, in India, truly the forerunner of modern industry.'

(Marx and Engels 1968a: 84)

Such an economic transformation would be simultaneously a cultural transformation:

'England has to fulfil a double mission in India: one destructive, the other regenerating – the annihilation of old Asiatic society, and the laying of the material foundations of Western society in Asia. . . . Modern industry, resulting from the railway system, will dissolve the hereditary divisions of labour, upon which rest the Indian castes, those decisive impediments to Indian progress and Indian power.'

(Marx and Engels 1968a: 82–4)

One central aspect of this transformation concerned the relations of production: independent peasant and handicraft producers engaged in subsistence and petty commodity production were, as a result of English colonial policy and the import of cheaper commodities from England, to be forced into relations of dependence upon landowners and tax collectors (1968: 40, 77–80).

But for Marx this is no simple dichotomy between British civilization and Indian barbarism because there were other contradictions at work. He also refers to the 'profound hypocrisy and inherent barbarism of bourgeois civilization' which is highlighted in the colonial context, behind which lay the 'inherent organic laws of political economy' which were creating the foundation for a new world (Marx and Engels 1968a: 86). The implication is that the barbarism of the bourgeoisie had a necessary and historically specific and progressive cultural role to play by advancing the spread of the capitalist mode of production which would, in turn, negate the 'backward' cultural characteristics of those rural populations which had been brought within its influence. In other words, both the British bourgeoisie and the Indian village communities were equally subject to the negative and positive cultural consequences of the laws of political economy.

In the light of these writings, some Marxists (Warren 1980; see also Brewer 1980: 44–60) argue that Marx expected the transformation that he had witnessed and analysed in Europe to reproduce itself throughout the world, converting precapitalist into capitalist relations in a progressive manner, albeit unevenly and with certain negative consequences (see Marx and Engels 1968a: 39–41, 51). The 'natural laws of capitalist production' therefore seem to imply an articulation of modes of production in which the capitalist mode necessarily predominates, destroying other modes and reproducing itself in their place, with only 'archaic' remnants remaining. However, Marx's late writings, especially those on Russia, give us reason to question this interpretation (Shanin 1984).

In these writings, there is recognition that the specificity of economic and social forms, particularly the peasant commune in Russia in the late nineteenth century, means that a model of socio-economic development derived from analysis of Western Europe has certain limitations. Indeed in unpublished draft letters Marx suggests that the commune might become a means for radical social change if a revolution was to occur in Russia. Yet, although Russia was a contributor to the world market, it had not undergone a thorough capitalist transformation (Shanin 1984: 16–17, 97–126). The implication is clear. In these later writings, Marx is considering the possibility that the conclusions drawn from an analysis of historical development in Europe might not necessarily apply to other parts of the world and that a conception of a linear, historical succession of modes of production (from feudal to capitalist to communist) might not correspond with the historical evidence. Unfortunately, there is no developed analysis of the origins and consequences of these Russian socio-economic forms in Marx's late writings. Consequently, although they may constitute a signpost to suggest the direction we might take after rejecting a strict evolutionist interpretation of Marx, the lacuna in Marx's writings appears even more vast.

Perhaps the most significant fact about Marx's late writings is that they (re)confirm that he took seriously the need for historical analysis. They show that he did not believe (or no longer believed?) that the analytical task was to draw conclusions as a result of applying mechanically a single 'law of capitalist development' to a multitude of historically distinct circumstances. Thus, although Marx provides an analysis of the nature and internal dynamics of the capitalist mode of production, we have to concede that he does not leave us with anything approaching a systematic analysis of the interrelationship between capitalist development in Europe and extant and newly created modes of production elsewhere in the world (including the colonial system). The historical analysis of this articulation of modes of production is left for others to undertake. Although we can approach that historical analysis with certain presuppositions about the form and consequences of that articulation, final conclusions about the interrelationship between the capitalist mode of production and other modes of production can only be drawn after the historical analysis has been conducted. What follows in Part 2 is a contribution to the recovery of the history of aspects of the articulation of modes of production.

Conclusion

We have seen that Marx's analysis of the historical origin and development of the capitalist mode of production is limited in scope and detail and even contradictory. Nevertheless, despite its limitations Marx's historical analysis does leave us with certain concepts and ideas with which to pursue further the issues of which he failed to provide a satisfactory account. First, if Marx's *concept* of the capitalist mode of production has analytical validity, it is necessary to demonstrate in any historical instance how these relations of production emerged. The manner in which they emerge can be expected to vary historically. The concept of *primitive accumulation* refers to this historically variable process which is necessarily continuous for as long as non-capitalist relations of production continue to be transformed into capitalist relations of production.

Second, Marx claims that the development of capitalism in England was historically dependent not only upon trade with non-capitalist modes of production elsewhere in the world, but also upon the rise of a slave mode of production in the Caribbean and North America. The international activities of merchant capital constituted a means for the accumulation of a sum of wealth that could function as capital as well as a method by which an increasing number of exchange values could be circulated. As for the slave mode of production, it supplied cheap cotton for commodity production in English factories. Thus in the case of the development of capitalism in England, its emergence and reproduction cannot be abstracted from production relations and circulation processes on a world scale. I have used the notion of *articulation of modes of production* to refer descriptively to the various interrelationships between distinct modes of production which, in Marx's view, facilitated, or were consequent upon, the emergence of the capitalist mode of production in England. Generalizing from Marx's discussion of the English case, one can suggest that the notion of articulation should be used to refer to a hierarchical but dynamic (dialectical) interdependence of modes of production both within and between different social formations.

Moreover, Marx's historical analysis of *primitive accumulation* in England presupposes the notion of *articulation of modes of production*. For example, the product of unfree relations of production in the Caribbean and the United States mediated the free relations of production in England over a long period of time. Thus this was an articulation in which non-capitalist relations of production were sustained rather than dissolved by the capitalist mode. It follows that the concepts of *primitive accumulation* and *articulation of modes of production* are interdependent. Primitive accumulation can be an instance of the articulation of modes of production in so far as, for example, a sum of wealth is accumulated in one mode of production and transformed into capital in another by being brought into contact with wage labour. The historical conclusion we draw and carry forward from this chapter is that the instance of this that Marx analysed in *Capital* (i.e. England) is only one instance and should not be viewed as a blueprint for all others.

3

Capitalism and unfree labour

Introduction

To this point, I have 'plundered' Marx's writings to specify concepts with which to analyse and explain the historical concurrence of the capitalist mode of production and unfree relations of production. In this chapter I attempt to show that this concurrence, combined with silences in Marx's writings, lead to theoretical problems which have been resolved by various writers who claim the mantle of Marx by utilizing a different conception of the nature of capitalism. Thereafter, I question the theoretical and historical adequacy of these formulations in preparation for a historical analysis of the relationship between capitalism and unfree labour.

On silences and limits

In the preceding chapter I argued that Marx's historical analysis of the articulation between the development of the capitalist mode of production in Europe and the development of the colonial system was perfunctory. This is not least because Marx's *Capital* is

> 'an analysis of the capitalist mode of production, conceived as a specific form of economy, in which historical descriptions of other economic forms enter only insofar as they illuminate aspects of the origin and development of this mode of production.'
>
> (Tribe 1981:4)

Marxist writers of the early twentieth century gave some attention to this silence, an attention which was given theoretical substance in the use of the concept of *imperialism* in the work of Luxemburg (1951:419–45), Lenin (1970:671–768), Bukharin (1972), Luxemburg and Bukharin (1972:136–50), and Hilferding (1981:364–70). But the attention of these writers remained primarily on Europe and North America, the places where capitalism had first developed and/or was most vigorous. In so far as anything was said about the colonies of capitalist Europe, Marx's assertions about the progressive spread of capitalism were repeated (Lenin 1970: 744; see also Brewer 1980: 127; Warren 1980: 48).

Marxists were preoccupied with the revolution in Russia in 1917, its subsequent failure to spread through Europe, and with the rise of fascism. After the Second World War, and once capitalism had entered another long cycle of vigorous expansion, serious analytical and historical work by Marxists began to be carried out on this articulation. The key idea that resulted was that of *underdevelopment*. The conception of the articulation of the capitalist mode of production and the colonial system focused on the large scale and long-term transfer of wealth from what was conceived as the *periphery* to the *centre* of a capitalist *world economy*. This emphasis was certainly in contrast to what is often considered to be the classic post 1945 analysis of the development of capitalism by Dobb (1963). To a large extent, Dobb's work reproduced Marx's silences. Dobb had little to say about processes outside England. Although he recognized the cruelty and plunder involved in colonial policy (1963: 208) and acknowledged that mercantilism 'played a highly important role in the adolescence of capitalist industry' (1963: 209; see also p. 88), his attention to these matters was brief and qualified by an insistence on the negative effects of monopoly under which the early trading companies operated (1963: 193).

The writings of the *underdevelopment* theorists challenged this tradition in a fundamental manner, analyzing the historical evidence of capitalist development with concepts and a method which denied the possibility of an explanation for the emergence of capitalism which focused on Europe alone. In so doing, they addressed directly the problem of how to conceptualize and explain the fact that production relations established in the colonies took the form of unfree labour (e.g. slave labour, indentured labour, sharecropping etc.) at the same time that wage labour was becoming predominant in Europe. They were therefore able to explain the historical fact, recognized by Marx, that the sugar and cotton, produced under unfree relations of production from the late seventeenth century onwards in the Americas, were increasingly processed by a combination of machinery and wage labour under factory conditions in Europe.

Additionally, the historical record demonstrates that the coexistence of forms of unfree labour, particularly to produce commodities for sale on the world market, with the development of capitalist relations of production was confined neither to the early colonial period nor to the colonial context (see Corrigan 1977; Long 1984: 2–17). This requires illustration. In the former case there is a variety of instances where, during the nineteenth century, on the one hand, the abolition of slavery did not immediately give way to wage labour but was replaced with a form of indentured labour (as in the Caribbean), and on the other, new or recent colonial settlement was followed by the partial introduction of unfree relations of production (for example, the use of indentured labour in Queensland). The case of Southern Africa is perhaps the most obvious. Colonization had been followed by the slow development of agricultural production for subsistence, although there were limited attempts at commodity production for the world market. But with the discovery of diamonds and gold, production for the world market became the imperative. As a result, the indigenous populations were forced to make their labour power available, and the consequent relations of direct domination were perpetuated in order to maintain that supply (e.g. van Onselen 1976; Levy 1982).

The parallel persistence of unfree and free relations of production was not only a dimension of the link between Europe and the colonial system. It was also evident within Europe. Within Britain, there were counter-tendencies to the spread of wage labour throughout the economy in the eighteenth and nineteenth centuries. It was not only that non-capitalist relations of production seemed resistant to transformation into relations between owners of capital and wage labourers, as in the case of serfdom in the Scottish coal industry (Ashton and Sykes 1964: 70–83; Duckham 1970: 240–53), but also that non-wage relations were extended, as in the case of the persistence (Hecht 1956: 1–34; Horn 1975: 1–13) and then increase (McBride 1976: 13–15) in domestic servitude in the nineteenth century.

Before it is concluded that these are trivial or minor instances, it should be remembered that

> 'By 1901 [domestic servitude] was not only the major employer of women in the country, but, with a total labour force of nearly one and a half million persons, it formed the largest occupation grouping of any kind – bigger than mining, engineering or agriculture. In this *female* servants were numerically predominant.'
>   (Horn 1975: 13; see also McBride 76: 14; Davidoff 1974: 409–10)

More recently there is the case of contract labour migration into Western Europe. A large majority of these migrants lack important civil and political rights despite having become permanent settlers (e.g. Thomas 1982a). As Corrigan has argued convincingly (1977), these unfree relations of production cannot be explained as 'feudal relics', as if they were like flotsam deposited by chance on the beach at high tide. The prevalence, scale, and longevity of unfree relations of production, and their apparent interdependence with free wage labour, require a positive explanation.

Similarly, it is necessary to explain the continued significance of unpaid labour in the household unit in social formations dominated by the capitalist mode of production. Domestic production, carried out largely by women, is essential to the reproduction of labourers and the production of new labourers who sell their labour power for a wage, and is therefore integral to the reproduction of the capitalist mode of production (e.g. Molyneux 1979). There are certain similarities between this process and the role that peasant production continues to play in many parts of the world in not only producing commodities for sale on a market, but also reproducing labourers who regularly or occasionally enter the labour market and sell their labour power for a wage (Bennholdt-Thomsen 1981; Meillassoux 1980, 1981). In both cases non-capitalist relations of production sustain the reproduction of labour power as a commodity, indicating another limit to the spread of wage relations of production. These, too, require explanation, although I make no attempt to provide it here.

In sum, Marx's, and classical Marxist, analyses are limited in at least two major, interrelated respects. First, by focusing upon the development of the capital/wage labour relationship, and the consequent class struggles within Europe, the role of the colonial system in the formation and reproduction of those production relations was largely ignored, as were the socio-economic consequences for the parts of the world that constituted that colonial system. The increasingly commonplace assertion that classical Marxism is Eurocentric (e.g. Robinson 1983:2) is therefore not without some validity. Second, there was a virtual silence about both the nature of the relations of production outside Europe in the colonial system and about the survival and apparent reproduction of unfree relations of production even in the heartland of the capitalist mode of production. I now consider how certain post 1945 Marxist writers have responded to these problems of theoretical and historical analysis.

Beyond the transition debate

Their response has been shaped to a large extent by the post 1945 debate about the transition from feudalism to capitalism (Hilton *et al.* 1978; Medick 1981; Tribe 1981; Holton 1985; Aston and Philpin 1985) which has centred on a conceptual dispute about the essential features of capitalism and on a historical dispute about the explanation for the transition. The origin of this debate lies with the publication of Dobb's *Studies in the Development of Capitalism* (1963) which prompted an exchange between various writers (Hilton *et al.* 1978). The debate was renewed partly as a consequence of the formulation of *underdevelopment* theory (Frank 1971, 1978), to which there has been a wide-ranging critical response (e.g. Kay 1975; Taylor 1979; Laclau 1979; Warren 1980; Armstrong and McGhee 1985; 17–40). Wallerstein's work (1974; 1979; 1980; 1983) is both a defence and an extensive development of themes present in the work of Sweezy and Frank, and has been criticized by various writers (e.g. Brenner 1977; George 1980; Gülalp 1981) who reassert the central claims of Dobb's work, although not uncritically (Brenner 1978). The totality of this debate is not relevant here. For my purposes, it is necessary to consider only the interrelation between conflicting concepts of capitalism and reference to the idea of an internal or external disintegrative force in the transition (Medick 1981:125; Holton 1985:74–81), an interrelationship which leads us to the question of the relationship between capitalism and unfree labour.

Dobb followed Marx's conception of capitalism as a distinct mode of production characterized by the capital/wage labour relation (1963:7) and rejected the arguments that capitalism could be equated with any form of production for the sake of exchange, and that the transition to capitalism could be explained as the result of increased trade (1963:7, 26). Rather he claimed that there was a crisis within the feudal mode of production, beginning in the fourteenth century, which could not be resolved within the constraints of the existing relations of production (1963:20, 42–3). Dobb did not deny that the transition that resulted from this crisis was influenced by the growth of trade (1963:26, 38) but he did reject the view that the latter played an overriding, determinant role.

Sweezy's critique raised several issues (in Hilton *et al.* 1978:33–6, 46–51) but for our purpose, the most significant objection was to the argument that the primary impetus for the transition arose from processes which were internal to the feudal mode of production within England (in Hilton *et al.* 1978:40). This is one of the main threads which provides the link with the work of Frank and Wallerstein. Sweezy's emphasis upon trade (the *external* factor) is consistent with his claim that feudalism in Europe, although not static, contained no *internal* dynamic capable of stimulating a transition to capitalism. In a second contribution to the debate, Sweezy reformulated this *internal/external* dichotomy as follows:

> 'Historical factors which are external with respect to one set of social relations are internal with respect to a more comprehensive set of social relations. And so it was in the case of Western European feudalism. The expansion of trade, with the concomitant growth of towns and markets, was external to the feudal mode of production, but it was internal as far as the whole European-Mediterranean economy was concerned.'
>
> (in Hilton *et al.* 1978:105)

Sweezy subordinates the feudal mode of production to a wider and more inclusive economic object (the European-Mediterranean economy), creating a new unit of analysis which permits trade to be described as the *internal* factor. Thereby the feudal mode of production is said to be dependent upon this spatially defined economic unit. In this way Sweezy shifts the analytical object away from relations of production to processes of circulation and exchange, with the result that the sale and purchase of commodities become the determinant influence, and production relations are, at best, only of secondary significance.

Sweezy's identification of a 'more comprehensive set of social relations' is elaborated in Frank's work. In an early text (1971), Frank was concerned with the characterization of the societies of South America as either feudal or capitalist. Frank characterizes them as having been capitalist from the sixteenth century. He explains the transition to capitalism by reference to the geographical spread of a commercial network:

> 'until the entire face of the globe had been incorporated into a *single organic* mercantilist or mercantile capitalist and later also industrial and financial capitalist system whose metropolitan centre developed in Western Europe and then North America and whose peripheral satellites underdeveloped on all the remaining continents.'
>
> (1971:39)

This worldwide economic unit is defined as capitalist, and is analysed using the dichotomous categories of *metropolis/satellite* and *development/ underdevelopment*. Yet precisely what distinguishes it as capitalism is unclear (Laclau 1979:22; Brenner 1977:28–9) and, in so far as a definition can be derived from his work, he equates capitalism with commodity production for the market (Taylor 1979:88–9).

The concept of *mode of production* is deprived of existence in this early text by a denial that the nature of relations between owners and labourers constitutes the defining feature of feudalism or capitalism (1971:267) and so no attention is given to the nature of the relations of production. All that the reader is offered is an undefended claim that the concepts of *feudalism* and *capitalism* refer to distinct economic systems, and a suggestion that a feudal system is always *closed*, an echo of Sweezy's more complex claim about fifteenth-century Europe. And because Frank denies that South American societies were closed in this period, he rejects their designation as feudal and argues that they were the creation of 'a single merchant-capitalist system embracing . . . the world as whole' (1971:268). Thereby the concept of a *capitalist mode of production* is replaced by a concept of a *world capitalist system* made up of a complex hierarchy of metropolis/satellite relations which reproduce development and underdevelopment at each of the two poles respectively (1971:119, 268). Within this world capitalist system, the role of the satellite is as an export economy serving the metropolis, and any development is limited by this dependent role (1971:53, 85, 92).

Frank has responded to his critics in various places (e.g. 1978a:xii–xiii; 1978b:238–59), but the main object in his analytical framework remains the world capitalist system or, more specifically, the process of accumulation on a world scale. He has periodized this process into three phases and for each phase has analysed the effects on the relations of production in the satellite (1978a:xi, 6). The *internal/external* distinction is discussed (1978a:2–11) and he refers to both the internal dynamics of world capitalist accumulation (1978a:6) and to the colonies' internal production and external exchange relations (1978a:2–3), but without any clear consequence. Elsewhere he argues that the question of internality or externality is irrelevant because there is only a single world capitalist system (1978b:252–53). Moreover Frank has continued to avoid offering a formal definition of capitalism and yet has denied that the presence or absence of wage labour is the crucial criterion by which to identify the capitalist system (1978b: 250). He repeats that his principal objective is to explain underdevelopment in the periphery (1978a: 20).

In sum, apart from a new concern with production relations in the periphery, there are no concessions to his critics. Frank continues to argue that the capitalist world economy has been in existence since the sixteenth century and his primary analytical interest remains with the trade patterns and international division of labour within that system. Concerning the transition, Frank has little to say. Where he does consider it (e.g. 1978b: 239–48), and following his implicit conception of capitalism as production for exchange and of capitalism as a world system, the transition problem tends to be reduced to the origin and development of the world market and world trade. Frank concludes by making a virtue out of uncertainty: 'The question of when and how original precapitalist, primitive accumulation of capital became (the starting point of) the capitalist process of capital accumulation remains substantially open' (1978b: 245).

Capitalism as a world economy

Wallerstein explicitly identifies with the tradition established by Sweezy and developed by Frank, although this is often ignored by commentators who consequently overestimate the theoretical originality of Wallerstein's work (e.g. Ragin and Chirot 1984). He defends Frank (Wallerstein 1974: 126–27; 1979: 7–10) against Laclau's (1979) critique and claims:

> 'I believe both Sweezy and Frank better follow the spirit of Marx if not his letter and that, leaving Marx quite out of the picture, they bring us nearer to an understanding of what actually happened than do their opponents.'
> (Wallerstein 1979: 9)

Wallerstein, like Sweezy and Frank, cites passages in Marx's *Capital* (volume 3) concerning the disintegrative influence of merchant's capital in order to support the view that his conception of capitalism follows that of Marx but, as we shall see, elsewhere he explicitly rejects Marx's concept. Moreover the above quotation indicates that Wallerstein rejects certain key analytical distinctions employed by Marx because they do not assist historical explanation. Thus although it is easy to demonstrate that Wallerstein's concept of capitalism (like that of Sweezy and Frank) is different from that employed by Marx (e.g. Gülalp 1981), this does not address the real challenge posed by Wallerstein, namely his claim that his theoretical framework better explains the historical development of capitalism than the critics of Sweezy and Frank. And, in doing so, his analysis directly addresses the silences and limits identified in the preceding section, and consequently transcends both Marx and the transition debate as previously understood.

Wallerstein's self-defined task is to analyze capitalism as 'an historical system, over the whole of its history and in concrete unique reality' (1983: 7). His conception of capitalism follows from his rejection of the individual society or nation-state as the unit of analysis. Emulating Sweezy's and Frank's references to a supranational economic unit, Wallerstein's alternative object of analysis is the *social system*:

> 'What characterises a social system in my view is the fact that life within it is largely self-contained, and that the dynamics of its development are largely internal.'
>
> (1974: 347)

He claims that for most of human history the social system has taken the form of a *world system* (1974: 7; 1979: 156). Of the two forms of world system identified by Wallerstein, the *world empire* and the *world economy*, it is to the latter that he devotes most attention. He describes a world economy as having a single division of labour, a multiplicity of cultural groups, and an absence of a centralized political authority. In the absence of a political mechanism to distribute the economic production within the system, this task is said to be undertaken by the market (1979: 5–6, 156–61). Significantly Wallerstein concludes that 'Capitalism and a world-economy . . . are obverse sides of the same coin. One does not cause the other. We are merely defining the same indivisible phenomenon by different characteristics' (1979: 6). The capitalist world economy is characterized by

> 'production for sale in a market in which the object is to realise the maximum profit. In such a system production is constantly expanded as long as further production is profitable, and men constantly innovate new ways of producing things that will expand the profit margin.'
>
> (1979: 15; see also p. 120)

Thus for Wallerstein capitalism exists when production takes place for the purpose of exchange and when profit is realized for the purpose of capital accumulation and, hence, for the continuing self-expansion of the system.

Wallerstein is less consistent in identifying capitalism as a mode of production (compare 1979: 16, 66 with 1979: 140ff). His references are formal and are subordinate to the primary requirement that production be for the purpose of exchange, from which it follows that *how* commodities are produced (the mode of *production*) is of secondary analytical interest. This is confirmed when he argues that a mode of production is capitalist when 'production is for exchange; that is, it is determined by its profitability on a market, a market in which each buyer wishes to buy cheap . . . but in which each seller wishes to sell dear' (1979: 159). This refusal to consider the specific nature of the *relations of production* as an essential, defining feature of capitalism is purposive. Indeed he denies, like Frank, that the presence or absence of a particular set of production relations, i.e. wage labour, is a defining characteristic of capitalism (1979: 17, 218). Rather he argues that capitalism

> 'is a mode of production that combines proletarian labour and commercialised land with other forms of wage payment and land ownership. The existence of non-proletarianised labour and non-commercialised land is quite essential for the optimisation of opportunities for overall profit in a capitalist world market for several reasons.'
>
> (1979: 147–48)

And, as if to remove all doubt, he continues: 'it is the combination of free and 'unfree' labour and land that in fact characterises the capitalist world-economy' (1979: 149).

Thus when Wallerstein discusses the development of a division of labour within the emergent capitalist world economy between 1450 and 1640 (1974: Chapter 2), he emphasizes the co-ordination of slave, serf, and wage labour, along with tenant farming, in a single capitalist system. These are all considered to be proletarian positions, and the various legal apparatuses and forces of production that accompany these relations of production are defined as capitalist. For example, slave owners are defined as capitalist because they supplied the world market and he characterizes slavery as 'a capitalist institution, geared to the early preindustrial stages of a capitalist world-economy' (1974: 88). Similarly he defines the hacienda in Spanish America as a capitalist institution because it supplied the world market (1980: 147–56).

These different forms of capitalist exploitation are considered to be economically and spatially ordered into a hierarchical relationship. Elaborating on the metropolis/satellite distinction, Wallerstein conceives the capitalist world-economy to be divided into three zones: *core, semi-periphery*, and *periphery*. These different zones are distinguished by different forms of labour exploitation: 'The division of a world-economy involves a hierarchy of occupational tasks, in which tasks requiring higher levels of skill and greater capitalisation are reserved for higher-ranking areas' (1974: 350).

Within each of these regions of the world economy, labourers in various guises are exploited by capitalists in various guises and, additionally and following Frank, the core region appropriates a surplus from the periphery (1979: 18–19, 293). Thus Wallerstein considers the capitalist world economy by 1640 to have consisted of north-west Europe as the core area, specializing in agricultural production involving high levels of skill and utilizing wage labour and forms of tenant farming; the Mediterranean as the semi-periphery, specializing in high-cost industrial products and using share-cropping as the predominant means of labour exploitation; and eastern Europe and part of the Americas as the periphery, producing grain, bullion, cotton, wood, and sugar for export, using slave and cash-crop labour (1979: 18, 21–3, 38–9). He claims that this spatial division of labour is synonymous with an 'ethnic' division of labour, the latter being distinct from class divisions (1974: 87, 351; 1979: 24, 196, 200–1; 1983: 76).

Wallerstein distinguishes between these divisions of the world economy as necessary structural positions and the particular nation-states that might occupy each position at any single point in time. Over time, the composition of the core changes, along with the relationship between the different nation-states which constitute the core (1980: 8–9, 179, 241). The bulk of Wallerstein's historical analysis (1974, 1980) describes the formation and changing composition of core, semi-periphery, and periphery between the fifteenth and mid-eighteenth centuries. Consequently the emphasis is upon the changing patterns of trade and inter-state rivalry and warfare.

Wallerstein's explanation for the existence of different forms of labour exploitation at different spatial and economic positions in the capitalist world economy follows from his assertion that, throughout the history of capitalism, the total number of people who have become fully proletarianized is small relative to the total number of people whose work is nevertheless part of the process of capital accumulation, but who are not rewarded with a wage. In other words, what requires explanation is not proletarianization, but its relative absence. The argument is that, other things being equal, capital benefits most where the proletarian is a member of a household unit which is able to generate at least part of its total means of subsistence. The consequence is that the proletarian is paid a wage which is lower than where the household unit has no additional source of 'income'. In the latter circumstance, wages must be higher, so increasing costs and reducing profits (1983: 27).

This argument suggests that capital has a permanent interest in obstructing full proletarianization in favour of maintaining the conditions which permit members of households to engage in various forms of subsistence production by means other than the sale of labour power. Having acknowledged this, Wallerstein explains that capitalism develops by means of alternating periods of expansion and contraction, and that in periods of crisis, groups of workers have attempted to improve their material circumstances by increasing their wages and withdrawing from other forms of production. Certain capitalists, believing that they might gain advantages over competitors, have conceded to such initiatives and have furthered the proletarianization of their workforces. This, Wallerstein notes, would in the absence of any counter-tendency reduce profits further. However capitalism is a self-expanding system, incorporationg new zones within its framework as a world system, so that the increased costs of labour in the core can be offset by the inclusion of new groups of labourers who are only partially proletarianized (1983: 34–9).

Finally, Wallerstein does offer an explanation for the emergence of the capitalist world economy. He describes fourteenth-century Europe as feudal and therefore has to explain the transition to capitalism. His argument is that during the fourteenth century, feudalism entered a period of crisis which continued into the fifteenth century, out of which emerged the capitalist world economy between 1450 and 1640 (1974: 15–37, 67). For Wallerstein, this was not a revolutionary transformation in any political sense. Rather

> 'the modern world-system took the form of a capitalist world-economy that had its genesis in Europe in the long sixteenth century and that involved the *transformation* of a particular redistributive or tributary mode of production, that of feudal Europe . . . into a qualitatively different social system.'
>
> (1980:7–8)

The feudal ruling class, facing peasant revolt, declining real income, and intra-class warfare, opted for a different form of exploitation:

> 'there was a sort of creative leap of imagination on the part of the ruling strata. It involved trying an alternative mode of surplus appropriation, that of the market, to see whether it might serve to restore the declining real income of the ruling groups. This involved geographical expansion, spatial economic specialisation, the rise of the 'absolutist' state – in short, the creation of a capitalist world-economy.
>
> (1979:161; see also 1980:31; 1983:105–6)

Thus Wallerstein returns to the transition debate, but only to transform it in a manner which is consistent with his conception of the nature of capitalism.

'The periphery was peripheral'?

Wallerstein's theoretical and historical analysis offers an account of an explanation for the relationship between Western Europe and the colonial system, and of the survival and reproduction of unfree relations of production. But although he articulates Marx's silences, Wallerstein's resolution of these problems is itself highly problematic. In this section I review and expand upon the critical response to Wallerstein.

I begin with theoretical problems. First, Wallerstein rejects Marx's view that the origin of the capitalist mode of production is to be found in the origin of wage labour (Brenner 1977:31–3). In rejecting this, Wallerstein is not only rejecting Marx's formal definition of capitalism as a mode of production, but also Marx's understanding of the inner nature and dynamic of the capitalist mode of production, grounded as it is in the hidden appropriation of surplus value by means of the wage form and the transformation of that surplus into new capital which then confronts the worker as an even greater power. As I have already shown, the specific character of the relations of production (i.e. the capital/wage labour relationship) are, for Marx, an essential feature of the capitalist mode of production. A number of additional theoretical problems arise from Wallerstein's rejection of this conception (e.g. Brenner 1977:31–3, 61, 66–7; DuPlessis 1977:33).

Wallerstein's rejection of the capital/wage labour relation as an essential feature of the capitalist mode of production is a specific aspect of his more general rejection of Marx's conception that the social relations of production constitute an essential and determining feature of any mode of production (Skocpol 1977:1079; Hunt 1978:60; George 1980:91). It follows that Wallerstein does not locate the 'prime mover' within a mode of production at the level of class relations, but in market processes, which are viewed, in turn, as the direct expression of ruling class interests (Skocpol 1977:1079–81; DuPlessiss 1977:32–3). The dynamic element is located in the sphere of circulation, and not production. DuPlessiss comments:

> 'What Wallerstein has done is to describe the formation of a greatly enlarged trading unit; he shows the transition from one market system to another. . . . The world system outlined by Wallerstein was a commercial network, more sizeable than but not yet fundamentally different from earlier world systems found around the Mediterranean and in northern Europe.'
>
> (1977:37–8)

Second, Wallerstein's conception of a structural tendency within capitalism which discourages proletarianization and which sustains a combination of wage and non-wage forms of labour exploitation suggests a failure to understand, or even a rejection of, Marx's understanding of the operation of the law of value in relation to the price of labour power. This is evident in various versions of the underdevelopment thesis (Kay 1975:50–5). Considered in relation to capital in general, it does not follow that an increase in wages necessarily leads to an increase in the costs of production and a decrease in profit.

The worker receives a wage from the value created by the combination of labour power with the means of production owned by the capitalist. The proportion of the value thereby created which is returned to the worker in the form of wages has its lower limit set by the cost of the reproduction of the worker (Marx 1976:655). The 'secret' of capitalist production is that the worker produces value which is greater than that required to ensure the reproduction of labour power. It is from this total surplus value that capital is accumulated and profits are distributed. Therefore what matters is whether or not an increase in wages is accompanied by an increase in the total value created in the course of the utilization of labour power. Ordinarily such an increase can be obtained by combining labour power with a greater quantity of constant capital, thus increasing the value equivalent to the cost of labour power in a shorter period of time:

> 'Increased productivity and greater intensity of labour both have a similar effect. They both augment the mass of articles produced in a given time. Both therefore shorten the portion of the working day which the worker needs to produce his means of subsistence or their equivalent.'
>
> (Marx 1976:666–67)

In such circumstances, the capitalist can potentially realize an increased quantity of surplus value, despite having to pay a higher nominal wage and to devote a greater proportion of capital to its constant component.

For Marx, as previously indicated, this is part of the dynamic of the capital accumulation process, such that constant capital increases in magnitude relative to variable capital. Although this is an uneven process (see Chapter 9), Marx argues that the overall process of accumulation ensures that an increasing proportion of a population becomes proletarianized:

> 'As simple reproduction constantly reproduces the capital-relation itself, i.e. the presence of capitalists on the one side, and wage-labourers on the other side, so reproduction on an expanded scale, i.e. accumulation, reproduces the capital-relation on an expanded scale, with more capitalists, or bigger capitalists, at one pole, and more wage-labourers at the other pole.'
>
> (1976: 763)

Thus Marx's conception of the accumulation process leads him to identify a structural tendency for an absolute increase in the size of the proletariat.

But what is true for capital as a whole is not necessarily the case for individual units of capital in all historical circumstances. Noting Marx's insistence that the determination of wages depends upon changes in the relative magnitudes of surplus value and the price of labour power (1976: 683) and that the relative magnitudes of these two elements vary according to the length of the working day, the intensity of labour and the productivity of labour, it follows that

> 'Very different combinations are clearly possible, since one of the three factors can be constant, while the other two vary, two factors may be constant while one varies, and finally, all three may vary. In addition, the number of possible combinations is augmented by the fact that, when all these factors vary simultaneously, the amount and direction of their respective variations may differ.'
>
> (1976: 655–56)

The complexity can be magnified by considering the impact of the two additional variables that Marx intentionally ignored, the varying cost of developing labour power and the 'natural diversity of labour-power' (1976: 655).

For individual units of capital, the interrelation between the level of wages and the level of surplus value (from which profit is derived) is therefore historically variable and can only be determined by empirical investigation. Thus one can envisage circumstances where an individual capitalist can gain an advantage over others by employing workers whose subsistence is partially met by family production, and to whom a lower wage can be paid as a result. Other things remaining equal, an increased surplus would be realized from the exploitation of labour power in such circumstances. The analytical task is to determine the specific historical circumstances in which this happens. But for Marx this could never be a general tendency because of the interrelationship between the accumulation process and the law of value, an interrelationship which ensured an increasing level of proletarianization.

More specifically, but on the same theme, Wallerstein's argument about partial proletarianization is contradictory. He claims that in periods of stagnation, some employers initiate a full proletarianization of a part of their workforce in an attempt to gain an advantage over others (1983: 37). But if Wallerstein's claim that full proletarianization necessarily means an increase in wages and a fall in profit is correct, there can be no advantage to be gained from such an action, especially in a period of stagnation.

Third, for Marx the process of proletarianization involved not only the commodification of labour power, but also the creation of a market for commodity consumption. This was necessitated by two things. First, it is by means of a wage that the labourer can purchase the means of subsistence and reproduction. Second, it is only in the process of commodity circulation and exchange that surplus value can be realized in a money form, after which it can be transformed into capital to sustain a new phase of production and accumulation. Thus although wages can be reduced if subsistence partially originates in a non-commodity form, this restricts the size of the market, and therefore sets limits to commodity production and the realization of a surplus. The dynamic of capital accumulation and increased commodity production therefore necessitate a constantly expanding market (the development of which Wallerstein documents), a process that sustains the tendency towards universal proletarianization.

There are also historical objections to Wallerstein's analysis. Inevitably, given the scope of his analysis, there are criticisms concerning his selective use of the historical record (Kellenbenz 1976; Janowitz 1977: 1094; George 1980: 87–8; Stinchcombe 1982: 1391). More serious are those criticisms which suggest that Wallerstein's interpretation of at least some of the evidence is mistaken and that his theoretical claims are therefore contradicted empirically (e.g. Zolberg 1981b). For example it has been argued that the historical evidence suggests the existence of a trade-based world system, in which there was a redistribution of surplus between core and periphery, prior to the development of what Wallerstein calls the capitalist world system (Schneider 1977: 25).

In addition several writers have focused on Wallerstein's explanation of the 'second serfdom' in eastern Europe, which he interprets as evidence of the enlargement of the capitalist world economy through the incorporation of eastern Europe and the utilization of unfree relations of production as the most efficient method of producing and directing a surplus from periphery to core (1974: 304–5). It has been argued that enserfment and the growth of trade in grain cannot be causally linked in the way that is vital to support Wallerstein's thesis because the former was under way long before the latter (Skocpol 1977: 1082; Hunt 1978: 53–9; Brenner 1976). More generally, Anderson has concluded:

'We have seen that the pull of the more advanced Western economy on the East has often been exaggerated in this epoch, as the sole or main force for the manorial reaction there. . . . Any wholesale integration of Eastern Europe into a Western European circuit . . . is thus inherently implausible.'

(1979: 196–97)

Historical evidence also questions one of the central claims of 'underdevelopment' theory, and of Wallerstein's work in particular, concerning the transfer of surplus from periphery to core. Wallerstein (1979: 18–19) along with Frank (1978: 255–57), claims that commerce with, and production in, the periphery realized large surpluses which were accumulated in the core and utilized in such a way as to advance capitalist development there. In other words, profits gained from the colonial system were a major component in the process of primitive accumulation in Western Europe.

O'Brien (1982) argues that these writers do not provide adequate evidence to sustain their claims. Moreover, his own attempt at verification does not amount to unqualified support. In particular he shows that trade between core and periphery was on a very small scale between 1450 and 1750, and that for Britain for the period 1781–1850, and assuming the most positive interpretation, only about 15 per cent of capital investment originated from the periphery (1982: 3–7). This, together with additional evidence, leads O'Brien to conclude:

'Except for a restricted range of examples, growth, stagnation, and decay everywhere in Western Europe can be explained mainly by reference to endogenous forces. The "world economy", such as it was, hardly impinged. If these speculations are correct, then for the economic growth of the core, the periphery was peripheral.'

(1982: 18)

De Vries, too, contextualizes colonial trade and concludes, first, that certain intra-European trade routes were more significant than trade between periphery and core; second, that monopolistic trading companies often failed to realize a surplus; and third, that any expansionary effect was not automatic but depended upon conditions within the European social formations (1976: 141, 145).

I draw two conclusions. First, Wallerstein's conception of the nature of capitalism departs from that of Marx, from which follows a different interpretation of the essential processes and dynamics of capitalism. This would not be so problematic if, second, key arguments of Wallerstein were not contradicted by the historical evidence. But these conclusions do not, by themselves, resolve the problems arising from Marx's analysis which were identified in the opening section of this chapter. In particular there remains the problem of explaining the historical reproduction of non-wage/unfree relations of production since the seventeenth century both in those parts of the world which were influenced by and connected with the development of capitalism in Western Europe as well as within Western Europe (and within parts of the world where capitalism was to develop subsequently). For Wallerstein, this is neither theoretically nor historically problematic because he defines the combination of wage and non-wage relations of production as an essential feature of the capitalist world economy. But if we reject Wallerstein's theory, we are left to formulate an alternative explanation for the maintenance and reproduction of unfree relations of production in parallel with free/wage relations of production, and one which does not contradict Marx's conception of capitalism as a mode of production.

In seeking to formulate an explanation, I wish to retain one important emphasis in Wallerstein's theory. His historical evidence and theoretical conception of the nature of capitalism suggest that, even if we define unfree labour as antithetical to the capitalist mode of production, its widespread occurrence might be explained as being somehow historically *interdependent* with or *contingent* upon the capitalist mode of production. I have already argued that this interpretation is evident in Marx's writing. An analysis of that interdependence might then demonstrate an affinity of production and/or exchange relations which in turn exposes the historical and material conditions for the formation and reproduction of the capitalist mode of production. In other words, the capitalist mode of production may depend on unfree relations of production because its existence is always historically and materially specific.

Mode of production and unfree labour

Attempts to theorize the articulation of modes of production are grounded in a simultaneous concern with the nature of capitalism and of its international, historical development, and they offer a theoretical approach which is distinct from that offered by Frank and Wallerstein. An analysis using a conception of *articulation of modes of production* permits the rejection, on theoretical and historical grounds, of the claim that a capitalist world system had been established by 1640. It accepts the historical evidence that a system of world trade existed by the mid-seventeenth century (De Vries 1976: 113), but it argues that this system was limited in scope and was not synonymous with the existence of a capitalist mode of production. The latter, following Marx, was emergent, initially in England from the seventeenth century. It follows that the theoretical and historical task is to explain and document the effects of the development of this mode of production in Western Europe not only on other modes of production in Western Europe but also elsewhere in the world. The problem is, therefore, fundamental to all analysis of capitalist development as long as we assume a distinction between the concepts of *social formation* and *mode of production* (Taylor 1979: 105–42; Wolpe 1980: 19–27, 34–42; Armstrong and McGhee 1985: 28–9) and between *economic system* and *mode of production* (Laclau 1979: 42–3).

These distinctions are central to the historical analysis in Part 2. The concept of *social formation* refers to a particular combination of economic, political, and ideological relations and practices (cf. Taylor 1979: 106–07; Fine and Harris 1979: 12–15). The boundary of any social formation is set by the socio-spatial limits of the exercise of power by the dominant class or class fraction. Historically, even before the emergence of the capitalist mode of production, the state became the main instrument by which political domination was achieved and maintained within each boundary. This historical development is synonymous with the emergence of the nation-state as a political unit and with the gradual division of the world into nation-states, each of which constitutes, to varying degrees, a distinct cultural unit. Within each, political power is exercised and political domination is achieved through various specific mechanisms which have a distinct cultural content e.g. language, symbols, myths of origin, etc. Thus the formation and reproduction of a state is both a legal/political and an ideological process.

Within the spatial limits of each social formation (and this has become increasingly synonymous with state formation) different modes of production may coexist, sustaining an often complex combination of classes. The concept of *economic system* refers to this combination of different modes of production within a single social formation, but also to the interrelation of modes of production located within different social formations. Such an interrelation has become simultaneously economic and political because of the key role of the state within each social formation. The development of trade has been an integral part of the development of social formations as nation-states and of establishing and sustaining an articulation of modes of production in different social formations. Historically, the initiatory role of merchant's capital has been transcended by the formation of industrial capital which has increasingly organized production on a scale to supply and extend this world market.

Using these distinctions, we need not assume that the emergence of the capitalist mode of production is synonymous with the abolition or transformation of other extant modes of production within either a social formation or an economic system (e.g. Bradby 1975; Hall 1980: 320). Hence the problem is to determine the effects of the capitalist mode of production (which includes the capital/wage labour relation), and its reproduction, upon relations and forces of production within the same social formation as well as relations and forces of production in other social formations. Moreover the particular relations and forces of production in those other social formations will influence the effectivity of the capitalist mode of production (Bradby 1975: 152–53). It follows that the concept of *articulation* can be used to refer to

'the relationship between the reproduction of the capitalist economy on the one hand and the reproduction of productive units according to pre-capitalist relations and forces of production on the other.' (Wolpe 1980: 41)

The process of articulation should not be assumed to be determined by the reproduction of the capitalist mode as if it had a universal and timeless 'demand' or 'need' or as if it is necessarily predominant. Such analyses are functionalist and displace the role of human beings as creators and transformers of the material and social world. The maintenance or disintegration of non-capitalist modes must be analysed in part as the 'effect of the struggle of agents organised under differentiated relations and forces of production' (Wolpe 1980: 40). The assumptions of this perspective create the analytical space within which to take account of, for example, the reaction of 'agents' in non-capitalist modes of production, and to the struggles that may result from that reaction. Such struggles may lead to the prevention or partial obstruction of the introduction of capitalist relations and forces of production. These assumptions point again to the importance of the historical analysis of specific conjunctures.

The value of the concept of modes of production is not only that it is consistent with Marx's fragmentary comments on the interrelation between distinct modes of production. Of greater significance is that it offers a theoretical framework within which one can begin to explain the maintenance and reproduction of unfree relations of production. This is because if it is possible to explain why and how non-capitalist modes of production are conserved within a social formation or economic system, within which a capitalist mode exists and/or dominates, one can then explain the continued existence of unfree relations of production. The reproduction of non-capitalist modes of production involves the reproduction of unfree relations of production and so the analytical task is to trace the nature of and the reasons for the articulation with the capitalist mode of production. If the explanation requires an analysis of class struggle, and not simply of economic interests, then it follows that there is an element of historical contingency involved in such an explanation.

It is in relation to this point that Corrigan's schematic analysis of unfree labour (1977) is susceptible to criticism. An explanation for the reproduction of unfree relations of production within the framework of an analysis of the articulation of modes of production can accept his central claim that unfree labour is not a feudal relic but it leads to reservations about his view that unfree labour is 'part of the essential relations of production' (1977: 438) and/or is one of the 'specific effects of capitalism's expansion' (1977: 441). These reservations are intensified by his reference to capitalism being a 'world-market phenomenon' (1977: 441) which suggests the acceptance of the Sweezy/Frank/Wallerstein conception of the essential features of capitalism, an interpretation which is sustained by the absence of any reference to capitalism as a mode of production.

Corrigan's suggestion that unfree labour is an essential feature of capitalism is an *a priori* and ahistorical resolution of the problem that he has correctly identified. It is *a priori* because he offers no explanation for unfree labour being a necessary feature of capitalist production relations and it is ahistorical because the circumstances of capitalist expansion are not specified. If the reproduction of non-wage/unfree relations of production are *conceptualized* within the idea of articulation of modes of production, it is necessary to offer a *historical* explanation for that reproduction, from which it might be concluded that the reproduction of such relations of production are, given certain material circumstances and the balance of class forces, historically necessary for the reproduction of the capitalist mode of production.

In moving towards the historical analysis in Part 2, a reservation concerning its scope is necessary. Following Marx, the relations of production are not the only constituent feature of a mode of production because the latter has been defined as a complex of forces and relations of production (see Chapter 1 and Laclau 1979: 34). My specific concern is to seek an explanation for the continued existence of unfree relations of production in economic systems and social formations influenced or dominated by the capitalist mode of production and not to advance a theory of articulation of modes of production. The focus of the historical analysis will be primarily upon the relations of production, and hence I make no claim to offer a complete analysis of either distinct modes of production or of articulation. Arising in part from the work of French Marxist anthropologists on Africa (for an overview, see Seddon 1978; Van Binsbergen and Geschiere 1985: 1–38), there is now a substantial literature on these topics which focuses specifically on Africa (e.g. Crummey and Stewart 1981; Coquery-Vidrovitch 1985; Van Binsbergen and Geshiere 1985) but also extends beyond it (e.g. Hindess and Hirst 1975; Wolpe 1980; Meillassoux 1981).

My use of the concept of *articulation* of modes of production is as a general heuristic, analytical device because it provides a conceptual framework which contains a distinction between different relations of production within a social formation or economic system and, following Marx, a conception of a combination and hierarchical interdependence of, and transaction between, modes of production. It is acknowledged that the wider significance of the conclusions of this analysis depends on establishing and sustaining the validity of the distinctions between modes of production and of their articulation (see Banerjee 1985).

This reservation ensures that I avoid the error, noted by Banaji, of identifying a distinct mode of production by the simple presence of a particular set of relations of production (1977: 5–9, 11). To sustain his case, Banaji points out that wage labour has been present in various different forms of social production before the capitalist 'epoch' (1977: 6), with the consequence that capitalist production cannot be equated with the mere presence of wage labour. This echoes Wallerstein's historical observation concerning the simultaneous and sustained coexistence of distinct relations of production, from which he, too, concludes that modes of production cannot be 'read off' from the formal existence of particular relations of production, although his reasoning and conclusion are rather different from that of Banaji.

But if Banaji's argument is correct, his conclusion that the relations of production are of no relevance in the determination of the character of modes of production is certainly contrary to the view taken by Marx (Wolpe 1980: 33–4). Following Marx, the capitalist mode of production is characterized by a particular combination of forces and relations of production (of which the capital/wage labour relation is an essential, constitutive feature) and by the existence of generalized commodity production. Wage labour can exist within any given social formation or economic system without the additional, associated relations and forces of production dominating economic and social relations within that formation or system. What remains problematic is to determine the criteria by which one can decide whether or not a capitalist mode of production dominates over other modes of production. This involves determining not only the point at which wage relations of production have been sufficiently generalized but also the point at which commodity production as a whole (and other essential features of the capitalist mode) has been sufficiently generalized.

Nevertheless there is a good theoretical reason for an emphasis upon the relations of production. As I have shown, Marx argued that the nature of the means by which a surplus is obtained has a determinant but dialectical relationship with class formation and class struggle, and with the nature and role of the state. Distinct relations of production therefore sustain distinct patterns of political and ideological relations. It follows that by distinguishing between the predominance of either free or unfree relations of production, one distinguishes between correspondingly distinct social formations. This is not because the 'economic base' determines the 'social superstructure' but because the mode of production is simultaneously a means of material and cultural reproduction; the relations of production include not only a process of surplus appropriation (exploitation) but also a whole complex of political and ideological relations which constitute essential moments in the conditions for, and reproduction of, the class relations established by the mode(s) of exploitation.

Thus in prioritizing the relations of production, one is not prioritizing 'economics' over 'politics' but rather the complex of economic, political, and ideological relations essential to the (re)production of a particular form of surplus appropriation in any particular historical context. One should expect that complex to show distinct patterns of variation according to the free or unfree nature of the relations of production. The objective here is to seek a historical explanation for the reproduction of unfree relations of production in the context of a spread of capitalist relations of production both within social formations and as a component part of the formation of a world economic system.

Conclusion

If capitalism is understood as a mode of production, and if social relations of production between capital and wage labour are considered to be an essential feature of that mode of production, a historical explanation for the survival and reproduction of unfree relations of production concurrent with the spread of free wage labour within the world economic system is necessary. In seeking a historical explanation, a preliminary theoretical and conceptual framework is required, and the first three chapters have been preoccupied with its formulation. I have elaborated on Marx's contrast between free and unfree labour, drawing an additional distinction between *unfree non-wage labour* and *unfree wage labour*. I have also discussed the significance of the concepts of *primitive accumulation* and *articulation of modes of production*.

In Part 2 I offer a historical analysis of four instances of the coexistence of unfree labour with the development of capitalist relations of production. This historical analysis specifically recognizes that the development of the capitalist mode of production within the various social formations of Western Europe was interdependent with the growth of an international economic system which linked the social formations of Western Europe with those in other parts of the world. This colonial system was an arena not only for the circulation of commodities, but also for the production of commodities. But commodity production did not necessarily involve either the formation of capitalist relations of production or the elimination of non-capitalist relations of production at all locations of the developing world economic system, as we shall now see. In Part 3 I shall use the concepts identified in Part 1 to explain the historical regularities identified as a result of comparative historical analysis.

Part 2

Historical studies of unfree labour

'History' is not a determining force in its own right . . . mere inheritance of ideological and political forms is a necessary, but not a sufficient, explanation for their persistence, particularly in times of radical change in the structure of the ruling class. We have to discover how capital came to terms with the existing structure, and more importantly perhaps, what the forces were that lay behind its decision to do so.'

(Bozzoli 1981:211)

'The exiles transplanted to the United States send sums of money home every year as travelling expenses for those left behind. Every troop that emigrates one year draws another after it the next.'

(Marx 1976:862)

4

The Caribbean

Introduction

Although the history of involvement in the Caribbean of English (and, after the Act of Union of 1707 between England and Scotland, British – for the specificity of Scottish involvement, see Sheridan 1977) merchants and plantation owners is synonymous with the use of slave labour, this was not the only form of labour exploitation. Indeed, bearing in mind first that English involvement in the region began in the late sixteenth century; second, that production using slave labour only predominated from early eighteenth century; and third, that slave labour was abolished in the mid-nineteenth century; the temporal limits to the use of slave labour are clearly evident (cf. Mintz 1977:260). Because slave labour was preceded and superseded by other modes of labour exploitation, one has to explain the utilization of and the transition from different relations of production in the Caribbean, and this constitutes an important complexity in the analysis of British colonization of this region. Thus the main aim of this chapter is to document the historical variation in modes of labour exploitation in the British Caribbean.

European colonization

Spanish merchants and settlers were the first Europeans to arrive in the Caribbean, and the Spanish Crown laid claim to all the islands. Settlement was prompted by the discovery of gold and later sustained by successful attempts to grow sugar cane (Williams 1970:23–9). Given the economic, political, and ideological rivalries between the different European feudal ruling classes of the sixteenth century, Spanish activity in the Caribbean and the American continent was soon challenged (Dunn 1973:25, 289). Dutch merchants were present before the end of the sixteenth century, trading with the local population, and later raiding Spanish bullion ships. Dutch merchants also began the colonization of part of the north-east coast of South America (Scammell 1981:384–86). French merchants were attacking Spanish shipping and ports even earlier, while trade and settlement followed in the early seventeenth century, notably in St Kitts, Martinique, and Guadeloupe (Scammell 1981:438–40).

British intervention was motivated similarly by the prospect of capturing Spanish bullion ships and trade (Williams 1970:73–5; Davies 1974:24–31, 308–10). The activities of Drake and Hawkins in the late seventeenth century included piracy and an early attempt to participate in the commercial trade in Africans (Deerr 1950:268; Haring 1966:29–32; Dunn 1973:10). They were not the only pirates to benefit materially from robbery and pillage. Between 1585 and 1604 'the English captured over 1000 Spanish and Portuguese vessels, plundered many of other nationalities, and obtained prize goods worth about 15 per cent of the country's then imports' (Scammell 1981:471). These activities were often actively supported by the English monarchy (Haring 1966:31; Scammell 1981:465).

The Anglo-Spanish War of 1585–1604, of which piracy was a constituent element, concluded with the Spanish Crown and fleet unable to control the activities of European rivals in the Caribbean. The way was then open for the establishment of English and French settlements in the region, and for the Dutch to expand their trade (Dunn 1973:16). But this did not mean an end to the activities of the buccaneers whose numbers increased when a proportion of Cromwell's troops objected to the uncertainty and rigours of land cultivation and took to piracy, along with indentured servants fleeing bondage and ill-treatment (Haring 1966:79, 91). Their activities were legitimated by the office of the Governor of Jamaica who drew them into conflict with Dutch and Spanish commercial interests (Haring 1966:128, 142, 299), a policy that was to have negative consequences when it was decided in London that direct force was no longer necessary to gain concessions from the Spanish state. Thereafter, the buccaneers regarded all shipping in the Caribbean as potential sources of plunder, and English ships were also attacked before they were finally subdued in 1697 (Haring 1966:230–31, 266).

Thus early English intervention took the form of piracy and warfare. This was followed in the seventeenth century by settlement, a development that was bound up with continuing conflict with Spain (Davies 1974:36). St Kitts (jointly with the French), Barbados, Nevis, Antigua, and Monserrat were all settled between 1623 and 1632, while Jamaica was captured from the Spanish in 1655. Under the Treaty of Paris in 1763, the British state retained control over the islands of Dominica, Grenada, St Vincent, and Tobago which had been captured in the previous two years. War with Spain led to the capture of Trinidad by British forces in 1797, while Guiana was exclusively occupied from

1803. But Spanish, French, and Dutch merchant interests in the region remained. Within all these spheres of interest, a mode of production was established to produce agricultural crops (predominantly sugar, but also coffee, cotton, cocoa, and pimento) for sale in Europe. It is this shift from piracy to agricultural production for exchange that constitutes the first theme of this chapter.

It is clear that English colonization was not initially synonymous with large-scale sugar production using the labour power of Africans who had been forced into slavery. Rather

'To begin with, the peopling of the New World was a confused affair. Only after experiment and some failures were winning formulas evolved. In part this confusion sprang from inexperience, in part from the mixed purposes with which different interests approached and evaluated the new lands.'

(Davies 1974: 86)

During the reigns of James I and Charles I, some 30,000 people went to the Caribbean from the British Isles (Dunn 1973: 16). Those who went freely were motivated by the availability of land, but the earliest English settlers certainly did not arrive with clearly formulated plans to produce and sell sugar for a profit. By the end of the seventeenth century, however, plantation sugar production was becoming dominant throughout the Caribbean. There was, therefore, a transition from pioneer, subsistence production, through a period of diversification in agricultural production, to extensive monoculture of sugar (Sheridan 1974: 119). This transition involved a shift from subsistence production to commodity production, and a change in production relations.

Present amongst the early settlers were merchants or individuals from merchant families who considered the Caribbean to be an appropriate arena to which to extend their trading activities (Sheridan 1970: 11–12, 58–9). Many sought to establish estates using a labour force bound by the restrictions that characterized manorial or seignorial properties (Harlow 1926: 16), and they had sufficient wealth to meet the high costs involved (Davies 1974: 61, 86; Galenson 1981a: 6). Their intention therefore was to maintain relations of production that were being displaced in England as capitalist agriculture developed.

But the motivation for English settlement was not only economic. There were also political determinants. For the first two-thirds of the seventeenth century, the English state exported to the Caribbean its 'surplus population' (Jernegan 1931: 46–7; Smith 1947: 7; Sheridan 1974: 75–6). For example, an order was issued by the Council of State in 1656 for the apprehension of dangerous persons, vagrants, and idlers, and for their removal to the Americas (Haring 1966: 126). In turn these determinants of Caribbean migration had their origin in changing relations of production in English agriculture which involved dispossession and enclosure, and the creation of a section of the population with no access to the means of production (Mantoux 1961: 136–85; Dobb 1963: 124–25, 224–27). These changes were one part of a wider economic crisis that affected not only England (Hill 1969:73) but Europe more generally and which was a crucial period in the transition from feudalism to capitalism (Hobsbawm 1965). Additionally, political and religious conflicts led to voluntary migration on the part of people who therefore sought a new life elsewhere, although this was a more important motive for settlement on the North American mainland (Scammell 1981: 489–90).

The introduction of indentured labour

It was in Barbados that the shift to commodity production occurred first. Between 1627 and 1640, subsistence production gave way to the production of tobacco, cotton, and ginger (Harlow 1926:21). This was largely controlled by yeoman farmers using the labour power of other migrants from Europe (Sheridan 1970:26–32; 1974:131), recruited and retained under relations of indenture. Indentured labour was a form of servitude which was widely used in the Caribbean and on the American mainland (Smith, 1947; Galenson 1981a; Souden 1984). Indeed, the number of indentured European labourers crossing the Atlantic exceeded the number of Africans until the last quarter of the eighteenth century. Estimates of the total number of British migrants to North America and the Caribbean range from 380,000 to 500,000 between 1630 and 1700 (Souden 1984:21–2), a large proportion of whom were indentured migrants (Davies 1974:97). Between one-third and three-quarters of indentured migrants were male and a similar proportion were aged between 15 and 24 years (Galenson 1981a:23–33; Souden 1984:23). A large proportion seem to have been agricultural producers or labourers (Souden 1978:26–7).

Under the indenture system, an individual entered a legal contract which bound him or her to a master for a fixed number of years, usually four. The individual was obliged to make labour power available to the master who appropriated the total product of the labourer's labour power and who, in return, was responsible for the costs of transport, subsistence, and reproduction. At the termination of the contract, the labourer was provided with a small plot of land from which to produce subsistence, or with a quantity of sugar. The intending migrant would first enter a contract with an agent, usually a merchant shipowner, who upon arrival in the Americas would sell the contract, and hence the right to the individual's labour power, to the highest bidder. Alternatively, the migrant was allowed to travel on the understanding that a contract of indenture would be entered upon arrival, following which the new master would pay the cost of the passage (Harlow 1926:293; Smith 1947:16–22; Jernegan 1931:47; Galenson 1981b:447–48).

Formally, the individual was free to choose to sign a contract of indenture. In practice, the degree of choice was often circumscribed. The dispossessed peasantry were induced to sign by having been freed from access to the means of production and by the prospect of punishment for vagabondage (Rusche and Kirchheimer 1968: 59; Weisser 1979: 89–105). Moreover, when a merchant wished to ensure a full cargo, there was often resort to kidnapping (Rusche and Kirchheimer 1968: 58) which was well organized and widely practised, especially in English ports, from the 1650s, and continued for much of the seventeenth century, despite attempts by the state to prohibit it (Smith 1947: 52–6, 69–82; Jernegan 1931: 48–9).

The degree of compulsion was even greater in the case of convicted prisoners transported to the colonies under terms of indenture as punishment. People labelled by the English state as rogues and vagabonds were transported from 1619 (Gray 1941: 345; Smith 1947: 139–42) while those convicted for crimes for which the penalty was death were transported from the early seventeenth century (Shaw 1966: 23–4; Rusche and Kirchheimer 1968: 59). Additionally, an unknown number of military and political prisoners were transported to the American colonies, including Scots and Irish defeated during Cromwell's campaigns, and many of those involved in the unsuccessful rebellions of 1685, 1715, and 1745 (Gray 1941: 346; Smith 1947: 152, 162–64, 188–97).

Once having entered indentured servitude, the individual had limited freedom to act independently of the will of the master. Most fundamentally, the use of the individual's labour power was alienated to the master, in return for which the master was responsible for the provision of the means of subsistence. Hence in so far as the servant had no cash income or savings, there was no scope for the exercise of personal autonomy as a consumer. The master was free to sell the indenture to another, thereby transferring the right to the use of the individual's labour power (Jernegan 1931: 54; Smith 1947: 233). Additionally, the indentured servant could not marry without the master's consent (Galenson 1981b: 452) and could neither vote nor engage in trade. The master was entitled to use corporal punishment for a variety of offences. Yet servitude and dependence were not absolute. Servitude lasted for only a stipulated number of years and the individual was not owned as property and did not become a commodity. Moreover, the indentured servant did have the right of appeal to a court (Davies 1974: 107) and could hold property.

In so far as there was an incentive built into the system of indenture, it was not monetary but took the form of a grant of land, 10 acres in the case of Barbados (Dunn 1973: 52). Thus the long-term consequence of indentured migration for the character of colonization and for the nature of class relations was an expansion of the class of small-scale, independent producers. There seems not to have been any conscious intention of stimulating settlement in order to form a pool of labourers with only their labour power to sell, a feature of later phases of colonization (Marx 1976: 931–40). But there was a limit to the process of colonial settlement proceeding on this basis. Once all the workable land, relative to the techniques of production then available, had been disposed of, an indenture system which aimed to attract at least a proportion of self-elected migrants was likely to break down. Such a situation was reached in Barbados by the end of the 1630s (Dunn 1973:51; Sheridan 1974:81), although land remained available on St Kitts, Nevis, Antigua, and Monserrat.

For a number of reasons indentured labour was increasingly used by settlers organizing the production of tobacco on small farms. First, if the settlers brought to the Caribbean English institutions, law, and religion (Dunn 1973:46), then they were bringing with them a historical tradition which included unfree labour (Craton 1974:161). In English agriculture, the sale of labour power for a wage dated only from the early seventeenth century (Dobb 1963:125) while the production of textiles continued largely on the basis of the 'putting out' system and, therefore, was not dependent upon wage labour (Dobb 1963:138–43). The main supply of labour power in English agriculture up until the eighteenth century was provided by servants who were contracted for one year and lived in the master's house, receiving board and lodging. With modifications, this provided a model for landowners in the Caribbean (Galenson 1981a:5–10).

Moreover, despite the disappearance of serfdom in England in an earlier period, various other forms of unfreedom remain. A male head of household could sell his wife and children while a form of servitude called villeinage could be imposed on debtors and on individuals convicted for vagrancy and vagabondage who were unable to pay their fines (Handlin 1948:4–6). Additionally, the customs and laws regarding apprenticeship provided a precedent, for under them the apprentice received knowledge of a skill and subsistence from a master who, in return, had considerable rights and powers of control over the apprentice (Gray 1941:342). With wage labour barely in its infancy, and against the background of these precedents, it would have required very special circumstances to seek to utilize anything other than unfree relations of production.

Second, there were the material circumstances of the settlers, and the alternative sources of labour supply available to them. When these settlers arrived, the islands were populated by Carib and Arawak Indians. The Arawak Indians were quickly eliminated by genocide, the introduction of previously unknown diseases, and enforced hard labour, but the Carib Indians resisted European intervention into the eighteenth century (Higham 1921:122–42; Deerr 1949:153–56; Davies 1974:261–69). Consequently, the indigenous population proved unsuitable as a source of labour power. As for the settlers from Europe, they were unlikely to form a pool of labour when land was freely available for cultivation. Given the distances involved and the conditions in the early days of settlement, wages were, in themselves, little inducement to travel to the Caribbean and, anyway, those recently 'freed' from the land had few means to meet the cost of the passage. In a new and uncertain environment, indentured labour guaranteed the organizer of agricultural production access to and control over labour power for a defined period of time and, moreover, provided a means for the transportation of labourers to the Caribbean and thereafter for permanent settlement.

From indentured to slave labour

Significant changes in the methods and relations of production, first in Barbados and then throughout the Caribbean, followed the introduction of sugar cane from Brazil. Like tobacco, sugar was a commodity produced for sale in Europe. Its use was initially limited to the ruling class, but consumption spread to the labouring classes during the eighteenth century (Sheridan 1974: 21–7; Mintz 1985: 45, 147–49), providing an expanding market. However, unlike tobacco, the extraction of sugar required the use of machinery (a crushing mill and the means to ensure the crystallization of sugar). Moreover, the ratio between land and product increased, with the result that the producer required access to a larger area of land. Finally, growing, cutting, and processing sugar cane on large plots of land required a large supply of semi-skilled labour (Mintz 1985: 26). Hence the conditions for the expansion of sugar production included a concentration of land ownership, access to money to acquire the necessary machinery, and an increase in the labour supply.

Sugar production developed first, and fast, in Barbados from around 1640. Land prices rose and a smaller number of people came to own a larger proportion of land (Sheridan 1970: 27; Dunn 1973: 66, 96). The small farmer remained, but on the poorer quality land and under the widening economic and political shadow of the sugar planter organizing production on 200 acre units (Dunn 1973: 88–9, 96). There was an exodus of small-scale producers to other parts of the English Caribbean (Harlow 1926: 306–7), and the proportion of the population of European origin began to decrease absolutely and proportionately from mid-century (Davies 1974: 137; Sheridan 1974: 132).

However, the total population increased dramatically from this time, due to the arrival of Africans who had been unwillingly captured and transported to the Caribbean to be sold as property. The owner thereby gained access to the total product of the enslaved person's labour power, in return for which subsistence (or the means of subsistence) was provided. Enslaved African labour joined indentured European labour in the cane fields during the expansion of sugar production in Barbados (Sheridan 1974: 131; Dunn 1973: 67–8). They also joined together in acts of resistance (Beckles 1981: 6–15). These changes proceeded in Barbados in less than two decades. They occurred subsequently elsewhere in the Caribbean, although the speed of transition was not so fast (Davies 1974: 180–82; Goveia 1965: 83). For example in Jamaica, sugar production did not expand until the second and third decades of the eighteenth century (Craton and Walvin 1970: 51). But the combination of indentured and slave labour on the developing sugar plantations in Barbados was not permanent. Slave labour gradually replaced indentured labour first in unskilled field work and later in skilled work (Galenson 1981a: 117, 126–28), although indentured labour continued to be used well into the eighteenth century (Galenson 1981a: 163–64). There are a number of reasons for the transition to slave labour.

First, the supply of indentured labour was difficult to maintain (Williams 1964: 18; 1970: 102–3). On Barbados land was no longer available for servants who reached the end of their contract, while reports circulated in England of poor conditions on the voyage and at work in the Caribbean (Rice 1975: 56). Both discouraged voluntary indenture. Moreover by the 1680s the English state was less willing to permit a continuing flow of emigration and had been discouraging kidnapping for a decade or more (Gray 1941: 349). From the last quarter of the seventeenth century, an increasing proportion of emigrants were either political prisoners or convicted criminals (Smith 1947: 95–8, 188–97; Goveia 1965: 105).

Second, there was knowledge of, if not direct acquaintance with, slave labour as an alternative form of unfree labour. Slave labour already had a long history by the seventeenth century (Patterson 1982; Phillips 1985), and had been introduced into the Americas by the Spanish and the Portuguese by the end of the fifteenth century (Williams 1970: 41). Against the background of this long history, there was no tradition of immorality associated with its use and so there was no general objection to slave labour (Rice 1975: 7). In so far as a justification for enslavement was sought at all, it was found in the claim that those enslaved were heathens (Rice 1975: 21). The introduction of slave labour into the English Caribbean was therefore a matter of extending an extant method of labour exploitation into a new context and of establishing the necessary trade networks to ensure a continuing supply of people who could be enslaved.

A trade in human beings between Africa and the Americas had been initiated by Spanish and Portuguese merchants during the sixteenth century (Phillips 1985: 184–87), and it was this trade which English merchant adventurers unsuccessfully attempted to enter later that century. Further attempts were made in the following century, but the decisive step was the formation of the Company of Royal Adventurers in 1663 as a monopoly, following pressure from London merchants and state officials. The Company failed, and was replaced by a new monopoly, the Royal African Company, in 1672, but amidst growing agitation from merchants excluded from the slave trade who were anxious to abolish monopoly privileges (Davies 1957: 57–63, 97–152). The Royal African Company was unable to meet the growing demand for a labour force in the English Caribbean (the Navigation Acts had excluded ships of rival states from supply the English colonies) as sugar production increased, and in 1698 its monopoly was abolished

(Williams 1964: 30–3; Dunn 1973: 230–32; Craton 1974: 55–64). From the 1660s, and especially after 1698, the trade in human cargoes from Africa increased in line with the growth of sugar production, and between 1701 and 1810 over 1.4 million Africans were imported into the British Caribbean (Curtin 1969: 265).

Third, slave labour had cost and control advantages. The price of indentures increased at a time when the price of slaves was constant (Bean and Thomas 1979: 398). Moreover, the owner of a slave had access to the total product of labour power for life. From the total value created, a deduction had to be made for the purchase price and for the costs of reproduction, but the longer period of servitude ensured a higher marginal surplus when compared with the shorter contract entailed in indentured labour. The material living standards of slaves were depressed below the level of indentured labourers in so far as plantation owners reduced their expenditure on clothes and food for slaves (Smith 1947: 29; Sheridan 1974: 238). As for food, slaves were usually provided with land upon which they were required to grow their own, using their own labour power (Bennett 1958: 104; Mintz 1978: 92–4). By reducing the costs of the reproduction of labour power, the plantation owner was able to increase the surplus product. Consequently the transition from indentured to slave labour was accompanied by a comparative deterioration in the conditions of the labourer (Patterson 1967: 74; Dunn 1973: 238–45).

This transition from indentured to slave labour was not a constituent element of a grand design to introduce slave labour or sugar production (Courtenay 1965: 20), but was the consequence of *ad hoc* responses to particular circumstances. The English colonizers did not bring with them an already formed body of law and tradition concerning slave labour. Rather, out of the more generalized tradition of unfree labour that was exported and given substance in the Caribbean, and in order to maintain social control in the face of the possibility of revolt, the legal status of slave was created in an *ad hoc* manner in order to meet the needs of the sugar planters for, and to control, a labour force (Rice 1975: 68, 74).

A complex body of law was developed over time which regulated many aspects of the lives of those enslaved and their relations with the planter class (Goveia 1965: 152–202, 320). These laws were often contradictory, and they varied from island to island, both in content and extent of coherence (Patterson 1967: 70–1; Craton 1974: 170–73). But generally these laws established a judicial basis for human beings to be held as property, as a result of which the slave could be bought and sold, set out minimum provisions for clothing, food, and shelter, and controlled the movement of slaves (e.g. Patterson 1967: 80–3; Dunn 1973: 239–42). Thus the landowning class with interests in sugar production, as a result of its control of the local state, shaped and maintained in law the relations of domination.

The organization of sugar production

The history of the development of sugar production on plantations in the Caribbean is well documented (e.g. Deerr 1949, 1950; Dunn 1973; Sheridan 1974; Mintz 1985) and is of only secondary interest here. The Caribbean planter class intended to realize a surplus from their transfer of money into land, slaves, and machinery, and their combination and organization to produce sugar as an exchange value on plantations. The concept of *plantation production* refers to the large-scale production of an agricultural commodity for sale, using a large labour force of primarily unskilled workers (Courtenay 1965:7; Beckford 1972:6; also Mandle 1972). But historically there have been important variations in the particular character of the relations of production on plantations.

Sugar production was organized under the hegemony of merchant capital (cf. Kay 1975:98–9). It required considerable financial expenditure relative to the period in question (Sheridan 1970:31–2, 46; Mintz 1985:53) as well as a continuing dependence on merchant activity in order to ensure supplies of labour power, food, raw materials, etc. and to transport partially processed sugar to European markets. Where financial assistance was necessary to establish and run a plantation, there were two possible sources. On the one hand London merchants provided trade credit to allow the planter to buy supplies for which payment would be made after the crop had been harvested and sold; alternatively, there was the commission sytem and agent; *inter alia*, the agent received the product and arranged for its sale, purchased plantation supplies, chartered and insured ships, and granted loans. For all of these duties performed, the agent made deductions and received certain percentages from the total sum of money realized from the sale of each crop (Sheridan 1974:270–71; Ragatz 1971:99–101). The consequence was the widespread indebtedness of planter to agent (Davies 1974:153–54).

Hence the commission agent was not simply a lender of money to the planter, important though that was. The commission agent was a merchant acting on behalf of the planter who gained a percentage share of the surplus realized from the exploitation of the labour power of enslaved Africans. Their central importance and power was revealed when sugar profits were in decline and the planter was required to meet all the debts owed to the agent. In such circumstances the ownership of the plantation could pass to the agent (Ragatz 1971:10). In sum, although the planter organized production (either directly, or indirectly through an attorney), the commission agent provided the money and services and thereby made the planter subordinate to merchant capital (e.g. Goveia 1965:106–10).

We can now consider the implications of the relations of production for the organization of the labour process. We have already seen that sugar production involved a concentration of the means of production in the hands of a planter class who extracted a surplus product from a labour force over which it had unmediated domination through ownership. The exploitation of labour power therefore depended on the purchase of human beings who functioned as fixed capital (Hall 1962: 305–8). This relation of direct domination had implications for the character of the labour process.

Plantation production of sugar was characterized by the utilization of a large quantity of semi- and unskilled labour organized into two or more gangs and using simple tools (Craton and Walvin 1970: 100–4; Craton 1974: 122–24; Dunn 1973: 198). Men, women, and children were distributed to these gangs on the basis of their health and strength, and each gang was assigned to a particular range of tasks. Skilled manual tasks, however, were carried out mainly by men (Craton and Walvin 1970: 128, 138–41). During the cane-cutting period, a variety of processing tasks were added to fieldwork. Of the total labour force on the plantation, more than half was permanently assigned to fieldwork, the remainder engaged in other work such as domestic tasks, herding, and craft labour (Ragatz 1971: 25; Higman 1976: 36). Immediate control over the labour process was placed in the hands of overseers empowered to use violence. Hours of work were long, invariably from sunrise to dusk (even longer during cane-cutting), and there was a six-day working week. On the final day of the week, labour was required on the provision grounds (Craton 1974: 126–27; Patterson 1967: 69).

This organization of work remained largely unchanged from the late seventeenth to the early nineteenth century (Ragatz 1971: 57; Goveia 1965: 120). Few changes were made to the technology of cane-growing and processing during this period, even though there were important advances in technical knowledge (Ragatz 1971: 63; Sheridan 1974: 108). Planters made little attempt to increase the productivity of labour by combining labour power with more complex and powerful tools and machinery or by applying scientific discoveries (Ragatz 1971: 12). This unchanging labour process was exemplified by and embodied in books and manuals which aimed to teach the 'art' of sugar production (Higman 1976: 188). Thus the widening market for sugar was met by the absolute spatial expansion of sugar production (Mintz 1985: 36).

The absence of an incentive to rationalize the labour process was reinforced by the trend towards absenteeism. The rise and scale of absenteeism differed from island to island, but was common by the second half of the eighteenth century (Craton and Walvin 1970: 120; Ragatz 1971: 44) and perhaps earlier (Dunn 1973: 200). For many, the objective of ownership was to maintain an aristocratic lifestyle and to fund a political career (Williams 1964: 95; Craton 1974: 141; Sheridan 1974: 360), and hence the plantation owner departed for Britain as soon as possible. Putting to one side the problem of the extent to which profits from sugar production (Ward 1978) constituted a key component of the primitive accumulation of industrial capital (Pares 1937; Williams 1964: 51–2; Engerman 1972), there is no doubt that profits from plantation sugar production were used in part for the purchase of landed estates and conspicuous consumption (e.g. Craton and Walvin 1970: 183–84).

With the owner absent the management of the plantation was left in the hands of overseers and an attorney. The latter was invariably responsible for several estates and was able to transfer estate funds to their own accounts (Craton and Walvin 1970: 169), so that effective daily control was in the hands of overseers who received a small salary and whose interests did not coincide with the absentee owner (Craton and Walvin 1970: 146–47). The owner required only that the plantation produce a steady income. Hence there was little or no incentive to improve the efficiency of the operation because any improvement (e.g. by spending money on the development of new forms of processing and on the subsequent construction and use of new machinery) would have increased current expenditure and reduced the immediate surplus (Ragatz 1971: 55–63; Craton 1974: 201–5). In other words, the monetary costs of improving efficiency would have reduced, in the short term, the profits remitted to Britain.

There were further reasons why the labour process remained largely unchanged. One must also consider the consequences of the relations of production. Considerable sums of money were necessarily committed to the purchase, reproduction, and replacement of men and women as slaves (Goveia 1965: 122–23). Having committed expenditure on the purchase of human beings, the planter had to provide the necessities of life, even if only at the most basic level. With subsistence guaranteed, the enslaved labourer had no material incentive to make labour power available. This was well understood by the plantation owners:

> 'We PLANTERS, by providing our NATIVE AND NATURALISED SLAVES with all the NECESSITIES of life, have left them few or no natural wants, and consequently no natural incentives to labour, and therefore, of course, the WHIP must be employed to compel them.'
> (cited in Hall 1962: 311; see also Craton and Walvin 1970: 195)

Force, or the threat of force, was therefore a major inducement which ensured that labour power was expended (Craton and Walvin 1970: 137–38), yet this negative inducement made for reluctant labourers. In such circumstances the misuse and sabotage of tools and machinery were perhaps the most effective form of active resistance short of rebellion (Dunn 1973: 201).

The nature of the relations of production set a further constraint on rationalization of the labour process. In the absence of a labour market and wage labour (although some planters hired out their slaves [Bennett 1958: 63–5]), the plantation owner had to purchase a sufficient number to meet the peak demand for labour during cane-cutting, even though this meant that the total number was in excess of what was required for much of the rest of the year. Thus once labour had become an element of fixed capital, there was little scope to vary the acquisition of labour power in relation to changes in seasonal demand, let alone changes resulting from the application of new tools and machinery. The labour process on sugar plantations therefore had to be organized to allow for the maximum utilization of human labour power throughout the year (Goveia 1965: 127), and this largely ruled out the replacement of labour power with tools and machinery (Goveia 1965: 129; Tinker 1974: 9).

Finally, by the early eighteenth century there were well-established merchant interests in the supply of Africans as slaves. For parts of the eighteenth century, merchants involved in the slave trade realized a profit from the transportation of human beings (Williams 1970: 147–48; but see Thomas and Bean 1974; De Vries 1976: 141–42). As a result not only was there a mechanism to replace and add to the stock of human fixed capital, but the trade also became part of a wider pattern of exchange in the form of the triangular trade (Williams 1964: 51–2). The material interests of merchant capital therefore sustained and reinforced the relations of production on the plantations.

In sum, Caribbean planters were engaged in the organization of commodity production from which, for at least certain periods, they were able to realize a surplus (see Ward 1978). But this form of commodity production had three characteristics which gave it a particular content and dynamic. First, merchant capital had a dominant, if not controlling, part to play in the organization of sugar production. As merchant capital, it functioned by buying cheap in order to sell dear, and the immediate object of this function was the owner of the sugar plantation who was obliged to transfer a proportion of the surplus to the commission agent. From the mid-seventeenth century to the end of the eighteenth, these interests of merchant capital were protected by the state (Richardson 1968: 22–7). Second, but for different reasons, the planter had a speculative intention in so far as many aspired to the class position of the landed aristocracy. Sugar production was viewed as a short-term activity which would provide the financial resources to purchase land and property. The consequence was conspicuous consumption. Third, the relations of production obstructed the rational-ization of the labour process. There was therefore no process that approximated that of capital accumulation.

From slave to indentured labour

The eighteenth century was the period of greatest prosperity for the British planters in the Caribbean. Jamaica was the leading sugar colony (Williams 1970: 152): the production of sugar, rum, and molasses was at its height from around 1740 to the outbreak of the American War of Independence (Patterson 1967: 22; Sheridan 1974: 222). The outbreak of the war had a negative impact because it disrupted trade in necessary supplies (Bell 1917), and was one of several factors which led to an economic crisis. In London the political position of the Caribbean planter and commission agent was under increasing pressure from the growing influence of an emergent fraction of industrial capital.

Moreover, there was an increasingly vociferous campaign against the slave trade and slave labour, one which combined humanitarian arguments with claims about the inefficiency of slave labour when compared with wage labour (Rice 1975:152; Temperley 1977).

Within the British Empire, and in the face of opposition from the planter class, the slave trade was abolished in 1807 and the use of slave labour in 1833. Some explanations of abolition are unduly economistic (e.g. Williams 1964:136, 154; Ragatz 1971:383), and a more generous interpretation of the influence of the abolition movement (i.e. of political and ideological factors) does not deny that a crisis of profitability and the economic interests of the industrial bourgeoisie created conditions within which the abolition movement could exercise influence (Goveia 1965:46, 326, 335–36; Rice 1975:153–55, 233–36).

Of greater significance here are the consequences of abolition for the continuation of plantation production of sugar in the Caribbean. Critics of William (e.g. Temperley 1977) are correct to point out that the abolition movement drew upon arguments of bourgeois economists who asserted that wage labour was more efficient than slave labour but, significantly, free wage labour did not replace slave labour in the Caribbean. From the crisis that preceded and followed abolition, other unfree relations of production emerged in a number of British Caribbean islands.

The abolition of the slave trade was intended to stop the sale of human beings, but given that plantation production was dependent upon a continuous supply of human beings to replace those who died, abolition also threatened the use of slave labour to produce sugar. An initial response of the planter class was to organize an illegal inter-island trade in Africans, supported by the connivance of island administrators (Brereton 1981:52–8). However there was an awareness that this response would be insufficient if slave labour were to be abolished, and discussion centred on the source of an alternative workforce and the relations under which it would work.

The essence of the problem was well understood, both in the Caribbean and in London. Where land was readily available, those freed from slave relations of production would not willingly sell their labour power to plantation owners (Burn 1937:105). Consequently a means was sought of forcing people to make their labour power available. Lord Hawick, Under Secretary of State for the Colonies, wrote in an official memorandum in 1832:

> 'The great problem to be solved in drawing up any plan for the emancipation of the slaves in our Colonies, is to devise some mode of inducing them when relieved from the fear of the Driver and his whip, to undergo the regular and continuous labour which is indispensable in carrying on the production of Sugar. . . . I think it would be greatly for the real happiness of the Negroes themselves, if the facility of acquiring land could be so far restricted as to prevent them, on the abolition of slavery, from abandoning the habits of regular industry. Accordingly, it is to the imposition of a considerable tax

upon land that I chiefly look for the means of enabling the planter to continue
his business when emancipation shall have taken place.'

(cited in Richardson 1968:109–10)

By denying the freed slaves access to the land by state-imposed
taxation, it was intended that they would be required to work for the
plantation owner to obtain the means of subsistence.

Political pressure ensured that abolition did not immediately lead to
the termination of unfree labour, and slave labour was initially replaced
by a temporary system of 'apprenticeship' (Burn 1937:118–19; Kloosterboer 1960:3), under which the 'freed' slave was required to work for the
plantation owner for four or six years under less harsh conditions (but
without cash payment). Political pressure in Britain forced a premature
end to apprenticeship in 1838 (Burn 1937:333–361), requiring that the
plantation owners determine new conditions for the exploitation of
labour power. On the smaller islands this was not a major problem
because most of the land had long been transferred to private
ownership and was under cultivation. Consequently where sugar
production continued there were few alternatives for those without
access to the means of production other than to make their labour
power available to the plantation owners (Courtenay 1965:27). Only
small-scale trading and the selling of skilled labour power constituted
alternatives for small numbers (Riviere 1972:2–4). Where sugar production ended plantations were replaced by smallholdings and a peasantry
emerged engaged in petty commodity production (Courtenay 1965:
27–8).

But in Jamaica, Trinidad, and British Guiana there remained substantial
areas of uncultivated land offering the prospect of an independent
existence for a significant proportion of the newly freed labourers and
reducing the power of the planter class to control labour power (Bolland
1981:598–600). In Trinidad some three-quarters of the ex-slaves entered
subsistence or petty-commodity production, mainly by leasing or
squatting on land, only periodically providing plantation owners with
labour power in return for a wage when they needed an additional cash
income (Brereton 1981:80). Similarly in Jamaica and British Guiana, a
peasant class was formed (Hall 1959:19–20, 26–8; Adamson 1972:34–8;
Post 1978:30–1) which was able to reproduce itself with only a periodic
dependence upon a wage income from the plantations.

Faced with a widespread withdrawal of labour the economic position
of the sugar plantations became even more precarious. The prospect of
the abolition of the protective duties which benefited Caribbean sugar
became a reality in the Sugar Duties Act, 1846, intensifying the crisis
and underlining the fact that the complex structure of protection for
merchant capital was in ruins. Sugar production fell (Craton and Walvin
1970:213). Plantations which had accumulated substantial debts were
unable to bear the imposition of new and increased costs and were sold
or abandoned. This was a crisis from which the sugar planters in

Jamaica never fully recovered, even though production on a reduced acreage did continue (Hall 1959:118; Post 1978:31; Green 1984:24, 28). The outcome was rather different in Trinidad and British Guiana where the plantations were not so heavily in debt and where the problems arising from soil exhaustion had yet to develop.

In British Guiana bankruptcy and abandonment were followed by a transfer of ownership and the creation of larger plantations from 1841 (Adamson 1972:172–213). These larger units were owned by individuals with additional, extensive interests or by emergent joint-stock companies (Beckford 1972:102–4). The methods of production inherited from the eighteenth century, including the gang system and the simple technology of crushing and boiling, continued during this period of transition. By the 1860s the traditional problem of soil exhaustion was becoming apparent, but this was met with uncharacteristically swift action on the part of the new owners. The increasing use of manures and fertilisers was indicative of a significant change in organization and intention. In the following decade there were a variety of improvements to the production process and an increasing application of science. Thus

'It is hardly an exaggeration to characterise the 1870s as the decade during which sugar manufacture in British Guiana cast off what remained of the primitive methods inherited from slavery and entered the modern industrial period.'

(Adamson 1972:184–85)

These changes were accompanied by an ongoing concentration of ownership and the vertical integration of the various operations, so that by 1884 just seven companies owned or controlled nearly half of the sugar production of British Guiana.

A similar process occurred in Trinidad. In the 1850s there was a recovery from the intensified crisis brought on by the Sugar Duties Act, with both cultivation and production expanding. The 1860s saw the initial introduction of technical improvements and the beginning of a concentration of ownership, leading to a situation in which by 1897 most of the sugar was being produced by eleven units owned either by British corporations or individual capitalists (Brereton 1981:82–6).

These developments were themselves dependent upon a resolution of the interrelated problems of establishing new relations of production and finding a new source of labour power. These problems were resolved only after a number of initiatives following the termination of apprenticeship. The first was to offer a wage to hire labour. This was attempted in Trinidad, and combined with the provision of rent-free accommodation and other allowances. Wages remained relatively high until the crisis engendered by the Sugar Duties Act (Brereton 1981:78–9). A second initiative took the form of negative inducements. In Jamaica planters introduced high rents for huts and land used by the freed labourers in an attempt to force them to work for the low wages on offer.

The reaction was a refusal to pay (Craton and Walvin 1970:217) or an exodus from the plantation as the freed labourers sought an independent existence elsewhere, and this initiative was ended in 1842 (Hall 1959:20–3). In Trinidad some plantation owners attempted to force a system of tenancy at will. Under this system the labourer resident on the plantation was exempted from the payment of rent but was obliged to make labour power available by the threat of eviction (Brereton 1981:79). These negative inducements were, again, a major cause of the withdrawal of labour from the estates (Hall 1978).

A third initiative was to import a new labour force into the Caribbean. A Parliamentary Committee reported in London in 1842

'That the one obvious and most desirable mode of endeavouring to compensate for the diminished supply of labour is to promote the immigration of a fresh labouring population to such an extent as to create competition for employment.'

(cited in Deerr 1950:363)

Various schemes were considered and attempted (Saha 1970:12–20). In Jamaica there was an unsuccessful initiative to encourage migration from Europe in order to populate land in the interior, forcing the freed labourers of African origin to remain or move to the lowlands where they would then have little option other than to work on plantations (Deerr 1950:384; Hall 1959:21–2; Craton and Walvin 1970:218). In British Guiana individuals were encouraged to recruit workers on a bounty system, a scheme which led to the arrival of labourers not only from elsewhere in the Caribbean, but also from Madeira and Africa (Deerr 1950:385; Adamson 1972:43–4). The bounty system was also adopted in Trinidad to obtain labour from elsewhere in the Caribbean, and was similarly a failure because so many of those recruited quickly left the plantations to engage in subsistence production on their own account. Small numbers of labourers were also induced to migrate to Trinidad from the United States, France, and Germany, but this did little to solve the labour shortage (Brereton 1981:96–100).

In their different ways these initiatives seem to have been designed to create a labour force that was free to sell labour power for a wage. The fact that they failed and the fact that the plantation owners were unwilling or unable to offer sufficiently high wages to attract ex-slaves limited further the options available to the plantation owners. The failure to turn labour power fully into a commodity left them to find an alternative and politically acceptable form of unfree labour and a population which could be induced to accept such relations of production.

The recently freed population of African origin was never a serious candidate because of its anticipated resistance and the likely opposition of the British government (Laurence 1965:10). One remaining option was to recruit a new labour force from outside the Caribbean and to bind that labour force to the plantations by restricting its economic and political freedom to dispose of labour power. The consequence was the introduction of indentured labour in a new form, the labourers being recruited from China (Deerr 1950:399–400), India (Tinker 1974), and Africa (Schuler 1980).

A system to supply Indian indentured labour had been established for the French island of Réunion in the 1820s and was quickly extended to Mauritius after the British abolition of slave labour (Kloosterboer 1960; North-Coombes 1984; Tinker 1974; 61–4). Plans to introduce indentured labour into the British Caribbean from Sierra Leone and St Helena (where Africans liberated from the slave trade were settled) were formulated in the late 1830s. Agreement was reached and between 1842 and 1867 some 31,900 Africans were taken to the Caribbean as indentured labourers. At the outset individuals were free to elect to enter contracts of indenture but when this failed to provide sufficient numbers of recruits, elements of compulsion were introduced (Schuler 1980:23–9). The conditions on the plantations quickly deteriorated and many left as soon as their contracts expired and established themselves as petty-commodity agricultural producers (Brereton 1981:98; Schuler 1980:63). From the planters' perspective this initiative was largely a failure.

From the mid-1840s indentured labour from India increased to constitute the bulk of the labour force on the plantations of Trinidad, British Guiana, and Jamaica, although a small number of Chinese were recruited under indenture by planters in Trinidad (Brereton 1981:100). The history of the development and operation of indentured migration from India to the Caribbean is complex because the British government, the Indian government, the Caribbean administrations, and the Caribbean plantation owners were all involved and had changing and often conflicting demands. I highlight four aspects of this migration and new form of indentured labour.

First, the migration was induced by rural poverty and the decline of important manufacturing industries within India. Concerning the former, there was in certain areas an interrelation between the inability of rural producers to maintain subsistence production and the growth of indebtedness to moneylenders which coincided in the early nineteenth century with landowners seeking the payment of rents in cash. Indebtedness, often accompanied by bonds of servitude to money-lenders, encouraged rural labourers to seek some means of gaining a cash income. Additionally, the development of mechanized cotton production in Britain was followed by the export of cheap cotton commodities to India which undermined village economies where they were dependent on part-time spinning. The destruction of the textile industry in large parts of India further intensified rural poverty and unemployment, as did periodic famines. Thus those engaged in the recruitment of labour under conditions of indenture were able to operate in favourable circumstances (Cumpston 1953:6; Saha 1970: Chapter 2).

Second, although the migratory indenture system was organized by the state on behalf of the interests of the plantation owners, these were not the only interests to which the state responded. For example, the Colonial Office in London was sensitive to continuing agitation by the anti-slavery movement, and so the British state wished to prevent kidnapping, poor living conditions, and ill-treatment (Kloosterboer 1960:9; Weller, 1968; Tinker 1974:69). There were further conflicting interests. For example when reports of ill-treatment of indentured labourers became widespread the British and Indian governments intervened to stop migration, a decision to which the planters were opposed (Tinker 1974:69–70). There was also conflict between the Colonial Office and the planters over the proportion of women who were to be taken to the Caribbean when permanent settlement began (Tinker 1974:89–90). And there was periodic conflict over who was to pay the administrative costs of the migration. Labourers had to be transported from India and officials were appointed to prevent kidnapping and other abuses, both necessitating expenditure (Weller 1968:2–3, 7). For much of the period most of the costs had to be met by the planters, and only in exceptional circumstances were they able to obtain a contribution from the state in London. However, the planters' control of local legislatures ensured that they could spread the burden to include the peasantry and the indentured labourers themselves by means of their indirect taxation (Adamson 1972:239; Ramesar 1984:69).

Third, the migratory indenture system was not a duplication of that used in the seventeenth century. Although in both cases the migrant entered a contractual relationship with a specified individual to whom labour power was made available for a specified period, the central difference was that the nineteenth-century planter was required to provide regular work for a designated wage, along with accommodation and medical attention. Additionally, the labourer had the option of reindenture or a free return passage at the end of the period of contract. There was therefore the formal appearance of wage labour, an appearance that was essential to allow the London government to present this migration of labour as being of 'free men' (Deerr 1950:363). But labour power was only formally commodified. The political relations of exploitation restricted the freedom of the labourer to sell labour power, a pass system restricted freedom of movement, and a structure of extra-economic compulsion laid down penalties for negligence, absence from work, etc. which were defined as criminal offences (Tinker 1974:191–92; Haraksingh 1981:7–8).

Fourth, the degree of unfreedom increased over time. The planters engaged in a constant struggle to increase their control over indentured labour in order to increase the rate of exploitation (Laurence 1965), for example by extending the length of contracts or by withdrawing from their obligation to provide a free return passage (Tinker 1974:82–6). In British Guiana planters agitated in the mid-nineteenth century for the introduction of ten-year contracts and for the imposition of a requirement that indentured labourers contribute to the costs of the return passage. Adamson comments: 'No matter what construction was placed upon them, it was clear that they reduced to zero what little social and economic freedom the immigrant had previously possessed' (1972:54). In the light of strong objections from the Colonial Office in London, the planters were forced in 1854 to accept initial contracts of three years with the requirement that the labourer complete five years of servitude by extending the first or entering a new one. A free return passage was only available if the migrant had worked for ten years in Guiana (Adamson 1972:55–6).

In addition, planters in Guiana made extensive use of the courts to force labourers to increase productivity. Work quotas were set unrealistically high and the planter had the power to prosecute for unfinished work or a refusal to work. Between 1866 and 1870, 18 per cent of indentured labourers faced these and related charges annually (Adamson 1972:113). An Ordinance of 1868 increased the planters' power further by allowing them to withdraw wages for work they considered to be inadequate or badly done. Simultaneously the rights of indentured labourers were reduced by administrative decisions which limited the movement of immigration agents around the estates, reducing the chances that an indentured labourer might draw attention to abuse, and their rights of intervention (Adamson 1972:122–25).

From the planters' point of view the effects of these restrictions were not limited to increasing the rate of exploitation of Indian indentured labourers. Wage labour had made an appearance in the Caribbean following the abolition of apprenticeship and had been used in Trinidad and Guiana to recruit casual labour, especially during the cutting season. Moreover, in so far as indentured migration led to permanent settlement, something that the planters had not envisaged at the outset (Wood 1968:60), the pool of labour power for hire began to increase. In Trinidad from the 1870s the planters were successful in reducing the wages of non-indentured labourers and increasing the work tasks of indentured labourers (which amounted to a wage reduction) (Weller 1968:47; Brereton 1981:106–8; Ramesar 1984:60). In Guiana the increasing size of the Indian population without access to land in the 1870s was a major factor encouraging the planters to reject reindenture, a view that was further encouraged by the mounting costs of the indenture system. Moreover 'As the populaton of unbound, legally free workers rose, so did the supply of labour. The discipline of indenture was replaced, *pari passu*, by the less visible, but often equally rigorous, controls of supply and demand' (Adamson 1972:146).

A dual process was occurring (Haraksingh 1981:10–13). First, by virtue of extra-economic compulsion the planter class was able to intensify the exploitation of indentured labour, which had downward pressure on the wages of free, wage labour. But second, where Indian migration was followed by permanent settlement (a process actively encouraged in Trinidad) in a context where independent production became more difficult, the planters could begin to replace indentured labour with wage labour. In those circumstances the development of a reserve army of labour could have the same effect over the provision and conditions of labour as extra-economic compulsion.

Conclusion

For most of the period between 1600 and 1900 British colonization of the Caribbean was synonymous with commodity production for export and unfree relations of production. This was not intended by the English merchants who first intervened in the region, but it was nevertheless a consequence of that intervention. One of the major problems facing those settlers who intended to organize commodity production was the absence of a labour force which therefore had to be recruited and brought to the Caribbean from elsewhere in the world. In dealing with this problem landowners drew upon a tradition of unfree labour long established in Europe, where wage labour was an emergent rather than a dominant relation of production. But tradition, in itself, is an inadequate explanation because it tells us nothing about the economic and political context in which production had to be organized.

Two features of that context were of particular importance. First, until the land had been fully settled any migrant to the Caribbean formally had the option of independent production for subsistence and commodity exchange. Second, where migrants did not possess the financial means to meet the costs of their migration, some method of subsidising the costs was necessary. Moreover where the prospective exploiter of the migrants' labour power met those costs initially, it was necessary to ensure that that labour power could be so exploited in order to produce a surplus from which payment could be made. Hence there was an overdetermination of the significance of the first feature. Some form of contractual servitude met both conditions because it prevented an independent existence and hence, in principle, offered the prospect of the creation of a surplus from which the costs of production (which included the costs of labour recruitment and migration) could be met. Both of these conditions were reproduced in parts of the British Caribbean in the nineteenth century, following the abolition of slave labour, as a result of which indentured labour replaced slave labour.

But between these two relatively short, historical phases of indentured labour were some 150 years of slave labour. Its origin also lay in the two factors identified, but it was sustained by a continuing supply of human beings and by the growing demand for the commodity that slave labour produced. It was, in other words, sustained by the activities of merchant capital which dominated trade in sugar and human beings and which extracted a surplus from the revenue of the plantation owners.

5
Australia

Introduction

The colonization of Australia occurred more than a century after that of
the Caribbean. Similarly, colonization was not motivated initially by
the interests of merchant capital or commodity producers. But as in the
Caribbean, following European settlement there emerged a search for
an item which could be produced for the world market. A complex of
reasons ensured that much of the labour power required to produce that
commodity came from Britain, where the capitalist mode of production
was predominant, although there were significant exceptions. But there
was no simple transfer of free relations of production from Britain
to Australia. Although capitalist relations of production emerged,
they were not predominant in the early phase of colonization and
were not immediately universalized throughout Australia during the
nineteenth century. Unfree, convict labour dominated the early period
of colonization and a form of indentured labour, dependent upon a
migration of labour from the South Pacific, was established in
Queensland in the latter half of the nineteenth century. Additionally the
labour power of the indigenous population was retained and exploited
using unfree relations of production in particular periods and locations
after military subjugation.

Thus the colonization of Australia during the nineteenth century
included the use of different forms of unfree labour. The predominance
of these production relations means that the issue of 'whether the
structure of social relations at the time was strictly "capitalist" or not'
(Connell and Irving 1980:66) is not a purely 'academic' matter, but a
matter of historical fact requiring explanation. The central aim of this
chapter is to show how these forms of unfree labour emerged and were
reproduced, and how they related to the development of the capitalist
mode of production in Australia.

The colonization motive

The Australian continent had been known by the Aboriginal population long before European merchant capitalists became aware of its existence in the early sixteenth century (Clark 1962: 12–131). The latter showed little interest because it

> 'seemed to grow no bush or flower or grain which Europe wanted. It seemed to yield no animal or fish for which European merchants were willing to risk their ships in long voyages. Its Aboriginals were not ocean seafarers, nor were they traders or collectors of precious stones, and they could show visiting seamen no commodity of value.'
>
> (Blainey 1983: 3–4)

Consequently in the absence of use values with the potential to enter circulation in European markets merchant capital had little reason to press for state intervention to secure domination of the region (cf. Fitzgerald 1982: 54–5). Although there was discussion of the possibility of commercial gain (Clark 1962: 59–60, 70), these interests did not significantly influence the decision to establish a settlement in Australia (Frost 1980: 185–95). The key motive for colonization was to establish a penal colony, although international military considerations had an important, secondary influence while commercial factors were a casual afterthought (Carrothers 1929: 24; Clark 1962: 69–70; Shaw 1966: 50–1; Crowley 1974: 1–3; Frost 1980: xii–xv).

Thus colonization did not conform to the general trend of British state policy and practice (Fieldhouse 1969: 26–9). Behind the decision lay a history of penal transportation which originated, as we have already seen, in the early seventeenth century. During the eighteenth century some 30,000 people were transported from Britain (Robson 1965: 5), so when transportation to the American colonies ceased as a result of the American War of Independence (Sellin 1976: 97), the British state was faced with a major problem. A number of alternative sites for transported criminals were discussed and in late 1776 the government decided to re-establish transportation by sending convicts to New South Wales. The colony was established in January 1788.

The significance of convict labour

Transportation to the Australian colonies continued until the middle of the nineteenth century, although there was some variation between colonies in the date of termination, reflecting uneven development. Transportation to New South Wales was stopped in 1840, and to Van Dieman's Land in 1852. In Western Australia, transportation began in 1850 and ended in 1867 when the British state abolished the whole system. Between 1788 and 1868, approximately 163,000 people were transported to Australia, the vast majority going to New South Wales and Van Dieman's Land (Robson 1965: 4; Shaw 1966: 148). Both men and women were transported, although the former predominated (Robson 1965:4; Shaw 1969:107). The majority of transported convicts were convicted of theft and assault (Robson 1965:30 ff), the remainder of political offences (Rudé 1978:1–2, 10).

As conceived by the British state, the purposes of transportation were to remove 'dangerous criminals' from Britain and to achieve their 'moral regeneration'. The latter was to be effected by means of regular, productive labour. Thus convict labour was used to establish and ensure the reproduction of the colony by growing food and providing a material infrastructure (Clark 1962:113–15). But the inefficiency of convict labour persuaded the governor of the colony to call for the settlement of non-convicts (Madgwick 1937:9–12). It was argued that free settlers would have a positive interest in the development of the colony and could exploit the convicts' labour power (Clark 1962:118–27). This idea was not endorsed in London until the 1790s. However the flow of free settlers was very small in these early years (Madgwick 1937:17–25; Shaw 1966:64) and so convicts remained the main source of labour power in New South Wales until the 1830s when the system began to be more widely condemned as inefficient and when demands for the abolition of transportation increased (Clark 1969:79).

Concerning the consequences of transportation, Rudé has concluded that 'whatever the original intention, once the convicts arrived in the colony they were cast for an economic role and if they became reformed in the process so much the better' (1978:166). Shaw has claimed that the system 'provided a labour force, which if less efficient than free workers was far better than no workers at all. It made private investment more profitable and caused very substantial government expenditure in the colonies' (1966:358). If the labour power of convicts established the colony (e.g. Crowley 1974:51), it is important to determine the nature of the social relations of production by which this was achieved. Under the terms of transportation the governor had the legal right to determine the use of the convicts' labour power during the period of their sentence. In the context of a population of convicts and military personnel, there were two main options, although a third became available when convicts had completed their sentence and when free settlement commenced. Thus convicts could be forced to work for the colonial state apparatus, for the state officials in a private capacity, or for free settlers or ex-convicts. All these options were used.

What they had in common was that those for whom the convict worked had the right to dispose of the total product of the convict's labour power, in return for which they were required to provide the basic necessities for subsistence. As a result of conviction the convict had been deprived of any right to determine the disposal of labour power. Therefore the convict's labour power was subject to direct procurement by the state or its assigned agent. The history of the early settlement of Australia indicates that access to and control over this form of unfree labour shifted significantly during the early decades of colonization, although before this could happen a process of differentiation of private and state interests had to take place.

This began in 1788 when the governor granted land to military and civil officers (Clark 1962: 113) and was fully achieved in 1793 when it was decided to grant land to all ranks of the military and to allow officers to engage in trade. Officers established a monopoly in trade and made considerable financial gains (Clark 1962: 132–35; Steven 1969: 120–22). And by being granted land, they gained control over the major means of production. But production could only occur if labour power could be appropriated and this was achieved by means of an assignment system, founded in 1789, whereby private individuals were allocated convicts to labour for them. Initially the costs of reproduction of the assigned convicts were met by the colonial state but this responsibility was later transferred to whoever gained control over the convict's labour power (Madgwick 1937: 36). In the case of assignation to private individuals, from 1804 the master was required to sign an indenture committing them to meeting the costs of reproduction. But in neither case were convicts responsible for their reproduction through independent commodity consumption because the means (a wage) were not available.

Thus both the colonial state and its officials in a private capacity attained the right to control and appropriate the product of the convict's labour power. By 1810 the terms under which they did so were similar (Clark 1962: 202, 245–46). The colonial state or the individual master was responsible for the provision of food, shelter, and clothing. The convict was required to work a ten-hour day between Monday and Friday, and for six hours on Saturday, but no money wage was paid. A pass system regulated and restricted the movement of convicts. Contravention of the pass system, disobeying orders, and neglecting work tasks could all be reported to the local magistrate, and the most common punishment was the lash (Clark 1962: 247).

During the early years of colonization the colonial state organized the construction of the economic and social infrastructure in New South Wales, using the labour power of convicts (Clark 1962: 240). The role of convict labour under state control was particularly important during the governorship of Macquarie who initiated a major public works programme. However, this programme increased the expenditure of the colonial state and by 1820 complaints were being made in London and New South Wales about the cost of maintaining the colony (Clark 1962: 269–70, 303–04, 347–48). The issue was addressed in three reports commissioned by Earl Bathurst, Secretary of State at the Colonial Office, and presented in 1822 and 1823 (Fletcher 1976: 54–81). There was wide disagreement with the policy of the governor, particularly over the assignment system. The reports recommended that, instead of their employment on public works, as many convicts as possible be assigned to private individuals, especially to those who had established large sheep flocks. This disagreement over assignment was indicative of a wider disagreement over the nature and role of the Australian colonies. For the governor the main objective was to punish and reform convicts, and in this respect he was following the original state policy in London. But new privatized, economic interests had developed in the meantime and Bathurst endorsed these, partly in order to reduce the costs of the colony (Clark 1962: 367–73).

A compromise between penal objectives and the advancement of private commercial interests was effected in 1823 when Bathurst requested that all convicts considered amenable to reform be assigned to private individuals in country districts on the grounds that they would be removed from direct contact with criminal and immoral influences in the towns. Those convicts thought to be unamenable to reform were to be isolated in penal settlements. The result was the closure of state farms (Clark 1968: 35, 68, 77; 1969: 47–8; Shaw 1966: 254).

Although convict labour employed directly by the state or by private individuals was the predominant source of labour power, it was not the only one. First, under the ticket-of-leave system, a convict could be freed from the obligation of forced labour, although the individual remained subject to certain constraints, e.g. he or she had to gain permission to leave the area of residence, could not own land, and could not sue or be sued in a court of law. If the conditions of the ticket were broken, it could be withdrawn. Being freed of the obligation of forced labour, the individual was free to establish agricultural and commercial activity or to find a buyer for his or her labour power. Tickets-of-leave were issued automatically to convicts who owned property or who originated from the dominant class, but also to convicts who demonstrated good conduct (Clark 1962: 239, 247, 369, 372).

Second, a convict who had completed a sentence could revert to the status of a 'free person'. Expirees were entitled to return to Britain or to remain in Australia. If they did the latter they were eligible for a small land grant and to receive both the means of subsistence and various means of production from the state. If the expiree failed to become established as an independent producer, there remained the option of selling labour power (Clark 1962: 133, 249; Shaw 1966: 65–9). Third, a convict could be pardoned, creating an emancipist who had similar rights to those under the ticket-of-leave system. However, following the 1822/23 review it was recommended that emancipists should not be allocated land grants and that they should return to the status of labourer. This recommendation was effected in 1823, forcing emancipists on to the emergent labour market (Clark 1962: 125, 249, 356, 369; 1968: 35). Finally, convicts had a limited scope to make their labour power available after completing their daily period of compulsory labour. Where an employer was in need of additional labour, it could be obtained by temporary hire. Wage rates were established by state regulation (Clark 1962: 245; 1969: 18).

These four statuses did not constitute the foundation for a large pool of commodified labour power. This was partly because certain groups had, for at least a period, monopoly access to the leasing of land, if not outright ownership. In addition, payment in kind (especially rum) was common at least up until 1830 and barter was the usual means of circulation (Clark 1962: 149; 1969: 18; Crowley 1974: 66–7), obstructing the development of money wages. Moreover, in purely numerical terms convict labourers were in a majority. In 1820 there were 9,451 convicts resident in New South Wales, compared with 5,798 persons classified as expirees, emancipists, or holders of a ticket-of-leave. One has to add to the latter group those born in the colony and those who arrived as free settlers, but this gives a total of 8,600 with a non-convict legal status (Clark 1962: 382). Finally, those exploiting the labour power of others for a long time regarded the lower cost of unfree and assigned, compared with wage, labour as being of paramount importance, despite the acknowledged inefficiency of the former. It was commonly estimated that the unfree assigned labourer cost £40 per annum while a free, wage labour cost £70 per annum to hire (Clark 1962: 246). The shortage of labour power for hire ensured that wages were very high (Shaw, 1969: 110).

While the economic and political context allowed this view to predominate, it was an important factor in preventing a decisive move by the landowners to universalize free relations of production. This reading of the historical evidence concurs with Connell and Irving's assertion that, in the period up to 1840, there was only a very limited move towards the commodification of labour power (1980: 44). The significance of the use of convict labour lay in the fact that not only did it predominate as the means of labour exploitation, but also that, by means of these unfree relations of production, a material and political foundation was created upon which distinct relations of production could develop subsequently.

This conclusion is reinforced by brief consideration of the role of convict labour in Western Australia (Hasluck 1959). This colony was founded in 1829 in the light of pressure upon the British government by a small group of people eager to realize a surplus from the commercial exploitation of land (Clark 1973: 17–20). The British state refused to incur any of the costs involved in the extension of colonization but it was prepared to authorize the distribution of land to those wishing to participate. Participation was dependent upon the individual either investing money or paying for the expense of the transport of labourers. But the early years of the settlement proved to be a disaster, not least because of the small number of settlers. By 1837 there were only 2,032 people of British origin in the colony (Clark 1973: 35) and by 1843 the governor was warning the government in London that the colony was on the point of collapse (Clark 1973: 279).

Here again was evidence that the possession of money without labour power was insufficient to produce material subsistence, let alone a commodity for exchange. Various schemes to import labour from Germany and China were discussed, but each was thwarted and in 1846 a group of landowners reluctantly concluded that they should apply to London to request convicts (Fletcher 1976:131) whose labour power would be used to construct the economic infrastructure necessary for future development and to produce agricultural commodities for exchange. Concern about 'moral pollution' faded in the face of the problems arising from the severe labour shortage (Clark 1973:279, 359, 391–92; Rudé 1978:229).

This request for convict labour coincided with a crisis over penal policy in Britain. Concern about the effectiveness of assignment as a form of punishment had led to its abandonment in 1839, and transportation to New South Wales (but not Van Dieman's Land) was terminated in 1840 because free migration was providing an alternative supply of labour. The problem of what to do with convicts in Britain was intensified and, during the 1840s, a scheme to combine an initial period of imprisonment with a subsequent period of transportation was formulated. Despite an initially favourable response in New South Wales to this revised system (due primarily to a temporary lull in free migration), the arrival of convict ships in mid-1849 was met with hostility (the labour shortage having been subsequently resolved), and the convicts were refused. It was therefore with relief that officials of the British state could send convicts to Western Australia (Shaw 1966:272, 275, 313–26; Hasluck 1959:31).

Between 1850 and 1868 (when transportation ended), 9,669 convicts were sent to Western Australia. With the exception of those qualifying for ticket-of-leave status, all convicts were housed in a jail and were forced to expend their labour power on public works (particularly roadbuilding) organized by the colonial state (Hasluck 1959:71–3). The former were allowed to work for settlers for a wage (Shaw 1966:353–55; Clark 1978:194–95). Clark has concluded: 'Once again the European discovered to his regret that to transplant a civilisation it was necessary to use a slave or semi-slave labour force to lay its foundations' (1969:55; see also Burroughs 1967:7, 80). The 'civilization' that was being transplanted therefore had a contradictory quality. But it was a necessary use of unfree labour because 'Though it altered the social life of the colonies and retarded their political development, it provided a labour force before free migrants were able to do so' (Shaw 1986:247). It is to this latter migration that attention must next be turned.

Free migration, land, and the labour market

Up to 1810 approximately 400 people had migrated as free persons to New South Wales and Van Dieman's Land. By 1820 943 men and 333 women, in addition to 665 children, had done so, most of the women and children being dependents of convicts (Clark 1962:296). Despite support in the colonies and London for migration for settlement (Clark 1962:127, 133) and for the idea that these settlers should be granted land and access to convict labour (Clark 1962:203), initially only small numbers of people were willing to migrate. In so far as there was a political strategy shaping this migration, it was, up until the 1830s, that free settlers would become landowners and not sellers of labour power (Madgwick 1937:36–9, 50–2, 60–1). Certainly many of those who migrated prior to the 1830s took with them significant sums of money, many having been landowners, merchants, and even petit-capitalists (Macmillan 1967:79–117, 188–89; Fletcher 1976:68; Sherington 1980: 29–35). These 'men of property' were allowed to exploit the labour power of convicts, alongside the already established merchant capitalists (Steven 1969; 123).

The isolation of the Australian colonies (Blainey 1983:40–70), arising from distance and cost relative to the technical development of communication, was a relevant consideration for those contemplating emigration from Britain. On these criteria, North America had clear advantages. But although there were impediments to free migration, they tell us little about the pressures within Britain which were encouraging other sections of the population, and the state, to consider the possibility of emigration (Madgwick 1937:67–87).

Military demobilization after 1815 led to rural and urban pauperism, but this occurred in the context of a wider set of rural and urban changes which stimulated internal migration (Redford 1964; Baines 1985). Enclosures and land clearances arising from the further spread of capitalist relations of production in agriculture extended poverty and unemployment, especially in Scotland and Ireland (e.g. Richards 1982, 1985), while the introduction of machine production displaced large numbers of petty-commodity producers. The plight of handloom weavers typifies the latter developments (Johnson 1966:42–56; Carrothers 1929: 33–43, 76–9). One of the political consequences was increasing support for political radicalism, and the threat of revolt was a significant factor which influenced the British state to effect emigration of the dispossessed (Johnston 1972:32, 37, 48, 163).

The British state funded six experimental emigration schemes between 1815 and 1826 which resulted in the emigration of some 11,000 people to Canada and the Cape of Good Hope. The terms of these schemes varied, but by 1820 the state favoured financial assistance to ensure 'pauper' emigration (Johnston 1972:16–17, 30, 39), although subsequently it was rarely willing to provide direct financial assistance and played a secondary role in organizing emigration (Johnson 1966: 93). This contradicted the recommendations of two select committees which reported in 1826 and 1827 in favour of state aid and state direction of the emigration of paupers to the colonies (Carrothers 1929: 56). A rather different view about emigration to the colonies was held at the Colonial Office (Johnston 1972:30–1). Lord Castlereagh spoke in favour of 'Settlers . . . of responsibility and Capital who may set useful Examples of Industry and Cultivation, and from their properly and Education be fit persons to whose Authority the Convicts may property be entrusted' (cited in Crowley 1974:31). But these different conceptions about the most appropriate candidates for emigration were not mutually exclusive.

In the 1820s Wilmot Horton, Under Secretary of State for the Colonies, distinguished between emigration and colonization. He conceived the former as a movement of labour and the latter as a combined movement of labour and money. Under a scheme of colonization, he envisaged that wealthy settlers would be allowed to purchase large blocks of land while poor settlers would pay only a percentage interest on the cash price of land (known as quitrent). Horton's scheme attracted little support (Madgwick 1937: 80), not least because of an unwillingness to subsidize the costs of pauper emigration, but it partly anticipated the colonization scheme of Wakefield (Burroughs 1967: 12–34).

The latter argued that the main barrier to colonial development was the easy availability of land. His recommendation was that land grants be abolished and the price of land raised to the point where it was out of reach of a significant proportion of the population, which would then be required to sell labour power for a wage (1896: 322–44, 372–81). In such circumstances, Wakefield anticipated, those with wealth would be willing to invest it in land and use it to employ wage labour. Unlike Horton, Wakefield envisaged the concentration of the means of production in the hands of a minority and the simultaneous creation of a labour market. He also envisaged that the costs of emigration would be met by the state from the sale of land (Carrothers 1929: 95–7; Johnston 1972: 109–11, 163–66; Marx 1976: 931–40).

The British state founded an Emigration Commission in 1831 and in the following year the Commissioners recommended that emigration to the Australian colonies should be encouraged. In 1840, the Colonial Land and Emigration Commissioners were appointed with overall responsibility for emigration throughout the colonies (Madgwick 1937: 170; Fletcher 1976: 88). Although up to 1837 emigrants were taken to Australia at the state's expense, this was the limit of the state's direct intervention beyond encouraging emigration through this Commission. Its preference was to allow the various private initiatives to provide for the costs of emigration (Carrothers 1929: 103–5, 111), which were considerable, North America being a much cheaper destination (Baines 1985: 86). Although state intervention was limited and was terminated in 1869 (Baines 1985: 72), it was sufficient to have a major impact on emigration to Australia by reformulating the regulations governing the distribution of land. It was here that Wakefield's influence was most evident.

In the early years of colonization emigrants, expirees, and settlers were all entitled to grants of land, although the amount varied considerably. Some were granted very large areas (Clark 1962: 133, 249–51; Robinson 1969: 91–4). But there remained the problem of finding a labour force with which the land could be worked. In 1831 it was decided in London that land grants were to be abolished and that all land would be disposed of in future by sale by auction at a minimum price, the change being justified explicitly as the means to create a class of persons who would provide their labour power for sale (Burroughs 1967: 35–9; McMichael 1984: 85). The amount of land sold increased from 20,000 acres in 1832 to 272,000 acres in 1835, most of which was bought by those already owning large areas. It was also announced that the revenue from land sales would be used in part to pay for the passage of those unable to afford the cost. These emigrants were expected to make their labour power available to those owning land. In 1835 the British state resolved to pay a bounty equal or nearly equal to the cost of passage to individuals wishing to emigrate to Australia and able to take with them a mechanic or agricultural labourer, a scheme which continued until 1841 (Madgwick 1937: 150–69).

In 1836 the number of assisted migrants was 808, while in 1839 it had increased to 8,416 (Clark 1968: 104–5; 1973: 158–63). A larger proportion were rural or urban labourers or tradesmen, many of whom had been displaced by the introduction of factory production (Macmillan 1967: 263–303). Between 1847 and 1851, 59,682 people were given assistance from the Land Fund to emigrate to the Australian colonies (Carrothers 1929: 114) under regulations which required all adults 'to be capable of labour and intending to work for wages in the colony' (Madgwick 1937: 195). By these combined measures, a class of large landowners had been formed, and both land and labour power had become commodities for exchange, although the latter was far from being universalized. Nevertheless the increasing number of free migrants was adding significantly to the free population of convict origin. An 1841 census in New South Wales revealed that only one in four persons was unfree (Clark 1973: 163). Finally, as we have seen, assignment was abolished in 1839.

Thus these legal measures of the 1830s played a major role in promulgating an initial shift from unfree to free relations of production. For these reasons the crucial decade of transition was not the 1820s as is commonly argued (e.g. Clark 1969; Crowley 1974: 70) but the period between the mid-1830s and the early 1840s as Connell and Irving (1980) have suggested. I question the latter's characterization of the preceding period as 'fundamentally capitalist' (1980: 51) because it was only during this period of transition that both land and labour power were transformed into commodities. Moreover this transition was not immediately universalized throughout the Australian colonies and did not preclude the subsequent development of unfree relations of production. Indeed, even where wage labour relations of production did develop, part of the payment to labour often took the form of the direct provision of use-values rather than money (McMichael 1984: 130).

With the formation of an interrelated landowning and merchant class in the early years of the penal colony there developed a search for an item which could become a commodity (Crowley 1974: 26, 43). The product was wool (Burroughs 1967: 133–37; McMichael 1984: 54–75), a commodity whose supply in Europe had been disrupted by war. Wool production did not initially predominate and cattle grazing supplied the internal market for the first two decades of the nineteenth century. Wool production increased significantly after 1810 (Abbott 1969), encouraged by support from the British state (McMichael 1984:51) and by 1832 there were over one million sheep in New South Wales. This expansion was associated with the development of squatting as both ex-convicts and migrants rushed to occupy land beyond the formal boundary of settlement (Shann 1948:36–7, 100; Burroughs 1967:141–59; Crowley 1974:29–31; McMichael 1984:101).

Squatters paid an annual lease fee of £10 for grazing sheep on land declared to belong to the British Crown (Clark 1969:83). The expanding export of wool and the income from its sale increased their economic and political power. This was reflected in an Order in Council made in London in 1847 which allowed squatters to lease Crown Land for production for periods of up to fourteen years and when the lease expired, which gave them the option of purchasing the land at a minimum price of £1 per acre (Clark 1973:375–6). Clark concludes:

> 'This meant the accumulation of landed property in the hands of the few to the exclusion of the many. For the squatters acquired *de facto* their security of tenure and with it a monopoly of the grazing and agricultural land of Australia, for in New South Wales alone the Order in Council handed over 180,000 acres of land to about 1,800 people.'
>
> (1969:97)

But the problem of appropriating labour power was not so easily resolved.

Before the age of fencing, wool production was labour intensive and shepherds were essential (McMichael 1984:129). The Colonial Office in London abolished assignment in 1839 with the intention of replacing unfree with free labour. This was consistent with the interests of a section of wealthy urban interests who questioned the efficiency of unfree labour, but it added to the problems of up-country squatters who lost their only reliable supply of labour (Madgwick 1937:202; McMichael 1984:184). European settlers were reluctant to sell their labour power in distant rural areas when higher wages were paid in the urban areas (Clark 1969:75, 78–80; 1973:157). Labour shortage was a continuing problem during this period and served as a constraint on expansion, constituting a contributory cause of the depression of the 1840s (McMichael 1984:153, 155, 190).

When free migration from Europe proved unable to supply sufficient labour for the landowners and squatters, they considered recruitment from elsewhere and pressed the colonial state to sanction and fund the recruitment of indentured labour from India (Madgwick 1937:237–38; De Lepervanche 1975:74–5, 1984:36–55; Dwight 1976). After several official enquiries, the colonial state decided not to fund the recruitment of Indian labour but it did not prohibit private initiative and, in 1846, 51 Indian labourers under indenture were recruited. In 1847 65 Pacific

Island labourers were brought into the colony to work as shepherds and general labourers. These numbers could not solve the labour shortage, but the initiative revealed the seriousness of the problem (Clark 1969: 99–100, 1973:197, 369; see also Willard 1967:3–7).

In conclusion it is clear that the establishment of relations of production founded on wage labour was not easily or immediately achieved, despite the various state legislative initiatives of the 1830s. Even though wool had become a major commodity produced for export, considerable sums of money were being invested in the Australian colonies from Britain (Fletcher 1976:135), migration of free settlers was increasing, and land ownership had become further concentrated in the hands of a minority, this class remained unable to recruit sufficient labour by means of market forces. This encouraged a search for labour from elsewhere in the world. In certain parts of Australia these circumstances also encouraged attempts to recruit labour from amongst the indigenous population.

Colonization and partial incorporation of the indigenous population

The Australian continent, like the Caribbean islands and Southern Africa, was inhabited by a human population long before European settlement. Colonization therefore inevitably involved contact between these two populations and their respective modes of production and social life. The outcome was subjugation of the Aboriginal population. Although the mode of material production which sustained the Aboriginal population was largely eliminated in large areas of the continent along with a large proportion of the population, the destruction of economic and social relations was not total (Hartwig 1978:135). This was because of Aboriginal resistance, conflicting policies and interests amongst the colonizers, and because of the decision in certain parts of Australia at certain times to incorporate the labour power of Aborigines within the developing relations of production.

Uncertainty about how to characterize the mode of production which sustained the Aboriginal population at the time of European colonization is of limited significance in this context. Whether it is described as a primitive communal mode of production (Hartwig 1978:132) or a domestic mode of production (Reynolds 1982:140) is here subordinate to the wider agreement on its historical characteristics. Material subsistence was achieved by hunting and gathering, a means of subsistence which required spatial mobility and which largely excluded attempts to cultivate land or rear animals in order to produce use-values. The main social unit of consumption and reproduction was founded on kin connections, although there were broader, albeit loose, 'tribal' affiliations. These were not sufficiently extensive to constitute the foundation for a wider political and military organization. Relations within and between such groups were based on clearly understood norms of reciprocity.

This mode of production had implications for the outcome of contact with a population which initiated a form of commodity production (cf. Bradby 1975: 152–53). First, it produced no significant surplus and no use values which could enter the exchange relations which linked the colonizers to the rest of the world. The possibility of a trading relationship based on Aboriginal production was therefore excluded. Second, the social and cultural reproduction of Aboriginal life was dependent upon continuing access to the land and upon maintaining a balanced cycle of natural reproduction. Thus where access was obstructed or terminated and that cycle was disturbed, the Aborigines had little option other than to resist. However, and third, the dispersed and fragmented nature of Aboriginal spatial and political relations obstructed the development of co-ordinated resistance.

The European settlers' policy towards the Aboriginal population changed over time and varied from area to area. Where colonization occurred relatively late, as in the case of Queensland, there already existed a history of contact and resistance which shaped the European intervention in a different mould to that which typified intervention in New South Wales (Loos 1982: 23–4). Even within individual colonies, the often slow pace of colonization over large areas, combined with changing material interests and the fact that the separate colonies were not politically united until 1901, ensured that different policies were employed in different areas and different consequences followed (e.g. Biskup 1973: 29–30). The intention here is not to offer a full history but to demonstrate how, under particular circumstances, attempts were made to incorporate the labour power of the Aboriginal population into the developing mode of production introduced by the European colonists.

In order to do this, it is necessary to summarize the main effects of colonization. The first was the alienation of land and the introduction of private property relationships. The settlers made no attempt to purchase land, but simply occupied it, moving the Aborigines off by force where necessary (Rowley 1970: 54). The subsequent development of pastoralism disturbed the water and food supply, hindering the production of subsistence which led to starvation and malnutrition, and prevented access to sites of religious significance (Elkin 1951: 166; Reynolds 1982: 66–7, 157; Loos 1982: 74). Second, European diseases were introduced, further reducing the ability of the Aboriginal population to reproduce itself. Third, there was considerable disruption to the pattern of Aboriginal social relations as a result of sexual competition, the introduction of alcohol, and the disruption of the limited political hierarchy (Reynolds 1982: 70–1; Rowley 1970: 30–3).

Aboriginal resistance varied in its extent and duration, but it occurred throughout the colonies (Reynolds 1982). It was rarely immediate, and was not a reaction, therefore, to the European presence *per se*, but was usually a response to one or more of these consequences. The predominant method of resistance was guerrilla warfare in which settlers and their property were the object of calculated attack. In certain areas, at certain times, settlers and gold prospectors were driven out (Loos 1982: 47–8, 52–3, 75; Reynolds 1982: 111, 167–68). The response of the colonial state and the settlers was generally swift and decisive. In the face of resistance, the 'protection' of the settler and the 'dispersal' of the Aborigines became major priorities for the colonial states which established police forces partly for this purpose (e.g. Hasluck 1970: 69; Evans *et al.* 1975: 55–62; Loos 1982: 22). Where Aborigines were killed in a punitive expedition of settlers or policemen, a spiral of violence could develop until the European arms and numbers had their almost inevitable consequence. It was overdetermined by the effects of malnutrition and disease.

The Aboriginal population rapidly decreased in size during the nineteenth century (Reynolds 1982: 121). The destructive effects of colonization were refracted in a clear shift in official and unofficial settler opinion about the nature of Aboriginal social and cultural organization and the role of Aborigines in the 'civilized' society that they believed was being created. During the earliest phase of settlement, the dominant opinion was that the indigenous population should be protected and encouraged to 'benefit' from their presence (Elkin 1951: 179; Hasluck 1970: 47–55). Thus Governor Darling issued the following instruction in July 1825:

'And it is Our further Will and Pleasure that you do, to the utmost of your power, promote Religion and Education among the Native Inhabitants of Our Said Colony, or of the Lands and Islands thereto adjoining; and that you do by all lawful means prevent and restrain all violence and injustice, which may in any manner be practised or attempted against them.'

(cited in Reynolds 1972: 151)

In the face of evidence that the 'Native Inhabitants' did not wish to benefit from such imperial benevolence, their subsequent decline was interpreted in terms of the dominant racist ideology of the period (Evans *et al.* 1975: 67–90).

The scientific falsity of 'race' theories of the nineteenth century is not the only measure of the ideological character of this legitimation. Although, for the reasons stated, there was a substantial decline in the Aboriginal population, there was also a partial integration of sections of the Aboriginal population in the developing mode of commodity production. There was, in other words, a disjunction between the apocalyptic vision of scientific racism and the continuing demand for labour power in all the Australian colonies. The shortage of labour led to various initiatives on the part of the landowning class, and those engaged in organizing sea-based extractive activities, to exploit Aboriginal labour power. Indeed, such a possibility was envisaged during the early phase of colonization. Governor Macquarie said of the indigenous population in 1814:

> 'Scarcely Emerged from the remotest State of rude and Uncivilised Nature, these People appear to possess some Qualities, which, if properly Cultivated and Encouraged, Might render them not only less wretched and destitute by Reason of their Wild wandering and Unsettled Habits, but progressively Useful to the Country. According to their capabilities either as Labourers in Agricultural Employ or among the lower Class of Mechanics.'
>
> (cited in Reynolds 1972: 109)

Property-owning settlers did have a certain success in realizing this objective, notably in Western Australia and Queensland.

In the case of Western Australia, the shortage of labour in the early period of colonization has already been discussed. One of the sources of labour power considered was the Aboriginal population. In the 1840s the governor devised a scheme to encourage the settlers to utilize and 'civilize' Aboriginal labour power which involved offering a bounty for teaching agricultural skills to men and cooking and dressmaking to women, in return for which participating settlers would receive a remission in the purchase price for land. The initiative proved to be a failure, due largely to its coincidence with a phase of Aboriginal resistance, and was withdrawn in 1848 (Rowley 1970: 66–7; Hasluck 1970: 36–7).

More successful in this early period was the exploitation of Aboriginal convict labour. In 1846 a majority of the prisoners in the native penal establishment at Rottnest were transferred to the mainland from the island. The colonial state used their labour power to build roads and carry the mail, and assigned it to settlers, especially at harvest time. This system of forced labour was ended in 1855 when the supply of British convicts was established (Hasluck 1970: 80–3). From 1850 the labour supply problem eased in the south of the Colony and, combined with the experience of the failure of the 'civilization' policy, the result was a growing belief in the idea that the Aboriginal 'race' was doomed to extinction (Biskup 1973: 13–15).

But not all the settlers were able to resolve the 'Aboriginal problem' in purely ideological terms. In the 1860s pastoralism expanded into the northwest of the colony, but under conditions which included a ban on the use of the labour power of convicts and holders of tickets-of-leave. In addition, isolated settlements were particularly vulnerable to Aboriginal attack. Significantly, the 1864 Land Regulations established Aborigines' rights to enter 'unimproved' areas of alienated land to obtain subsistence, a measure designed to reduce resistance and sustain the Aboriginal population as a potential workforce. Aboriginal labour power was used for shepherding, cattle-herding, and harvesting, and by 1881, 2,346 Aborigines were employed by settlers in pastoral production (Biskup 1973: 16–18; Crowley 1970: 189).

But there was no labour market and rarely any exchange of labour power for a wage. The relations of production developed initially in an informal manner but were determined against the background of the effects of European occupation of the land which disrupted the subsistence mode of production and encouraged a dependence upon the pastoral station. Initially, there were informal understandings about an exchange of labour power for food, but this did not always meet the demand of the landowner for a regular and controlled supply of labour power. Sections of the landowning class attempted to organize an indenture system in order to formally bind labour power to the station and contracts were introduced during the 1870s. This system of unfree labour required the involvement of the infant state apparatus to enforce contracts. This apparatus, largely staffed and controlled by the land-owners, responded with the lash and periods of imprisonment for absconding Aborigines who were caught.

The importance of Aboriginal labour power was signified by the Aborigines Protection Act, 1886, which established conditions for contracting Aboriginal labour, indicating that the state desired to formalize and maintain this source of labour power. The Act required the employer to provide a contract which included a commitment to the provision of food, clothing, and medical attention, but was silent about the payment of wages. Rowley comments:

'The section on labour was, in fact, a form of words which could bind the Aboriginal indefinitely to a master. . . . Lack of provision for cash wages shows that no thought was given to the important matter of labour incentives – or to the future of the labour force as a market.'

(1970:190)

In other words, the role of the Aboriginal was to provide labour power under conditions of unfreedom and in return for the direct provision of subsistence.

The Act had limited influence. By 1905, a little less than half of the Aborigines were employed on contracts, the majority being retained by informal means. The common pattern was for the remnants of an Aboriginal group to be resident on a station, providing labour power in return for the means of subsistence which could not be obtained by hunting and gathering. Although labour power was provided in a context of a degree of mutual dependence, the landowner had to resort to both the law and physical force in addition to the monopolization of the use of the land. In the relatively isolated northwest region of Western Australia, formal contracts were not a necessary adjunct to the maintenance of unfree relations of production. With the 1905 Aborigines Act, a further attempt was made to require employers to formalize the acquisition of labour power. Significantly the Act also gave the state the power to remove any Aborigine who was not 'lawfully employed' to a reserve, thus formalizing the arrangement whereby Aborigines were segregated and only considered useful when their labour power was required (Biskup 1973:64–5; Hasluck 1970: 153–57; Rowley 1970:180–92, 196–99).

From the earliest days of settlement in the southern part of what became Queensland the pastoralists utilized unfree labour, including that provided by Aborigines (Saunders 1982:10–14). Pastoral settlement expanded in the colony from 1861, sustained by the widespread use of force (Evans 1984:137). But the policy of 'dispersal' (supported by squatters who initially wanted the land they occupied cleared) was not compatible with the utilization of Aboriginal labour power. Given the shortage of labour, 'dispersal' was counterproductive because the resulting Aboriginal resistance was a disincentive to settlement and served to drain investment as a result of the destruction of property that followed. Aboriginal resistance was certainly one of the contributing causes of the crisis in pastoralism that developed late in the 1860s.

However, once force had led to the establishment of an effective monopoly of land by the European settlers, squatters increasingly utilized Aboriginal labour power after 1870 (Rowley 1970:159; Loos 1982:32–60; Fitzgerald 1982:214–15). Accordingly Aborigines became a source of casual labour, recruited from camps located on the edges of the stations. This was a role that they also filled for miners, sawmillers, and sugar planters (Loos 1982:162). Recruitment often involved forced abduction, and even the sale of Aborigines as objects of property, although it was also achieved by a forced accommodation in the context of the disruption of the local ecology (Evans 1984).

The demand, and the search, for labour intensified in the 1870s with the development of mining and sugar production and the spread of cattle-rearing. A government report published in 1895 recommended the establishment of a system of reserves where Aborigines could be retained under conditions of self-sufficiency and which could provide a pool of unskilled labour. The 1897 Aboriginal Protection and Restriction of the Sale of Opium Act established sixteen reserves and legislated a philosophy of protectionism. It provided for the retention of Aborigines on reserves under the direction of the state and for a system of formal labour recruitment, laying down that an Aborigine could only be employed with a permit which was renewable every twelve months and that written labour agreements should specify the terms of employment, accommodation, and wages (Rowley 1970:173–84; Loos 1982:172–80; Fitzgerald 1982:207–9; Evans *et al.* 1975:120). In this way

> 'the government and employers gained control of Aboriginal labour while the Aborigines lost their freedom to change or leave employment for the duration of their agreement and gained a perfunctory supervision of their employment which could only detect the most blatant excuses.'
>
> (Loos 1982:179)

Hence the reserve system ensured that 'The interest of the station holders in retaining a supply of cheap labour was safeguarded' (Rowley

1970). It was for this reason that the pastoralists preferred Aboriginal to 'white' labour (Reynolds 1972: 47).

A similar development is evident in other Australian colonies, especially in the Northern Territory (see Duncan 1967; Stevens 1974), although away from the expanding frontier the dependence upon Aboriginal labour was much less due to the greater availability of labour (Crowley 1970: 118; Hartwig 1978: 135). In the case of New South Wales, Aboriginal labour was rarely used in the first five decades, and where it was, it was only for short periods (Rowley 1970: 34). But by the 1870s military defeat and the expropriation of land had made subsistence within the traditional mode of production extremely difficult and a government report in 1883 revealed that over half of the Aborigines in the colony reproduced themselves largely by providing their labour power to farmers, fishermen, and sawmillers on a seasonal or inter- mittent basis. Prior to the 1870s the state had made no attempt to underwrite the reproduction of the Aboriginal population but there- after, motivated by a concern to maintain social order and to ensure an efficient utilization of Aboriginal labour power, the state intervened to assist the reproduction of the Aboriginal population (Curthoys 1982).

In South Australia the early establishment of a flow of free migrants from Britain ensured that there was only a limited utilization of Aboriginal labour power. The sporadic nature of their employment is best illustrated by the consequences of the Victorian goldrush which denuded the pastoral regions of European labour, the jobs being filled temporarily by Aborigines employed on wages, although on lower rates. It was only in frontier regions of South Australia where there was a persistent shortage of labour that Aboriginal labour became more permanent (Rowley 1970: 31, 35).

There was one sector of the economy, extraction from the sea, where Aborigines played a particularly prominent role for a large part of the nineteenth century. Whaling and sealing made an important contribution to the economies of the Australian colonies in the first four decades of colonization (Blainey 1983: 115–16), while in the latter half of the nineteenth century the extraction of pearl shell and sea slug around the northern coast of Queensland and Western Australia made an important contribution to exports (Loos 1982: 113–20). Aborigines were well represented in all these activities (Hasluck 1970: 23, 31; Reynolds 1982: 175; Loos 1982: 119–23). Young men were employed directly on the boats and women were required to provide sexual services on shore (Loos 1982: 126–47; Reynolds 1982: 177–79).

The relations of production in these extractive industries were grounded in compulsion, evident not only in recruitment methods but also in the conditions of retention. Aboriginal recruitment was a result of 'choice', deception, and direct force. Of those who chose, a proportion were subject to the persuasion of elders or others in the Aboriginal population who received flour and tobacco in return for each recruit while others were attracted by the idea of adventure. But deception and force ultimately guaranteed the relations of engagement and employment. Even where a labourer agreed voluntarily to serve a master owning a boat, he was liable not to be returned to his or her place of origin at the end of the agreed period of service when the master needed to reduce costs and/or maintain an experienced workforce. Moreover those who engaged did so for specified periods of time, and were bound by a combination of verbal or written contract and the power of the master in what was an isolated work situation.

Reports of kidnapping, ill-treatment, and a high mortality rate were common and the colonial state eventually intervened in an attempt to regulate the relations of production. In Western Australia several Acts were passed. The 1837 Pearl Shell Fishing Regulation Act specified that an Aborigine had to have a twelve-month written contract endorsed by the police or a magistrate, that the employer was required to return the employee to the place of origin, and that the employer was responsible for the provision of food and clothing. Subsequently in both Western Australia and Queensland employers engaged in the extraction of pearl shell and the sea slug were subject to the provisions of the respective Aborigines Protection Acts (Rowley 1970: 188; Hasluck 1970: 43–4, 152–53).

That some writers (e.g. Connell and Irving 1980) remain largely silent about the utilization of Aboriginal labour power in the nineteenth century is difficult to justify. I have shown that there were circumstances throughout the Australian colonies in this century where Aboriginal labour power was actively sought and exploited in unfree relations of production. This was most extensive in Western Australia and Queensland, but it also occurred in the southern half of the continent. In the course of the century the colonial states increasingly intervened to legalize and formalize these unfree relations of exploitation with the interrelated objectives of eliminating abuse and attempting to guarantee the reproduction of Aboriginal labour power.

Indentured labour in Queensland

There was a further use of unfree labour in the Australian colonies in the nineteenth century. A system of indentured labour was established for the sugar plantations in Queensland. The colony was established formally in 1859, but settlement began in 1842, initiated by squatters who exploited convict labour under the ticket-of-leave system. This form of unfree labour was later supplanted by a combination of forced Aboriginal labour, European servants, and indentured Indian and Chinese labour, so that by the 1860s there was an established tradition of pastoral development dependent upon forced labour (Saunders 1982: 3–14, 1984b: 214–19). In addition to wool, attempts were made to produce cotton and sugar. Manchester cotton merchants were interested in developing a new source of supply and the governor of Queensland encouraged aspiring commodity producers.

Cotton was grown on small farms and plantations from 1853, but was replaced by sugar production from the early 1860s. Initially small farms dominated, but from 1870 large plantations were organized, funded by British investment and displacing the small farmer. Ownership and control of the land, buildings, and machinery were initially vested in a single individual or small group, but this structure was replaced by the joint stock company in the 1880s during a phase of speculative investment. An economic crisis in the mid-1880s led to the break-up of the plantation system and its replacement by a combination of tenant farming and centralized milling (Saunders 1982: 47–52, 144–53; Fitzgerald 1982: 179, 187).

A major obstacle to the development of agricultural commodity production in Queensland was a shortage of labour (Fitzgerald 1982: 105). The abolition of transportation prevented any extension of the exploitation of convict labour. As a result, landowners initially sought the recruitment of labour from India under indenture, but while the Queensland government was engaged in negotiation, a landowner initiated the recruitment of labour from islands in the southwest Pacific in 1863 (Docker 1970: 6–7; Saunders 1982: 15–16).

The Pacific had been the site of colonial rivalry between the British and French states in the eighteenth century and of merchant and missionary activity in the early nineteenth century. Merchants involved in the gathering of sandalwood and sea slug and the hunting of whales established contact with the population of many of the islands (Morrell 1960: 14, 28, 63–8; Corris 1973: 6–12). In 1838 a Sydney newspaper recommended the recruitment of Pacific islanders as shepherds, and in 1847 a small number went to New South Wales, as we have seen (Parnaby 1964: 6–7; Willard 1967: 13). For merchant shipowners the recruitment of labour was a logical extension of extant trading networks because contracted labourers could also be bought cheap in order to sell dear. As a result of this activity of merchant capital, intending commodity producers in Queensland were able to obtain a supply of labour power.

From 1840 the Pacific region became a major labour reserve, not only for plantation owners in Queensland but also in the Pacific itself (Newbury 1980, 1984). More than 280,000 Melanesian and Micronesian islanders were recruited as indentured labourers for Queensland, Fiji, Samoa, and other islands between 1840 and 1915. Between 1863 and 1906, about 64,000 islanders, mainly men, were recruited for Queensland alone (Corris 1973: 46; Saunders 1984b: 221; Graves 1984: 112). A significant proportion were recruited by force and deception (Docker 1970), but these were not the only methods. Kidnapping dominated only in certain periods (Saunders 1982: 29–31; Graves 1984: 117) and at other times, islanders exercised a greater degree of choice. However, the element of choice was not necessarily individualized because clan 'chiefs' and others acted as intermediaries or 'passage masters'. They encouraged young men to sign indentures, and for each recruit they received gifts from European merchants (Corris 1973:60–6; Graves 1984:117, 129). However, the opportunity to travel was a sufficient motive for some recruits while for others indentured labour offered the possibility of advancing their position in the 'gift exchange' economy (Graves 1983:98–106).

Moreover, individual choice cannot be analysed apart from the changing economic and political circumstances of the Pacific region (Newbury 1980:21–2, 25; Graves 1984:114–15, 118–23). From the early 1860s onwards there was an increasing amount of European investment to stimulate commodity production (of, e.g., sugar, copra) and this had a disruptive and disintegrative effect on the existing mode of production. Land was alienated, local village surpluses, especially of food, entered the new circuits of distribution established by plantation production and mining, and externally produced commodities entered the 'gift exchange' economy, encouraging a dependence upon indentured migrant labour. In the case of Fiji, Indian labour under indenture was recruited to provide the main source of labour power for sugar production partly because of fears about the negative impact of plantation employment upon the indigenous population (Lal 1984: 126–27; see also Naidu 1980). And as commodity production expanded within the region new sources of labour were continually being sought. The disintegrative effects of commodity production were invariably explained as the price of 'civilization', but the evidence of force and kidnapping in labour recruitment forced both the imperial and the colonial states to intervene to regulate recruitment and establish a legal framework for the operation of the indenture system in Queensland (Parnaby 1964:59–66).

In the earliest period of recruitment Pacific islanders were employed in domestic service and shepherding and on cotton and sugar farms on six- or twelve-month contracts (Parnaby 1964:54). From 1861 the relations of production were legally constituted by a Masters and Servants Act which established periods of service of from six months to two years as well as penalties for absconding, insubordination, and attempts to increase wages (Evans *et al.* 1975:168–69, 176–78). The Polynesian Labourers' Act, 1863, attempted a systematic regulation of recruitment and employment. It required that ships engaged in the labour trade had to be registered and licensed, that those recruited had to be returned to their place of origin at the end of the contract, and that those who signed up had to have a European witness to the event. It also established three year contracts and required the employer to provide food, clothing, accommodation, and medical care, along with a minimum wage of £6 per annum (Graves 1984:116; Saunders 1982:28; 1984b:225). In 1872, following pressure from London, government agents were appointed to observe the recruitment process (Parnaby 1964:83–4; Saunders 1982:29).

As with indentured labour in the Caribbean, the provision of a wage and the supposed freedom of the individual to enter a contract of indenture was cited as evidence of a production relation which dispensed with the force and unfreedom of slave labour. Yet again the move towards a form of wage labour was more formal than real. Of the value produced by the labourer, a portion was returned directly in the form of food, clothing, etc., and the contract bound the labourer for a period of up to three years. The relations of dependence were intensified by the practice of withholding wages until the end of the indenture and by the payment of wages as truck up to 1880. Even after the Pacific Island Labourers' Act, 1880, which introduced compulsory and officially supervised pay days at six month intervals, and the facility of a savings bank, labourers were not allowed to withdraw money deposited in the bank until their contract had ended. The truck and deferred pay systems reduced the nominal value of wages and functioned as a form of social control (Graves 1983: 108–22). In addition to obstructing the commodification of labour power, the truck and deferred pay systems also hindered the general development of commodity exchange because the labourers had little or no money to spend.

Moreover, the system of recruitment remained open to abuse and coercion. For example, the agents nominated to oversee recruitment were invariably selected upon the advice of those with merchant or plantation interests and, where they were not, they remained, in practice, subordinate to the ship's master. Whichever was the case, the likelihood of the agent reporting forced recruitment was not great (Parnaby 1964: 87).

Additionally, Pacific islanders were restricted specifically to employment in tropical agriculture. In 1877, regulations were introduced which required Pacific Islanders on their first contract to be employed in tropical agriculture within thirty miles of the coast. This effectively prevented the use of Pacific island labour by pastoralists and coincided with the widespread introduction of fencing and the use of itinerant shearers, both of which reduced the pastoralists' demand for permanently employed labour (Saunders 1984b: 223). The 1880 Pacific Island Labourers' Act, as amended in 1884, extended this restriction to apply to those re-engaging for a second period, although a limited number were exempt from this restriction. Those islanders who had been resident since September 1879 were allowed to engage for any type of work at mutually agreed wages. There were 885 persons in this category, and only a minority were contracted labourers, the majority being lease-holders or engaged in petit-bourgeois activity (Saunders 1982: 153–55, 1984b: 226–27).

Thus from 1884 Pacific islanders were not only required to enter a contract of indenture which bound him/her to a particular employer and permitted only a partial exchange of labour power for a cash wage but were also restricted to working in tropical agriculture. These measures were incompatible with the development of a labour market and commodity exchange. They were the outcome of a conflict of interests within the dominant class and between a fraction of that class with interests in plantation production and the growing number of wage labourers of European origin (a conflict which paralleled that in New South Wales in the 1840s over the use of Indian labour under indenture [De Lepervanche 1984:36]). That fraction maintained that plantation production was only possible using workers capable of manual labour in tropical conditions, but those with urban interests, who did not need to draw upon Pacific island labour, feared that the continued use of such labour would prevent the development of bourgeois political freedoms. Further, they were concerned about the increasing working class agitation which simultaneously complained about the economic threat of 'cheap labour' and objected to Pacific island labour on racist grounds (Willard 1967:161). Their objective was to end the recruitment of Pacific island labour and to encourage the employment of European labour in tropical agriculture, and they therefore supported the introduction of central milling and small scale farming in the 1880s which had been induced by the fall in sugar prices (Saunders 1984b:227–32). As a result the number of cane farmers increased from 480 in 1892 to 1,450 in 1897.

But the shift from Pacific to European labour did not occur. In 1892, there were 195 employers of Pacific island labour, but by 1898 this had increased to 1,264, while throughout this period approximately 8,700 islanders remained under contract. The decision taken in 1890 to terminate the recruitment of Pacific island labour had to be rescinded in 1892. The poor conditions of work and the low rate of wages were powerful disincentives for workers of European origin and so the dependence upon indentured labour from the Pacific region remained. Only when a depression hit the pastoral and transportation industries was there a limited movement of European labour into tropical agriculture as cane-cutters (Parnaby 1964:138; Willard 1967:178; Saunders 1982:157). Despite a continuing dependence on Pacific island labour, the Pacific Island Labourers' Act, 1901, ended recruitment in 1904 and provided for the 'repatriation', with certain limited exceptions, of all Pacific islanders resident in December 1906 (Birch 1961; Corris 1972). It also provided support and incentives for sugar producers to employ 'racially superior' labour of European origin (Saunders 1982:163).

Conclusion

I have shown that unfree relations of production predominated in the Australian colonies from the time of British settlement until the middle of the nineteenth century, in the form of convict labour, and thereafter were of regional importance in frontier and pastoral areas (where Aboriginal labour was exploited) and in Queensland (where Pacific island labour was exploited). The colonial context is, again, central to explaining the appearance and reproduction of these relations of production. The nature of the original settlement, combined with the free availability of land, dictated the use of forced labour in the period up to the 1840s. And throughout the nineteenth century land was available for settlement and for subsistence and commodity production, in circumstances where free migration from Britain was on a relatively limited scale. Thus although a labour market developed in urban areas and in more heavily settled rural areas in the latter half of the nineteenth century, those outside these areas wishing to organize commodity production continued to face the problem of labour shortage. That problem was resolved by attempting to retain Aboriginal labour by direct force and legal control, and by recruiting migrant workers under indenture and restricting by law the economic sectors where their labour power might be used.

6
South Africa

Introduction

It is to the historical specificity and even uniqueness of economic and political development in South Africa that Marxist and many non-Marxist writers refer in their various attempts to unravel what they see as a paradoxical instance of capitalism (e.g. Van den Berghe 1970: 3–4; Wolpe 1975: 248). Although the debate between Marxist and non-Marxist writers about South Africa (see Stasiulis 1980) is not of direct concern here, it is the historical specificity of economic, political, and ideological relations which must gain our attention, not that this should blind us to the importance of comparative analysis (e.g. Fredrickson 1981) and to those features which are common to the formation and reproduction of the capitalist mode of production (cf. Yudelman 1983: 13–51). That the uniqueness of the development of the South African formation is relative is emphasized by a comparison with the Australian colonies. In both cases, there were migration flows from Western Europe, and from what were then conceived as 'backward' regions which were part of the British Empire, to supplement the indigenous populations which were not immediately or easily incorporated into new forms and relations of production arising from colonial intervention. The incorporation of sections of all these groups was achieved by means of unfree relations of production in Australia and South Africa. In other words, it is the particular historical pattern of incorporation that distinguishes the South African example, and this will be described and explained in this chapter.

European colonization

The early European colonization of southern Africa is a history of unfree relations of production in a region with limited links with the world commodity market. European settlement was initiated by the Dutch merchant class which established a refreshment station at the Cape of Good Hope in 1652 for ships of the monopolistic Dutch East India Company engaged in trade with India and the Far East (Schutte 1979: 174–80). Production was intended to supply these ships as well as the reproduction of those who migrated to staff the colony, and so commodity production for export was poorly developed prior to British intervention at the end of the eighteenth century (De Kiewiet 1941: 26; Wilson and Thompson 1969: 193). The European settlers were officials of the Company, subsequently supplemented by a small number of independent settlers. The latter were permitted to lease land under an annual licence, but the process of land occupation was largely uncontrolled, and Dutch cattle-herders continuously extended the boundaries of the settlement, contrary to the wishes of the local government (De Kiewiet 1941: 11, 17; Wilson and Thompson 1969: 211). By 1752 the population of European origin resident in the colony was just 5,419 (Magubane 1979: 31).

Dutch settlement led to contact with the Khoikhoi and San (known collectively as Khoisan) peoples whose subsistence was gained by a nomadic pastoralism and hunting and gathering respectively, and whose economic and social existence were interactive (Elphick 1977: 23–42). The nomadic Khoikhoi maintained large herds of cattle and sheep and continually sought out suitable grazing land for their animals. They also engaged in gathering and hunting. The San lived in smaller, unstable groups, dependent exclusively on the success of hunting and gathering. The Khoisan therefore had a material basis for an independent economic and social existence which was not dependent upon the permanent possession or occupation of a specific area of land (Elphick 1979: 5–7). As was the case with the Aboriginal population in the Australian colonies, this had implications for the outcome of the contact with the mode of production initiated by the European settlers.

European occupation of land and the continual extension of the European frontier progressively disrupted the reproduction of these subsistence, redistributive modes of production by utilizing land required for migratory herding, and by disturbing the environment in ways which made hunting less productive. Although there were economic transactions between the settlers and the Khoikhoi herders involving the exchange of cattle and women for alcohol, tobacco, and trinkets (Elphick 1977: 162–70), there was also conflict over land occupation, grazing rights, and cattle raiding. The combination of conflict and the disruption of the economic structure of the Khoikhoi (along with the spread of new diseases) led to the break-up of the socio-political structure of their communities, murder, and an enforced dependence on European settlement on the part of those who survived (Wilson and Thompson 1969: 40–63, 67–71; Fredrickson 1981: 37–8).

The possibility of co-ordinated and sustained resistance was limited by the absence of a centralized political structure amongst the Khoisan due to the migratory nature of their material reproduction (Elphick 1979:34). The San produced or possessed little that was of interest to the European settlers and they tended to be marginalized at or beyond the frontier of settlement or exterminated. The extension of the European frontier to the east also brought the European settlers into contact with the Xhosa with whom there was a partial accommodation but then a succession of wars over land and cattle (Giliomee 1979). The resistance of the Xhosa had only limited success and they lost large areas of land (Wilson and Thompson 1969:237–52; Van der Horst 1971:7).

The break-up of the economic and social organization of the Khoikhoi during the seventeenth and eighteenth centuries was accompanied by the incorporation of their labour power into agricultural and pastoral production established by Dutch settlers (Elphick 1977:175–81, 217–39). They became herders, agricultural labourers, and domestic servants, directly exchanging labour power (as well as sexual favours) for subsistence (Marais 1957:7–8, 109; Wilson and Thompson 1969:184, 211; but see Legassick 1975:239). But these people were not the only source of labour power exploited by the Dutch settlers (see Boeseken 1977). There was a trade in human beings from Africa and Asia who were bought and sold as slaves from 1658 (Armstrong 1979:77; see also Greenstein 1973) and slave labour was the predominant means of labour exploitation throughout the eighteenth century (De Kiewiet 1941:21; Marais 1957:1–2; Wilson and Thompson 1969:204–5). By 1795 there were 16,839 slaves in the Cape colony (Armstrong 1979:90). The limited and primarily subsistence production of the Cape colony (Guelke 1979:67, 70) was therefore dependent upon the institutionalization of different forms of unfree labour, and particularly upon slave labour.

Colonial control over the Cape changed when a British force took over the colony temporarily in 1795 and more permanently in 1806, with the objective of protecting the trade of British merchant capital with the East (Madgwick 1937:3). There were, however, commercial and production implications for the Cape colony (Legassick 1975:237; Freund 1979:215–20) which was not producing on any significant scale a commodity for the world market (Giliomee and Elphick 1979:368). From the 1830s there was an increase in the export of wool, stimulated by the same factors as had influenced wool production in New South Wales (Frankel 1938:47–8; Wilson and Thompson 1969:290–91; Van der Horst 1971:25). Although there was a sixfold increase in trade between 1806 and 1820, the increase was from a very low base and the structure of production within the colony was largely unchanged (Freund 1979:214). It remained dominated by agricultural and pastoral activity and by the exploitation of labour power in the form of slavery and 'voluntary' servitude. Thus in 1849 the Cape colony continued to be listed in Treasury accounts in London as a *Military and Maritime Station* and not as a *Settlement or Plantation* (De Kiewiet 1941:38).

Additionally, the imposition of British control brought the Cape colony within the orbit of conflicting forces within Britain contesting the morality and economic utility of unfree labour (Freund 1979: 220–24). The slave trade within the British Empire was abolished in 1807, but as elsewhere, the relations of production based on slave labour were maintained, as was the exchange of slaves within the colony until 1834 (Simons and Simons 1969: 16). Between these two dates a series of regulations were effected which initially increased the power of the landowners and masters over their non-slave labour force (Kloosterboer 1960: 18–19). The most important of these was a proclamation issued in November 1809 which was intended to force more of the population descended from the Khoikhoi to make their labour power available to property owners by a form of contractual servitude (Legassick 1975: 239). This population was required to have a fixed place of abode and, when absent, to possess a residence certificate or pass, or face the possibility of conviction as a vagabond. When labour power was made available for periods of more than a month, a written contract was required, the contract stipulating that the master had to provide the means of subsistence for the servant and the remainder of the family. A proclamation issued in April 1812 empowered a farmer to apprentice children of servants raised on the farm for ten years from the age of eight.

However, these measures were contrary to policy in London which was moving towards the abolition of slave labour. The governor of the colony, anticipating pressure, issued a further proclamation in 1828 which, *inter alia*, abolished the pass system, limited contracts of service to the duration of one year, and permitted the apprenticeship of children only with parental consent (Marais 1957: 116–21, 156–58; Simons and Simons 1969: 16; Wilson and Thompson 1969: 303–05, 1971: 196).

But the landowning class seeking the legal regulation of the relations of production in the Cape colony had to take account additionally of the small but increasing migration from Britain of people who possessed little or no property and who had no access to the means of production. This began with the experimental schemes sponsored by the British state between 1815 and 1826 (see Chapter 5). The subsequent limited flow of migration included indentured servants. The problem facing the landowning class was the enforcement of the contract in a colonial context where there was an expanding frontier and a general shortage of labour. Their concern was therefore to increase their legal powers, and the governor obliged with a proclamation in June 1818 which established a sentence of two months imprisonment and a fine for any servant who defaulted on a contract (Simons and Simons 1969: 17).

The abolition of slave labour in 1834 reopened the problem of the recruitment and retention of labour power. The consequences paralleled those in the Caribbean in the same period (see Chapter 4). An ordinance in 1835 required that ex-slaves become apprentices to their previous owner who would provide the means of subsistence but no wages, and established a disciplinary code for desertion, negligence, indolence, damage to property, unlawful conspiracy, etc. When apprenticeship ended in 1838, there was a flight from the farms and then a shortage of labour. The immediate result was agitation for legal measures to restrict further the freedom of labourers (Marais 1957: 190–94).

There followed a Masters and Servants Ordinance in 1841 which applied to any person who entered relations of production as servants, the latter being defined to include any person employed for hire, wages, or other form of remuneration. The 1841 Ordinance (which repealed that of 1828) established criminal sanctions for breach of contract by the servant, extended the maximum length of contract from one month to one year in the case of oral contracts and from one year to three years in the case of written contracts (Wilson and Thompson 1969:309; Simons and Simons 1969:17–20; Legassick 1975:239). But none of these measures produced a solution to the problem of labour shortage. Consideration was given to importing convicts from Britain, but there was opposition within the colony and no action was taken. However, the labour power of convicts within the colony was used to build roads, alongside 'free' European settlers imported for the same purpose at public expense (Van der Horst, 1971:26).

The Cape colony was granted representative government in 1853 and three years later the government extended the provisions of the 1841 ordinance in the form of a Masters and Servants Act which was to apply to all servants, including those arriving from Europe (Marais 1957: 205–7). This Act established a form of contractual servitude under which labour power was exchanged for the means of subsistence and, on occasion, a small cash wage (Marais 1957:130, 185). It also established maximum lengths for contracts, one year in the case of oral contracts and five years in the case of written contracts. Breaches of the Act (breach of contract, indiscipline, and injury to property) were declared criminal rather than civil wrongs in order that masters could utilize the power of the state to hold and exploit a workforce. Masters were also subject to the legislation, but the penalties were minimal. The law was amended in 1873 to reduce penalties for offences by servants and to increase those by masters, although the fundamental purpose of the legislation remained unchanged. This Act structured relations of production well into the twentieth century (Doxey 1961:128–29; Simons and Simons 1969:23, 30; Van der Horst 1971:35–6).

The extension and consequences of colonial settlement

The abolition of slave labour was one of the factors which led to the extension of colonial settlement by farmers of Dutch origin who objected to the loss of the right to hold people as property (Fredrickson 1981:163–70). They migrated to the east and north east with the aim of gaining political and economic independence from the British-controlled Cape colony. Thus European settlement in regions later known as Natal, Transvaal, and the Orange Free State began, but only after the military subjugation of the African population. The state in the Cape colony was unhappy about the extension of the frontier, not least because of their fears of the consequences of conflict with the African population and of any attempt that might be made to force them into servitude (Welsh 1971: 7–10). Although annexation of Natal in 1843 was successful, the initial attempt to annex Transvaal and the Orange Free State in 1848 was not, partly because of a reluctance in London to provide the necessary resources (Wilson and Thompson 1969: 334, 423–24; Magubane 1979: 43–5).

The migration of farmers of Dutch origin was simultaneously a migration of the unfree relations of production that they wished to retain. They were primarily pastoralists who also grew their own vegetables and cereals. Most of what they produced was for subsistence, and very little entered the poorly developed exchange networks (Frankel 1938: 44–5). Almost all the labour power was provided by imported slaves and the descendants of the Khoikhoi, for the migrant farmers encouraged or forced many of the latter bonded servants to move with them.

In the latter case labour was made available not by isolated individuals but by family groups who, in return, were allowed access to a plot of land and were provided with various goods in kind. Only rarely was there an exchange of labour power for money. This form of production relation is defined as *labour tenancy* (see below). The dependency of the labourer was therefore direct and unmediated by money, and was reinforced by legal relations which prevented all members of the family providing labour power from owning land, horses, or firearms, or from moving around without a pass. These regulations were intended to prevent labourers from either establishing themselves as independent producers or from gaining access to the means of resistance, and hence to bind them to the landowner indefinitely (Wilson and Thompson 1969: 335–6, 366–7, 407–8, 425, 435; Legassick 1975: 242; Fredrickson 1981: 52, 89–90).

Following settlement, other means were used to procure labour power, especially in areas of sparse African settlement. In the course of conflict with African communities, military officers purposely captured young children with the intention of apprenticing them to farmers. These 'apprentices' were supposed to be freed once they had reached a certain age. In addition, parents could also voluntarily transfer their children into apprenticeship, although the relations of extreme dependence that they occupied meant that the scope for voluntarism was limited (Wilson and Thompson 1969: 335, 367, 437).

Overall, European colonization had various consequences. There is a complex history here and no space to document it. But for the African populations there were three main outcomes (FAO 1982: 9). First, as has been described, a proportion were encouraged or forced into providing labour power for Europeans who occupied the land. The relations of production ranged from labour tenancy to relations which approximated to slavery. Second, groups of Africans, often from different clans and tribes, found themselves living on land claimed by European settlers but not necessarily occupied or individually owned by them. Sections of such land were allocated or conceded to these groups. In the Cape Colony and Natal, Africans were free to purchase land either individually or collectively (Wilson and Thompson 1971:82). Third, certain African chiefdoms were allowed to maintain political control and to remain on ancestral land or land allocated for the purpose. In these reserves the traditional land tenure system was retained, alongside traditional political relations, but in return for some degree of subordination to the colonial administration.

Only one of thee outcomes was determined by the colonizers' demand for labour power. The objective of the latter two was to permit African communities to reproduce themselves independently of the European colonizers by allowing direct access to land as a means of production. Thus where African labour power was not required the communities were marginalized. This reflected the weak economic condition of the region: African communities produced little or no surplus which could enter international exchange and European farmers were engaged largely in subsistence production. Wool was the only significant export, exports rising to 25 million pounds per annum by 1862. Exchange relations were therefore poorly developed and there was little scope for the accumulation of wealth within the region (Frankel 1938:47–8; Wilson and Thompson 1971:1–4, 107; Hobart Houghton 1976:10). But this marginalization of large sections of the African population was to prove problematic when the demand for labour increased. The contradictions first became evident in Natal.

Plantation production in Natal

The annexation of Natal was determined by political factors, supported by commercial interests. The newly installed colonial administration was immediately faced with the task of organizing and administering the African population which was increasing in number as result of a return migration of those who had fled during earlier disruption. Governor Shepstone devised a system of indirect rule whereby the established tribal authorities remained in control over the African population which was settled on reserves where existing relations of production could be reproduced. Additionally, the imposition of taxation was intended to raise money for the colonial state and to force Africans to seek a cash income by selling their labour power. Finally, as a result of maintaining traditionalism, it was hoped that pressures for the formation of a resistance movement would be minimized and extant conflicts between African groups would be reproduced.

A series of contradictions arose from this strategy. In order to realize the political advantages, the material foundation of the extant political relations had to be successfully reproduced which meant that the conditions for the successful reproduction of African agricultural production had to be recreated. Two contradictions arose from this. First, the amount of land required to maintain the African population thereby reduced the amount available for colonial settlement. Second, the successful maintenance of African agricultural production, to the point where production of sufficient surplus allowed the payment of the hut tax, would minimize any economic pressures on the population to sell their labour power (Palmer 1977: 12). In other words the conditions for the successful reproduction of the African redistributive mode of production contradicted the demand of the colonizers for ever-increasing areas of land and for labour power (cf. Beinart 1979: 200). Yet not to attempt to guarantee the reproduction of the established political structures promised to lead to African resistance.

The contradictions were exposed, first, in the political opposition to Shepstone's scheme. The Colonial Secretary in London claimed in 1849 that it was both impossible to allocate sufficient land for reserves to permit economic self-sufficiency and inexpedient because it would not force sufficient Africans to provide labour power. The latter claim was contested within the colony by others who argued that there was an adequate supply but that its availability was affected by the conditions under which it was procured (Welsh 1971: 31–2, 177–79). They were exposed, second, by the course of events. Both the spatial area and the quality of the land allocated to the reserves were insufficient to support all of the African population in Natal and a majority lived either on Crown land as squatters or on privately owned land as tenants. Moreover, from the late 1870s productivity on the reserves declined dramatically as a result of an interaction between the poor quality of the land, climatic conditions, and ill-judged attempts to 'improve' production.

There were two consequences. First, European farmers were provided with a labour force which they exploited by means of labour tenancy. An attempt was made to encourage this by a decision in 1857 to exempt Africans resident on farms from paying the hut tax, but it had only limited success, suggesting that the African desire for self-sufficiency was strong and that large sections of the African population continued to be capable of independent production. Second, by the end of the century, an increasing proportion of Africans were opting to become migrant workers (Welsh 1971: 188–95).

But these two developments were themselves contradictory. The latter did eventually have the effect of increasing the proportion of the African population that was required by economic pressure to sell labour power for a wage, while the former served to increase the proportion that was bound in a semi-servile condition to a landowning class which had little interest in improving farming and increasing production (De Kiewiet 1941: 83). The former meant the formal transformation of labour power into a commodity whereas the latter involved the appropriation of labour power by the utilization of extra-economic means which nevertheless ensured that Africans remained capable of producing directly their own subsistence on land made available to them by farmers. In other words, the former facilitated the emergence of a labour market while the latter retarded it. Other factors reinforced this retardation.

First, much of the land in European ownership was not occupied, partly because of the failure to find an agricultural product which could be commodified. With the slow introduction of a cash economy, represented in this case by the introduction of rent, this land was increasingly made available to Africans in return for cash. Moreover, rents increased as African demand for access to this land increased. This development provided another avenue by which the African could avoid offering labour power for sale as the means of gaining subsistence. Second, in 1880 it was decided to sell Crown lands and Africans were numbered amongst the purchasers. Although there were only 1,548 registered African landowners in 1907, this nevertheless allowed a section of the African population to reproduce itself independently of the economic relations determined by colonial settlement.

These contradictions became evident with the development of commodity production to supply the world market. Included amongst the settlers from Britain were individuals wishing to organize agricultural commodity production in a context where world demand for sugar remained high. They were joined by a small number of sugar planters from the Caribbean (Tinker 1974:30). The main obstacle to the development of sugar production was the recruitment of a labour force. With the majority of the African population able to produce its subsistence from the land, it became necessary to recruit labour from outside the region. Hence the sugar planters called for the intervention of the state to recruit indentured labour from China or India. The export of labour under indenture from India was well-established elsewhere (Cumpston, 1953:173, 178; see Chapter 4) and so the colonial state was able to negotiate the introduction of extant procedures. The necessary legislation was passed in Natal in 1859 and in India in 1860, following which the Natal state appointed various officials to organize and monitor the recruitment of indentured labour (Thomson 1952: 3–4; Tinker 1974:96–7; Palmer 1977:14–20).

The supply of Indian indentured labour solved the immediate problem of labour shortage. The first phase of migration was terminated by depression in 1866, by which time approximately 6,000 Indians had entered Natal. This figure included women, who were to constitute 35 per cent of the total migration. Indentured migration began again in 1874, but only after complaints of bad treatment had forced the Natal government to improve supervision (Tinker 1974:244, 247–48). It continued until 1911 when the Indian government stopped the migration because the South African government refused to guarantee that Indians would be accepted as permanent citizens after the expiry of the period of indenture (Tinker 1974:290–314). During the early period of indenture, most recruits worked in the sugar industry, but the labour shortage affected the economy of Natal as a whole, and indentured labour was increasingly used on the railways and in dockyards, coal mines, municipal services, and domestic employment. Throughout the period of indentured migration, the Natal state subsidized from public revenue the costs of recruitment, and the employers never paid the full costs (Thomson 1952:32, 35–6, 65; Kuper 1960:2, 5; Palmer 1977:26).

The indenture system was established in its classic form. The recruit was contracted to provide labour power, first for three years and later for five, in return for food, accommodation, medical attention, and a small wage, all to be provided by the planter. Movement off the plantation was regulated by a pass system and fines and/or imprisonment could be imposed where the labourer was absent from work without legal reason. Indeed, desertion and absenteeism (along with sabotage and suicide) were the main means of resistance used by labourers (Tayal 1977:542–45; Bhana and Pachai 1984:17–20). When the period of indenture was completed, the contracted labourer had a number of options, including a return passage to India, entering a new contract, or remaining in Natal as a free individual and eligible to receive a small grant of land (Thomson 1952:13–14; Wilson and Thompson 1969:388).

The latter option was the result of two factors. First, the assumption that Africans would elect to work on the sugar plantations and replace the Indian labourers (Thomson 1952:16), proved to be unfounded. Second, the Indian government insisted that labourers be allowed to remain in Natal in the hope that this would help to relieve rural poverty and unemployment in India (Palmer 1977:27). Material deprivation was the key factor inducing Indians to enter contracts of indenture (Saha 1970:38–61) and was a disincentive to return. Consequently, a large proportion of indentured labourers elected to remain in Natal, many signing new contracts of indenture while the remainder entered semi-skilled labour or became shopowners or market gardeners.

The central contradiction arising from colonization of South Africa is now evident. The majority of the African population retained access to the means of production (Wilson and Thompson 1969:390) and this obstructed any sudden transformation into a labour force for European property owners concerned to develop commodity production. This was overdetermined by the unfree relations of production maintained by landowners engaged in mainly subsistence production. This set of circumstances reflected the limited penetration of economic and political forces which could transform the region by the introduction of large-scale commodity production and of free relations of production (Frankel 1938:48; Wilson and Thompson 1969:380–81; cf. De Kiewiet 1941:81–4). In turn, this explains the very low number of migrants entering the colony from Britain during the period of the major emigration from Western Europe to North America and Australia: in 1959 there were 8,000 people of European origin in Natal and 18,000 in 1870 (Wilson and Thompson 1969:380; De Kiewiet 1941:70). This contradiction was further exposed by the development of diamond and gold mining.

The development of mining

That the discovery of diamonds around Kimberley in 1867 and of gold in Witwatersrand in 1886 was the origin of a major transformation of economic and political relations in Southern Africa is indisputable (Frankel 1938:107; Legassick 1974a:260). At the time of these discoveries the region made only a very limited contribution to the world economy. Wool and sugar were the only significant agricultural exports, although on a small scale, and there was competition with other parts of the colonized world. Moreover, there was little evidence of an internally generated accumulation of wealth (Wilson and Thompson 1971:1). However, diamonds and gold were in high demand and fetched a high price, while the latter played a major role in the operation of the international capitalist economy (Magubane 1979:113–14). The development of the mining of these minerals had the following consequences. First, it stimulated an internal and an international migration to the mining regions. Second, it required the development of an adequate infrastructure in the form of road and railway links with the coast. This in turn increased the demand for labour. Third, it created a concentrated market for food, thereby stimulating the expansion of agricultural production in the colonies. Fourth, it created pressure for the political unification of the colonies.

Although the individual prospector played an important role in the very early phase of the mining of diamonds and gold, the fact that the most important sources of mineral-bearing rock were buried below the surface necessitated the formation and domination of large mining companies which were capable of funding deep-level mining. Other factors encouraged a move towards monopoly, including in the case of diamonds the pressure to eliminate competition in order to force up the sale price (De Kiewiet 1941:92–9, 115–19; Wilson and Thompson 1971:11–13). But these developments depended upon the initial recruitment of a labour force.

European diamond prospectors hired Africans for a wage and agitated to ensure that they did not have the right to gain a licence to dig for diamonds. A proclamation of 1872 set out the conditions governing the recruitment and retention of labour and effected measures intended to prevent the theft of diamonds by labourers (Simons and Simons 1969:37; Van der Horst 1971:74). First, it restricted the issue of licences to those persons certified by a magistrate or justice of the peace to be of 'good character'. Second, it stipulated that labour contracts had to be registered and those hired were required to produce certificates of registration on demand. Third, a labourer who left a mining area was required to carry a pass.

The consolidation of mines meant that this master/servant relationship became one between a management hierarchy and a large number of labourers rather than between a single individual and a few labourers. Moreover, the relations of production were increasingly structured by the compound system which was an attempt to prevent diamond theft and a means of control over labour power (Simons and Simons 1969:41; Doxey 1961:35). It also served to sustain a system of migrant labour by providing accommodation and food for labourers whose presence was deemed to be temporary. Thus labour was recruited using a contract system which entailed subjugation to a series of extra-economic controls ranging from the compound to the risk of criminal sanctions for breach of contract. In part these relations of production incorporated existing legal provisions determining the procurement and retention of labour.

When gold was discovered in Witwatersrand, the flow of investment into the colonies had already established a property-owning mining class (Bozzoli 1981:31-3). Sections of this class moved to the Rand, bringing with them the wealth necessary to finance the development of gold mining, and the experience of a form of unfree labour (Frankel 1938:72). But in order to explain the relations of production that they established, it is also necessary to understand the particular problems facing the development of gold production. First, the price of gold was fixed internationally, making it impossible to pass on automatically increased production costs. The corollary was that holding down the costs of production was vital to obtaining a surplus product. Second, the gold-bearing ore was generally of low quality and formed a seam which penetrated deep below the surface, necessitating the extraction of large quantities of ore from deep shafts which was a costly and labour-intensive operation. This implied a labour process which maximized labour productivity and minimized the return to labour (Johnstone 1976:19-20; Levy 1982:16).

The mining companies intended to recruit labour by means of a cash wage, presupposing the existence of a labour market and, hence, of a population which had been at least partially deprived of access to the means of production. Moreover, the demand of mining capital was for a differentiated labour market. There was no supply of skilled labour in the South African colonies, and so recruitment occurred from Western Europe, particularly Britain (De Kiewiet 1941:119). As for semi- and unskilled labour, recruitment was envisaged from within the South African colonies, and this required the mining companies to confront the marginalization of large sections of the African population and its continuing access to the means of production. As the development of diamond mining demonstrated, there was a section of the African population which was either deprived of land or wished to earn sufficient money to purchase land or a gun, but this was limited in size and did not meet the demand (Legassick 1977: 179). In effect the mining companies faced a labour shortage.

The problem was compounded by certain of the consequences of mining development. The creation of a market for food occurred in a context where both Africans and Europeans had access to the necessary means of production. An African peasantry had access to the land as owners and tenants and was capable of producing on a small scale to satisfy its own reproduction needs and to engage in exchange (Wilson and Thompson 1971: 50). Sections of this class experienced a period of relative prosperity after 1870 as a result of supplying agricultural goods as commodities in response to increased demand. Indeed, so successful was this response that a small class of African commercial farmers emerged (Wilson and Thompson 1971: 56; Van der Horst 1971: 104; Bundy 1979: 9–10, 66–7, 92). This development was most pronounced in the Cape Colony but was also apparent in the other three colonies.

The success of this peasant class intensified emergent contradictions within the African tribal economies and between European farming interests and the infant mining economy. Concerning the former, communal land ownership was threatened, along with traditional power relationships. Concerning the latter, European farming interests found themselves in competition with African peasant producers in a situation where they found it was increasingly difficult to obtain labour, a problem intensified by the increasing demands of the mining industry (Wilson and Thompson 1971: 117). Above all the very success of the peasant producer between 1870 and 1890 provided a section of the African population with a means of reproduction which protected it from incorporation in the mining industry as a provider of labour power (Bundy 1979: 78, 112–14).

The rise of this class was terminated by a combination of processes, which includes state aid to increase the competitiveness of European landowners, declining productivity of peasant agriculture (caused by factors such as drought, animal disease, and population increase), and increasing peasant indebtedness caused by the purposive over-extension of credit. Significantly, it was also affected by state measures which were intended to compel Africans to work for the mining companies (Wilson and Thompson 1971: 56–9; Bundy 1979: 110, 115, 127–30, 134). The consequence was that by the first decade of the twentieth century sections of the peasant class were being forced into the mines alongside other sections of the African population which had been separated from the means of production by state coercion.

State coercion required legislation and the administration of various procedures and sanctions. But the predominant interest represented within the state was that of farming (Levy 1982: 22–3, 74) and so a lobby of state representative was necessary. This, in turn, presupposed some unanimity between the mining companies. Although the companies established a co-ordinating body, the Chamber of Mines, in 1887 to represent their collective interests and to co-ordinate common production-related tasks (Johnstone 1976: 16), they continued to compete with each other in the recruitment of labour until the second decade of the twentieth century. Initially each company operated its own system of recruitment and decided its own wage rates. Recruiting agents were employed, each receiving a *per capita* payment for every labourer recruited. In the context of labour shortage, wages and recruitment costs tended to rise, reducing profitability (Levy 1982: 45–6; Jeeves 1985: 120).

Following political pressure the state intervened on behalf of the mining companies during the 1890s. The gold mining companies had opted for a migrant labour system similar to that developed for diamond mining. Single, male workers were recruited on contract for specified periods of time and were housed in compounds (where a male-dominated culture emerged, in which alcohol consumption and prostitution were central elements [Van Onselen 1982a: 5–6, 27]). Within the compounds, certain reproduction needs were met directly by the company, although a small wage was also paid. This sytem of recruitment and control depended on a mechanism to prevent and punish desertion. The Chamber of Mines drafted regulations in 1895 which were effected by the Transvaal government in 1896 (Van der Horst 1971: 133–34). These pass regulations were modelled on earlier regulations and required the African miner to possess documents legitimating travel to and residence in the mining area. These were later strengthened to increase their effectiveness (Jeeves 1975: 11–12; Levy 1982: 76–9).

Being concerned to increase controls over labour already recruited, these regulations did little to increase the supply of labour. The Chamber of Mines saw a solution to the latter problem in the imposition of taxation which, by requiring payment in cash, would force Africans to enter wage labour. Such legislation was introduced in other South African colonies but not in Transvaal. For example, the Glen Gray Act of 1894 imposed a ten shilling tax on all men in Cape colony who could not prove that they had been in wage employment for three months in every year. It was also intended to divorce agricultural subsistence producers from the land by introducing rules of hereditary succession based on primogeniture which would make the majority of dependants landless. In addition, as was explained in an official report at the time:

'The intention was to locate these resident natives on these surveyed allotments, and to make no provision for the natural increase of the population, the surplus to find work elsewhere: so that . . . during the coming generation a limited number will be agriculturalists, i.e. native farmers – and the rest will have to go out and work.'

(cited in Wilson and Thompson 1971: 65)

This was highly unpopular with the African population and was repealed in 1905 when it had failed to achieve these objectives (Van der Horst 1971: 149; Jeeves 1985: 16).

Faced with a continuing labour shortage (intensified by the development of deep-level mining in the last decade of the century), the Chamber of Mines sought to recruit labour from Mozambique which had been opened originally for labour recruitment by agents working for diamond companies. Between 1896 and 1898, 60 per cent of mineworkers employed by the Chamber of Mines came from Mozambique (First 1983: 16). In 1896 the Chamber of Mines gained the agreement of the mining companies to form a centralized recruiting agency, the Witwatersrand Native Labour Supply Association (WNSLA), which had a monopoly over the recruitment of labour from outside the four South African colonies (Johnstone 1976: 16). The objective was to reduce recruitment costs by eliminating competition between mining companies and by negotiating concessions from the Portuguese-controlled colonial state in Mozambique which obtained financial benefits from the arrangement (Levy 1982: 81–2; First 1983: 17–24; Jeeves 1985: 189–90). This objective was realized for it proved easier to recruit on annual contracts sufficient numbers of workers who retained access to the land in Mozambique, to which they returned on completion of their contract (Legassick and de Clerq 1984: 147–48).

Further attempts to increase the supply of African labour were postponed by the outbreak of the Boer War, the origin of which lay in conflicts over the promotion of the interests of the gold-mining companies and the concern of the British state to unify the South African colonies (De Kiewiet 1941: 138–39; Legassick 1974a: 260). After the victory of the British forces there was a greater willingness on the part of the Transvaal state to support the interests of the gold-mining companies (Jeeves 1975: 13; Levy 1982: 134). The prewar legislation concerning the recruitment and control over labour power was amended or incorporated into new legislation, reinforcing the contract system and the use of criminal sanctions to deal with breaches of contract. But the problem of finding sufficient recruits at the 'right price' remained:

> 'For a rapid development of the Rand, for a large accumulation of profits, an unlimited supply of cheap, docile and regular labour was necessary – but it was also wanting. That was the Rand crisis of 1903.'
>
> (Crawford 1923: 169)

The consequence was an increase in wages in an attempt to increase the supply of labour (Levy 1982: 137–38, 145, 151–52, 157; Richardson 1982: 15–16)

The response was to seek alternative sources of semi- and unskilled labour. One was unemployed workers of European origin, although it was widely recognized that this could be only a temporary measure because any long-term use of this source would lead to increased wage and reproduction costs. Other initiatives included an attempt to dislodge African 'houseboys' by the immigration of female domestics from Britain, with the intention that the former would then seek paid work in the mines (Van Onselen 1982a: 33–4) and the introduction of a more flexible wage scale in order to facilitate the retention of experienced workers (Denoon 1967: 481–82, 488; Levy 1982: 163, 170; Richardson 1982: 16). In the light of the continuing labour shortage, the Chamber of Mines concluded in 1903 that a more strategic initiative was necessary in order to expand the labour supply and drive down wages (Richardson 1977: 88; Levy 1982: 170). But the recruitment of labour from outside the Transvaal depended upon the support and intervention of the local state.

State support for the mining interests followed from the report of the Transvaal Labour Commission, established in 1903 to consider the labour shortage in the colony. Its majority report concluded that there was no adequate supply of labour in central or southern Africa, a conclusion that implicitly ruled out the use of unemployed labour of European origin. It rejected the idea of increasing taxation to coerce Africans into mine work on the grounds that the African population could respond by increasing agricultural output (as did happen) and that even if this did not happen, the supply of African labour would not increase quickly. It therefore recommended an extension of the migration of labour under contract (Simons and Simons 1969: 80; Levy 1982: 171–92; Richardson 1984a: 267, 1984b).

In the light of the report the Chamber of Mines requested in 1903 that the Transvaal state permit the import of labour from China which had served as a source of labour for other British colonies from the mid-nineteenth century (Crawford 1923; Farley 1968). Negotiations led to the Anglo-Chinese Labour Convention of 1904 and the Transvaal Labour Importation Ordinance of 1904 which established the legal and administrative framework for the import of labour under indenture (Richardson 1982: 29–38, 1984a: 269). The contract was for an initial period of three years with an option of renewal for two further years. Although a wage was paid, the relations of production were additionally structured by the terms of the contract which defined the labourer as a temporary resident with limited political and legal rights (Crawford 1923: 176–78). The contract ensured that the employer had considerable powers over the direction and retention of labour power and subjected the labourer to a pass system. Any breach of contract (such as desertion, inefficiency) by the labourer was defined as a criminal offence. The regulations also restricted the use of Chinese labour to unskilled manual labour in the mines in order to ameliorate the concerns of skilled labour and the commercial petit-bourgeoisie in the colony, both of whom feared the consequences of competition, a fear that was sustained partly by the evidence of the economic position achieved by time-expired Indians in Natal (Crawford 1923: 171–72).

Recruitment of labour was carried out by the Chamber of Mines Labour Importation Agency mainly in the north of China and was most successful where poverty was endemic (Richardson 1984b: 167–73). Only men were recruited, and all those considered unfit for work were excluded. A total of 63,695 Chinese labourers were landed in South Africa between 1904 and 1907 (Richardson 1982: 61, 140, 1984a: 271–73). The effect of this addition to the labour supply was largely as intended. The unskilled labour force in the mines was almost doubled between 1904 and 1907, fluctuations in the supply of African labour were ironed out, labour turnover was reduced, the experimental use of European labour was terminated, and the steep rise in African wages was halted. By 1905 the supply of labour exceeded the demand, and this allowed the mining companies not only to hold down wages, but also to extend the contracts of African workers to a year (Denoon 1967: 492; Richardson 1982: 176–78; Levy 1982: 228, 238–41). But this proved to be only a temporary resolution of the problem of maintaining a supply of labour for the gold mines (Jeeves 1985: 87–91).

The development of mining did not directly lead to widespread urbanization, partly because the compound system prevented family migration and partly because the migration system prevented settlement. And there was no significant pressure to develop manufacturing industry until the First World War when imports were restricted and, even then, manufacturing did not expand at a great rate until tariff protection was introduced in the mid-1920s (Hobart Houghton 1976: 121–22). Although there was pressure leading to changing relations and methods of production in agriculture, this sector remained weak at the turn of the century (De Kiewiet 1941: 183–85, 204; Wilson and Thompson 1971: 135) and was able to retain within its influence, if not control, large sections of the African population.

Mining, sustained by a massive import of investment from Europe (Kubicek 1979: 22), was the dynamic element, resulting in dramatic uneven development between mining and agriculture (Morris 1980: 223). One measure of this uneven development was the slow progress in breaking the link between the African and the land and this was the crucial factor which necessitated the recruitment of labour from outside the South African colonies. The recruitment of labour from Mozambique and China demonstrated that the measures taken to coerce Africans to make their labour power available as a commodity were inadequate to meet the increasing demand. Large numbers of Africans continued to retain access to land and were therefore able to produce their own subsistence and, where required, to meet taxation imposed on them (e.g. Beinart 1979: 200).

The significance of the land question

At the turn of the century Africans retained direct access to the land by three main means. First, although they had few resources to take advantage of this, Africans in Natal and the Cape colony continued to have the legal right to purchase land, a right that was extended to Africans in Transvaal and the Orange Free State at the end of the Boer

War. Second, in Natal areas of land had been set aside exclusively for African occupation. Third, whether landowners organized production for subsistence or the market, they wished to retain access to labour to do the necessary work, and so tenancy arrangements were maintained. The comparative importance of each means of access is difficult to determine. Significantly, one of the few detailed studies of agriculture during this period (Bundy 1979) offers no overall figures for African land ownership. But it is reasonable to assume that the process of land appropriation by settlers and the limited means of Africans to obtain money ensured that individual land ownership was confined to a minority of the African population and therefore that some form of tenancy predominated.

The predominant form of tenancy was *labour tenancy*: 'In return for residence, the right to cultivate a piece of land and graze a few animals, the landowner usually received the services of the tenants in the field and of his women in the household' (De Kiewiet 1941:203; see also Wilson and Thompson 1971:117). This relation of production governed relations between settlers and sections of the African population from the mid-nineteenth century. Up until the early part of the twentieth century the labour tenant often owned the implements (means of production) with which to work the land and could be called on to perform service at any point in the year. The total product of the labour tenant was appropriated by the landowner for consumption or exchange, but in return for access to land on which production for both subsistence and exchange could take place. Hence, labour tenancy immobilized the African labourer on the land (Frankel 1938:125–26). In certain areas, particularly the Orange Free State, this relation shaded into a form of share-cropping (called farming-on-the-half) whereby the landowner provided land and seed, the tenant provided labour power, and the product was shared (Bundy 1979:206; Wilson and Thompson 1971:128).

It was not only Africans who were bound to landowners by some variant of labour tenancy (De Kiewiet 1941:187–94; Wilson and Thompson 1971:120). Once European settlement on the land reached its geographical limit, the male members of a family became dependent on the subdivision of land for access to the means of production. Extensive subdivision created landlessness amongst the population of European origin and many of these gained access to land by making their labour power available to a landowner. Some received a small cash wage. The number of Europeans without direct access to land was increased by a continuing migration into the region (Horwitz 1967:31–3).

Landowners were opposed to any measure, whether economic or legal, which threatened to deprive them of access to labour power. It was partly for this reason that legal measures intended to coerce Africans into some variant of wage-earning under contract were rendered ineffective. For example Bundy has argued with reference to the Orange Free State:

'Anti-squatting laws and other legislation designed to promote the flow of labour were enacted year after year . . . yet the same years saw considerable settlement by African peasants on government and private lands. Anti-squatting measures remained dead letters as long as collection of tribute from African peasants remained the easiest means of appropriating surplus.'

(1979: 204)

There were also conflicts of interest between different groups of farmers over access to labour power, especially where some opted for production for exchange and wished to attract more labour. The latter were in favour of an extension of dispossession, especially of those Africans who continued to make a success of peasant production, but they were thereby also competitors with mining companies for access to such 'released' labour, and yet not necessarily capable of matching even the depressed wages in the diamond and gold mines. This was a conflict of interest that was to continue through the 1920s and 1930s (Lacey 1981: 13).

A major advance in the process of partial dispossession of the African population was achieved after the formation of the Union of South Africa in 1910 with the passage of the Natives Land Act, 1913. Its main provision was to prohibit Africans from owning or renting land outside what were defined as scheduled areas or native reserves which constituted just 13 per cent of the total land area of South Africa. The Act also prohibited share-cropping in the Orange Free State. The intention was to increase the supply of labour available for hire and to eliminate the class of African peasant producers (Bundy 1979: 213). Yet labour tenancy was specifically permitted by the Act, in the interests of landowning farmers who could thereby retain a supply of labour on the land. However, although the main pressure for the Act came from agricultural interests (Wilson and Thompson 1971: 129), there was no provision to require the dispossessed to make their labour power available exclusively to farmers. There was a continuing demand for labour in the mines and in the small towns, and the Act prompted an internal migration of Africans seeking a means of subsistence following their dispossession (Wilson and Thompson 1971: 132; Lacey 1981: 275).

The Natives Land Act initiated a longer-term strategy. By confining African access to the land to the reserves, a process of partial segregation was initiated so that an 'independent' material and cultural existence for the African was only possible in circumstances which obstructed any possible competitive threat (FAO 1982: 22). The inferior quality of the land and its limited quantity (De Kiewiet 1941: 206) ensured that, but also established conditions whereby a proportion of the African population resident in such areas would be increasingly unable to produce their subsistence, an outcome which would force it to seek an employer. The policy of segregation was to become, therefore, a key determinant of the maintenance of the migrant labour system within South Africa because the reserves became reservoirs of labour (Wolpe 1972: 432; Legassick 1977: 182). Although economic forces

operating within the reserves forced Africans to seek an employer outside their boundaries (Lacey 1981:41), their existence was dependent
initially on a politico-legal intervention by the South African state.

However, dispossession was not complete so long as a proportion of
Africans could continue as illegal squatters on unused land owned by
absentee landlords. Moreover, the legal act of dispossession, although it
created a landless class of Africans outside the reserves, could not in
itself guarantee to meet the demand immediately for labour in all
sectors. Indeed, the reserve system is better understood as a necessarily
contradictory phenomenon and not as an unproblematic and functional
means of ensuring a supply of labour power. Viewed in this way it is
easier to explain the continuing difficulties of the mining companies in
obtaining a labour force and their resulting dependence upon an
expensive system of competitive recruitment during the second decade
of the twentieth century (Jeeves 1985:3–6).

One important contradiction arose from the conflicting interests of
mining companies and farmers over access to labour power. Both
favoured dispossession as a means of compelling Africans to work for
them, but once this had been achieved, they became competitors (with
the small manufacturing enterprises in the towns) for the labour that
was 'released'. Moreover, the reserve system was in itself a benefit to
the mining companies but problematic for the landowners wishing to
produce for the market. The greater the proportion of the African
population located in the reserves, the less that would be available for
farmers who wanted a source of labour power resident permanently on
their land. The farming class therefore wanted to limit the segregation
of the African and to bind the African as securely as possible to the land
to prevent labour power being 'attracted' to the mines and the growing
urban areas. This contradiction was intensified by the continuation of
squatting. The mining companies tended to favour the forced removal
of squatters to the reserves whereas the farmers favoured dispossession
and their redistribution amongst the farmers (Lacey 1981:180–81).

This contradiction was mediated by the state in the interests of the
farming class. Financial support for agricultural production organized
by European farmers had been provided from 1910, partly by drawing
on the profits of the mining companies. Between 1910 and 1936 an
estimated £112 million was spent on the development of European
agricultural production compared with a little more than £600,000 on
agriculture in the reserves (Horwitz 1967:136; see also Frankel 1938:116;
De Kiewiet 1941:253–59). This financial support encouraged a rational-
ization of production which became increasingly more oriented to
production for exchange, but this led to an increased demand for labour
as well as a more systematic and rational use of labour power. The
labour problem therefore became more intense during the period 1923
to 1929. The landowning class feared, and was incapable of surviving
(because of low levels of mechanization), an unfettered competition for
labour because it would increase the very low wages on offer. It

therefore favoured a policy which would bind labour to the land and called for restrictions on the areas in which mine recruiting agents could operate (Morris 1980:219; Lacey 1981:149–50).

Various legislative measures were taken between 1924 and 1932 to entrench and rationalize the labour tenancy system in order to further bind the dependent labourer to the land (Lacey 1981:158–75). Labour tenants were bound to provide a six month period of service and farmers were given increased powers over pass law offenders. The poll tax paid by Africans was doubled to increase the pressure to offer labour power for hire. But the most far reaching item of legislation was the Native Service Contract Act, 1932. Under this law the unit of employment became the family unit and not the individual, and if any member of the family failed to fulfil the requisite obligations, the whole family was liable to eviction. In addition there was no requirement that there be a written contract nor that the required period of service be completed in one unbroken period. Freedom of movement and of contract were further limited by the requirement that all workers possess an identity document or pass book before they could be employed or issued with a pass to leave their place of residence. Finally, every African male was required to either work for a minimum of three months per annum or pay a tax of £5.

In sum the Natives Land Act, 1913 was an attempt to break the ability of large sections of the African population to subsist on the land, forcing Africans to make their labour power available for hire and reduce the dependence of the mining industry on migrant labour from outside South Africa. But the separation of the African from the means of production was partial, for neither the mining companies nor the landowning class opted for full commodification of labour power. In the former case, labour was recruited under the terms of a contract migrant scheme, the single male labourer leaving a family unit which retained access to the land from which reproduction needs were partially met. The migrant labourer was therefore a temporary 'proletarian', an unfree wage labourer whose labour power was produced and reproduced largely by processes structured by a different set of (non-capitalist) production relations. The migrant worker sold labour power for the length of the contract and then returned to participate in a form of peasant production in the reserve until material circumstances forced re-engagement and the sale of labour power under contract. Those who followed this cycle of productive activity were successively a proletarian and a peasant producer, a cycle that has precedents in other contexts (e.g. the Irish seasonal migrant labourer in the early nineteenth century [Miles 1982:126–8]). In both cases, extra-economic coercion was used to retain and exploit labour power. Moreover, the forces of production and the more complex labour needs of the mining industry led to further contradictions, as we shall now see.

Mining, manufacturing, and unfree labour

From 1911 the South African state made a co-ordinated attempt to confine the African population to a subordinate economic and political position. In addition to partial dispossession, the state set out to confine African labourers to semi- and unskilled positions in the mining industry and other sectors of the still slowly expanding economy. Under the terms of the Mines and Works Act, 1911, it prevented the African from occupying a range of skilled jobs in the mining industry (Wilson 1972a: 8) following the example of the previously discussed Labour Importation Ordinance, 1904. In addition the Native Labour Regulation Act, 1911, made breaches of contract by African labourers in the mining industry a criminal offence, thus criminalizing strikes (Van der Horst 1971: 180). But these initiatives had contradictory consequences. These became apparent in a context where a process of dispossession was affecting other sections of the population in South Africa and where migration from elsewhere in the world was filling other positions in the hierarchy of the labour process.

The mining companies recruited labour to fill skilled manual, supervisory, and administrative positions from Britain and elsewhere in Europe. The value of their labour power was higher and, given that they had no access to the means of production, they had to be paid at a level which met the full costs of their own reproduction and also that of their family. Moreover, they brought with them a tradition of trade union organization. But because cost minimization was essential in the gold mining industry, these skilled workers were particularly vulnerable to simultaneous de-skilling and replacement by African semi-skilled labour (Braverman 1974). The economic interests of these workers therefore lay with resisting any initiative by the mining companies to this end (Johnstone 1976: 50–8; Davies 1979: 51–2, 66–72).

These contradictory interests were the root cause of the 1922 Rand Revolt (Johnstone 1976: 70–80), although there were conjunctural determinants. An escalating crisis of profitability in the early 1920s forced the companies to move lower-paid African workers into certain positions occupied by European workers in order to reduce production costs. The result was a strike which took on insurrectionary characteristics and which was defeated using state power. Subsequently, African workers were moved into positions occupied by European workers, and profitability was restored. The significance of this outcome was accentuated by a court decision, reached in 1923, which declared that the restrictions on the employment of Africans laid down in the Mines and Works Act, 1911, were illegal (Horwitz 1967: 181–82; Wilson 1972a: 10–11; Johnstone 1976: 127–45; Davies 1979: 152–58).

The employment policy of the mining industry developed in the context of the spread of exchange relations throughout the economy. One effect of this was the separation from the means of production of a section of the landowning class of European origin as a result of subdivision of land and the abolition of share-cropping as land values increased. Additionally, the preference of landowners for African labour (becaues it could be procured more cheaply) limited alternative means of obtaining subsistence from the land. They therefore migrated to the towns to establish themselves as small-scale independent producers (Van Onselen 1982b:112) or as wage labourers. But the legislative dispossession of the African also led to an urban migration. Where the latter remained partially dependent on subsistence agriculture in the reserves, their labour power could be bought at a lower wage than the European labour, and this led to increasing hostility (De Kiewiet 1941:183–94, 216–22; Johnstone 1976:51; Davies 1979:55–60; Lavey 1981:181, 208–12).

This would have posed fewer problems if investment in primary and secondary production had been on a scale sufficient to incorporate all those separated from the means of production, but this was not the case and the major expansion of manufacturing did not occur until the state erected a tariff barrier and provided financial support during the mid-1920s (Van der Horst 1971:240; Hobart Houghton 1976:122–23). These conflicting economic interests were overdetermined by the qualified access of the European worker to the franchise and the effective disenfranchisement of the non-European population (Horwitz 1967: 76–8; Wilson and Thompson 1971:457). Thus the defeat of the Rand Revolt, the imposition of the mining companies' terms, and the growing economic and political conflicts in the towns led to the election of a coalition government in 1924. The result represented the defeat of the mining interest and the political supremacy of an emergent national bourgeoisie in alliance with sections of the labour movement (Davies 1979:167–69, 179–82; but see Yudelman 1983:233–43).

After 1924 there was active state support for the development of commodity production in agriculture and manufacturing, and state intervention to shape the labour market by reinforcing emergent patterns of discrimination between African and European workers (Davies 1979:201). This was achieved in a number of ways. First, African workers were again excluded from skilled jobs in the mining industry (Horwitz 1967:102). Second, the dispossessed European population, proletarianized in the urban areas and competing for semi- and unskilled work, was defined as 'civilized labour' and was paid a wage sufficient to achieve a 'European' standard of living (De Kiewiet 1941:275). As an employer the state operated a discriminatory recruitment policy, replacing African with 'civilized' workers on the railways (Hortitz 1967:196; Van der Horst 1971:251; Lacey 1981:223–24). Third, Africans were excluded by the Industrial Conciliation Act, 1924, from administrative arrangements to determine wages and conditions of work (Wilson and Thompson 1971:30, 439). The intention was to contain militant trade unionism, and the exclusion of the African labourer from its provisions underlined the ideological dimension of the political compromise achieved in the 1924 election (Du Toit 1981: 94–7).

The Rand Revolt, and the political realignments that its defeat promulgated, testifies to the existence of distinct fractions of capital, with distinct interests, and to the possibility of different patterns of development. From 1924, the South African state did not pursue the logic of earlier policies as if there had only ever been one direction open to it. The crisis of 1922 revealed that there were alternative strategies of development. This is also revealed by debates within the Chamber of Mines over the comparative advantages of a migrant, African workforce compared with one which was permanently settled (Jeeves 1985:31–2, 256), and by debates in the early 1920s over the hypothesised advantages of increasing the wages of African workers in order to increase consumption and, thereby, production and labour productivity (Bozzoli 1981:194–97). The strategy adopted after 1924, although it consolidated and built upon earlier political and legislative developments, represented a particular compromise with the free wage labourers and petit-bourgeoisie of European origin.

The post-1924 measures were intended to reinforce the unfree position of the African labourer as the provider of semi- and unskilled labour at low rates of pay, bound to an employer under a contract which was enforceable by the state. But the development of manufacturing and other forms of urban employment widened the use of African labour power, raising the question of whether the main features of the forced labour system in mining could be extended to the urban context. This problem had been recognized by the state prior to 1924, and after 1924 the state extended the solution adopted in the earlier Native (Urban Areas) Act, 1923.

Two official enquiries in the early 1920s problematized the increasing African presence in urban areas. The Stallard Commission of 1922 commented:

'The native should only be allowed to enter urban areas, which are essentially the white man's creation, when he is willing to enter and minister to the needs of the white man, and should depart therefrom when he ceases so to minister.'

(cited in Davenport and Hunt 1974:71)

Thus the Native (Urban Areas) Act allowed for any urban area to become subject to restrictions on the presence of Africans. Male Africans entering such an area were required to register with the state authorities and to obtain documentary evidence of having done so, and were liable to expulsion from the area if they had not found work within a given period of time. All contracts between employers and male Africans had to be registered. The Act also provided for residential segregation. The Act was amended in 1930 to exclude African women from these areas unless they could prove that they had accommodation (De Kiewiet 1941:229–31; Wilson and Thompson 1971:187, 197–99, 234). By these political measures the freedom of movement and settlement on the part of African labourers were severely constrained in an attempt to limit the African presence (meaning the single labourer and not the family unit as a whole) in urban areas by reference to the level of demand for their labour power.

Conclusion

Because 1924 constituted a major turning point I have terminated my analysis there, although I have referred to certain legislative measures introduced after 1924 which extended the unfree relations of production to which the African population was confined. Their further extension, and the consequences, have been analysed extensively by others (e.g. Desmond 1971; Wilson 1972b; Legassick 1974a, 1974b; Giliomee and Schlemmer 1985).

In sum the early history of colonization of South Africa was dominated by unfree relations of production during a period of time when there was very little commodity production. Given that the African populations were capable of reproducing themselves from the land, and that land for new settlers was available, some form of coercion was necessary to force people to work for those who appropriated but did not yet have a monopoly of it. The development of commodity production was accompanied first by the recruitment of labour from outside the region because few Africans wished or needed or could be compelled to enter mine work. Subsequently it was accompanied by the adaptation of unfree relations of production to recruit and retain sections of the African population, creating circumstances where their labour power was only temporarily commodified under contract and where a differentiated labour market was developed in which Africans were legally banned from certain sectors. This contrasted with the real commodification of the labour power of workers of European origin who also, by legal means, gained privileged access to certain kinds of work. By the end of the 1920s the development of commodity production in South Africa was dependent upon both free wage labour supplied by Europeans and the extension of unfree relations of production for the Africans who had become unfree wage labourers.

7

Western Europe

Introduction

By analyzing Western Europe since 1945 I am considering part of the centre of the world capitalist system, rather than the periphery, or peripheries which have been transformed into semi-peripheries. The social formations of Western Europe since 1945 are dominated by the capitalist mode of production. Within these social formations, the predominant form of labour exploitation is wage labour and production is primarily commodity production for exchange. Thus unlike the cases of the Caribbean in the seventeenth century, the Cape colony in the eighteenth century, or Australia in the first half of the nineteenth century, there is no reason to debate the hypothesised existence and nature of a precapitalist mode of production. And yet it is for this very reason that the reappearance of a form of unfree (migrant) labour within Western Europe warrants particular attention. This reappearance demonstrates that the conditions for unfree labour are not confined either to the historical past, to some previous period of primitive accumulation which was the prelude to the transition from a non-capitalist to capitalist mode of production, or to the periphery of the world capitalist system.

Migration flows within and into Western Europe since 1945 have different origins and have occurred under different and changing legal constraints (Böhning 1984: 47–57) and I am not concerned with them all. First, there have been a number of migrations stimulated by political factors such as decolonization and political repression (e.g. the Moluccan migration to the Netherlands in the 1950s (WRR 1979: 9–46; Van Amersfoort 1982: 101–35), the Vietnamese migration to various Western European countries in the late 1970s). Second, there has been an economically determined migration within the supranational economic and political unit known as the European Economic Community

(EEC) under the terms of the Treaty of Rome, 1957, which allowed for unrestricted movement of labour (Bouscaren 1969:11–17; European Communities Commission 1975). The most notable migrations that occur under these provisions are those of cross-border workers (e.g. Feldstein 1967:32; Tuppen 1978) and of various professional workers who migrate in accordance with the demands of multinational companies (e.g. Salt 1981:137, 153–56). Third, there has been a migration from the Mediterranean region and from colonies and ex-colonies of the Western European nation-states (United Nations 1979a:50–131, 1979b: 21–34) which has been economically determined:

> 'Especially large intakes of immigrants have been recorded in periods of economic prosperity, such as 1957, 1964–65 and 1970, while sharp cutbacks have occurred in years of economic recession such as 1959, 1967 and 1974–1975. Analyses for individual countries have shown that labour market indicators, such as trends in unfilled job openings, are particularly strong determinants of migrant flows.'
>
> (United Nations 1979a:129)

It is with this latter migration that I am concerned here. I describe the nature and scale of the migration into Western Europe and then analyse the position of the migrants in economic and political/ideological relations. It is this latter evidence which sustains the main argument of this chapter, that a significant proportion of these migrant workers constitute another form of unfree labour in the long history of capitalist development. In order to understand the origin of this form of unfree labour, I first explore the interrelation between capital accumulation and migration in post-1945 Western Europe.

Accumulation and migration

The interrelationship between capital accumulation and migration is an integral element of the major expansion of the capitalist mode of production that occurred in Western Europe, the United States, and Japan between 1950 and 1974 (Mazier 1982; Armstrong *et al.* 1984). In the postwar period it was not until after Marshall Aid from the USA and the defeat of the European labour movements that the conditions for capitalist expansion were created. By the end of the 1940s profitability was increasing and by the mid-1950s, after the Korean War, a consumer boom was in progress and the capitalist class became confident of its domination (Armstrong *et al.* 1984:24–49, 155, 163–64). The fourth 'long wave' of capitalist development was under way, based on a fundamental revolution in power technology and machinery (Mandel 1975:108–46).

One measure of this capitalist boom is that output in the advanced capitalist countries was 180 per cent higher in 1973 than in 1950 (Armstrong *et al.* 1984:167). Its main cause was an equally large increase in the quantity and quality of the means of production which was accompanied by major changes in the labour process (Mazier 1982:

43–60). As Marx observed for the nineteenth century (1969:573, 1973:399), this rapid accumulation was accompanied by both an absolute increase in the demand for labour and a decline in the quantity of labour power relative to the increase in the mass of machinery and other forms of fixed capital. Consequently there was an increased demand for labour, and where it was met an increase in the size of the working class.

These new wage labourers were recruited from a number of sources: the latent surplus population in agricultural production (particularly in West Germany and France) within Western Europe; women within Western Europe who were previously involved only in unpaid domestic labour; and from social formations outside Western Europe (Bernabé 1982:163, 166–69). This overall increase in the number of people engaged in wage labour was accompanied by important changes in the distribution across different sectors of the Western European economies. The decline in the proportion of employment in agriculture was more than matched by the increase in the numbers employed in services and directly by the state. Thus for example 'In both Britain and Germany the number of manual workers stayed virtually constant over the boom while white-collar employment rose by 50% in the United Kingdom and doubled in Germany' (Armstrong *et al.* 1984:238).

In the agricultural sector the percentage of the working population employed fell in the Western European social formations after 1945: for Belgium from 13 per cent to 5 per cent between 1947 and 1960; for France from 21 per cent to 10 per cent between 1962 and 1975; for West Germany, from 23 per cent to 8 per cent between 1950 and 1970; for the Netherlands, from 20 per cent to 6 per cent between 1947 and 1971; and in Switzerland it fell from 17 per cent to 8 per cent between 1950 and 1970 (United Nations 1979a:31–3). The proportion of women in the total paid workforce increased throughout the period of the long wave of capitalist development: in Belgium from 31 per cent to 42 per cent between 1947 and 1970; in France from 52 per cent to 58 per cent between 1962 and 1975; in the Netherlands, from 33 per cent to 35 per cent between 1947 and 1971; and in Britain from 43.5 per cent to 59.5 per cent between 1951 and 1971 (United Nations 1979a:36–7).

The relationship that particularly concerns us here is that between capital accumulation and labour migration (cf. Marshall 1973:3–38). The necessity for such recruitment is revealed by the fall in unemployment rates within European social formations during the 1950s, reaching an all-time minimum in the mid-1960s. In the period 1964–66, unemployment decreased to 1.9 per cent of the labour force within the countries of the EEC (Bernabé 1982:173). Data on job vacancies show a continuing high demand for labour by employers continuing up to the early 1970s (Armstrong *et al.* 1984:240–41). The sources for recruitment within the social formations of Western Europe (i.e. agricultural labourers and women engaged solely in domestic labour) proved insufficient to keep pace with accumulation.

When considered as a component part of the various measures taken to increase the supply of labour (Kindelberger 1967), the ability to internationalize the labour market and the success of so doing were both cause and consequence of the capitalist boom in Western Europe. As the demand for labour increased during the 1950s, and as supplies of labour within European social formations were gradually exhausted, capitalists who wished to expand production would have been forced to increase wages to attract labour from other sectors of the national economy if an alternative source of labour had not been available. The problem and its resolution is illustrated by a study of the British textile industry (Fevre 1984) which underwent a major reorganization of production in the 1950s.

The introduction of new machinery in this industry was an instance of capital accumulation induced by international competition. The new machinery permitted an increase in productivity as long as a labour force could be persuaded to accept the introduction of shift work, a less pleasant work environment, and a speed-up of the work process. This change in the labour process took place at a time when other manufacturing sectors were also expanding, many offering more pleasant working conditions and higher wages, with the result that many of those directly affected by the deterioration in working conditions moved out of the textile industry. The employers faced a number of options, which included increasing wages, but their solution followed the traditional strategy of recruiting a new workforce. In the past, women had been brought into employment at relatively low rates of pay, but as many left they were replaced by migrant workers from the Indian subcontinent whose experience of discrimination elsewhere in the economy left them with few options other than to accept low basic rates of pay, although shift work offered the possibility of substantially higher total wages. Thus although the introduction of migrant workers did not lead to an absolute decrease in the wage rate, in the prevailing conditions it did obviate the need for employers to increase wages to attract labour from elsewhere, and in this sense one can typify migrant labour as a source of cheap labour (Fevre 1984: 4–5).

This study of one manufacturing sector in one country is not typical of what happened in all economic sectors in all Western European social formations. For example not all migrant workers were recruited to work in manufacturing, and migrants from the Indian subcontinent were, during the 1950s, British Commonwealth subjects who had the right to settle permanently in Britain as full citizens. But it is a model of the articulation of capital accumulation and labour migration in post-1945 Western Europe: labour migration was not just the result of an increase in numerical demand but also of changes in the labour process which resulted from increases in constant capital intended to increase labour productivity (see also Duffield 1985). We can now consider the scale of the migration that the accumulation process stimulated.

Migration into Western Europe 1945–1980s

In this discussion of the nature and scale of the labour migration into Western Europe the phases of the migration, the numbers of people involved, their origins, and the development of permanent settlement will be reviewed. I demonstrate that this was a large-scale migration and that what was generally intended as a temporary rotation of contracted labour has led, contrary to the expectations of capital and the state, to the permanent settlement of a proportion of migrant workers. I shall consider collectively the migration to France, West Germany, Belgium, Switzerland, Netherlands, and Britain, although I shall also highlight certain features specific to migration to each social formation.

The recruitment of labour from outside national boundaries began at different times, reflecting the extent to which each social formation had an internal surplus population upon which to draw. In the case of Switzerland, France, and Belgium, international labour migration began in the late 1940s (McDonald 1969: 116–18; Hoffman-Nowotny 1974, 1985: 209; Freeman 1979: 69–73; Debbant and Declerck 1982: 13–14). In Britain too there was a brief period of state-organized labour recruitment immediately after the war (Tannahill 1968). In West Germany international labour migration began in the mid-1950s and was not on a large scale until the early 1960s (Rhoades 1978a: 563–65; Rist 1978: 61; Esser and Korte 1985: 170–73) when the flow of political refugees was terminated (Schechtman 1962: 287–340). By the 1960s the recruitment of labour, either by employers or by the state on behalf of employers, was in full swing and increasing in all the main Western European social formations (Salt and Clout 1976: 88). Migration policies and the methods and sources of recruitment varied in each social formation and over time.

There were two main sources of recruitment, from colonies and ex-colonies or from spatially proximate social formations elsewhere in Europe. There were flows of colonial migrants to France, Britain, and the Netherlands. In the case of France citizens of North and West African ex-colonies had a favoured legal status and unrestricted entry to France until the mid-1960s, while the islands of Réunion, Guadeloupe, and Martinique remained Départements of France and their populations were therefore full French citizens. All these regions have provided French employers with labour (McDonald 1969: 125–28; Freeman 1979: 69–90; Kennedy-Brenner 1979: 22–6; Adler 1981: 54–123). In the case of the Netherlands only a small proportion of migration from Surinam and the Dutch Antilles was a direct response to labour demand (Bovenkerk 1979; Entzinger 1985: 52–5).

Colonies and ex-colonies have been the main source of migrant labour for Britain. Since 1945 the vast majority of migrants to Britain have come from the Caribbean and the Indian subcontinent, this migration being facilitated by the legal framework created in the course of decolonization which permitted the unrestricted entry and settlement with full social and political rights of people who were, up until 1962, British Commonwealth subjects. Prior to the legislation of the 1960s (e.g. Layton-Henry 1984; Miles and Phizacklea 1984), the entry of British Commonwealth subjects was regulated largely by market demand for labour (Peach 1968). The state has played almost no direct role in labour recruitment, although the political and legal framework for a migrant labour policy based on the rotation of workers was established in the Immigration Act, 1971 (Sivanandan 1976). All this makes the British case distinctive when compared with all other Western European social formations (Castles and Kosack 1973:28–31; Phizacklea and Miles 1980:1–25; Castles *et al.* 1984:41–7), to the extent that some writers prefer to ignore the British case when analysing migration flows into Europe (e.g. Hoffman-Nowotny 1978:86).

The second source of migrant labour has been from other European and from North African social formations. Broadly speaking Western European states and employers recruited labour first from the European periphery on the northern edge of the Mediterranean and then, as the boom continued and supplies from this region became more difficult to obtain due to increasing competition (Salt and Clout 1976:88–9), from the southern Mediterranean and Turkey (e.g. Abadan-Unat 1976). For several recruitment countries Italy was the first main source of labour, but when the development of capitalism within Italy reduced emigration (Bouscaren 1969:27), recruitment from Spain, Portugal, and Greece increased. From the mid-1960s recruitment from Yugoslavia, Turkey, Morocco, and Tunisia was organized. Within Western Europe this has produced a migrant worker population composed of several different nationalities, the particular combination varying from one country to another according to the pattern of its bilateral recruiting agreements. The situation in West Germany is outlined in *Figure 7.1*. Thus migrant workers in Western Europe do not constitute a homogenous cultural category (cf. Booth 1984:29–30).

The method of labour recruitment depended largely on the source. In the case of recruitment from colonies and ex-colonies, migration flows have tended to be organized informally through kin networks (e.g. Watson 1977) but there are also instances of direct recruitment by employers (e.g. Brooks 1975:256–70). State involvement has tended to be limited because the migrants have had the right of entry, if not permanent settlement, at least until the state decided that those rights should be removed. In the case of recruitment from proximate European social formations, direct state involvement was from the outset necessary because the prospective migrants had no right of entry to work or to settle, and so the minimum requirement was for a legal and administrative framework to regulate entry and temporary settlement of people who were formally foreign nationals (Miller and Martin 1982: 53–8). However, the form and extent of state intervention has varied over time and place.

For example in Belgium a system of state-organized recruitment in

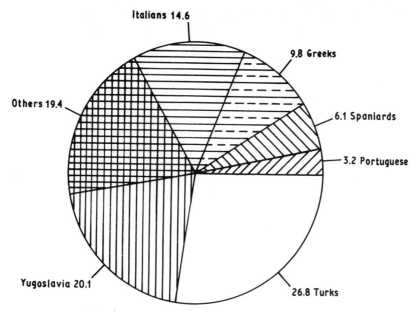

Italians 14.6

9.8 Greeks

Others 19.4

6.1 Spaniards

3.2 Portuguese

Yugoslavia 20.1

26.8 Turks

Figure 7.1 Migrant workers in West Germany

Source: Rist (1978:66)

the 1940s gave way to a system where people entered Belgium as tourists and obtained work and residence permits after they had found employment. The latter procedure was terminated in the late 1960s. Thereafter an employer had to obtain prior permission from the state to seek workers outside Belgium and, when permission was granted, recruitment could only take place from countries which had entered into an agreement to export labour to Belgium and where an employment office had been opened to assess potential workers for their suitability (Debbant and Declerck 1982: 13–19). Direct state regulation of the latter kind typified the recruitment of labour by the West German state throughout the period in question (Rist 1978: 61; Esser and Korte 1985: 187–88), using as a model the system of forced foreign labour established during the Nazi period (Rhoades 1978a: 560–63; Döhse 1981).

In France there had been a long tradition of labour migration prior to 1945 and a record of state intervention to provide a legal framework for entry (Dignan 1981; Cross 1983; Green 1985; Singer-Kerel 1986). After 1945 the state declared itself in favour of a policy of immigration leading to permanent settlement and established an administrative structure to organize the migration, although a large proportion of migrants entered France without reference to it until the early 1970s when administrative procedures were enforced (McDonald 1969: 118; Kennedy-Brenner 1979:

26–31; Thomas 1982b: 42; Verbunt 1985: 136–37). The Swiss case fell between the two extremes of West Germany and France in that the actual recruitment of workers was organized by employers, but within a legal framework established and strictly administered by the state (Hoffman-Nowotny 1974: 14–19).

In the case of West Germany, France, Netherlands, and Belgium, the state reached formal bilateral recruitment agreements with the states of the European and north African social formations from which migrants were to be recruited in order to provide an overall mechanism and structure for labour migration (Salt and Clout 1976: 98–100). These agreements established the conditions under which people were recruited and worked. Moreover they allowed the state of the social formation from which the migrants were recruited to have a regulatory role, not least because these states anticipated benefits from the export of their citizens.

They expected such export to decrease levels of un- and under-employment, and their citizens to return with industrial and other skills, and with sums of money which could function as capital. Labour migration was therefore viewed as an instance of primitive accumulation which would lead to, or further, the development of the capitalist mode of production, an assumption which allowed certain commentators to regard labour migration as a form of 'development aid' to the European periphery (e.g. Hume 1973). Significantly therefore there was a bilateral agreement on the need for a rotating system of migration so that, in this instance, migrant workers would return to allow the realization of these hypothesised advantages. The available evidence suggests that, at best, these objectives were only partially realized (e.g. Paine 1974: 91–8, 114–20; Baucic 1972: 43; Rhoades 1978b, 1979; Gmelch 1980: 146–55; Kubat 1984; Keles 1985; Nikolinakos 1973a; Toepfer 1985).

The recruitment of workers increased through the 1960s until the short recession of 1967–68 when recruitment was reduced (see *Figures 7.2* and *7.3* (see also Salt and Clout 1976: 90–1)) and some migrants were forced to return to their country of origin. But this was a shortlived restriction, and recruitment was again on the increase by the end of the decade, continuing until the early 1970s. Many of those who were forced to return to their country of origin in 1967–68 were able to re-migrate, their termination of employment being, in effect, a forced and extended holiday (Kayser 1972: 9–10). The collapse of the long-wave of capitalist expansion in 1973–74 brought a sudden and larger decline in recruitment (see *Figure 7.3*), forcing a re-evaluation of state policies and a major change in migration patterns (Salt and Clout 1976: 220–22; Kayser 1977; Salt 1981: 139–40). The recruitment ban proved that the social formations from which the migrants originated

'can have only limited control over emigration and foreign investment, since the potential volume of flows of both factors is dictated by the industrialised countries and the overall economic situation of the countries concerned.'

(Bourguignon *et al.* 1977: 37)

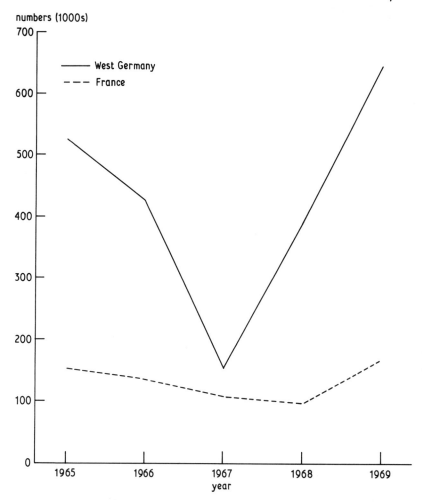

numbers (1000s)

— West Germany

– – – France

year

Figure 7.2 Recruitment of foreign workers (West Germany and France, 1965–69)

Source: Kayser (1972:7)

The consequence was

'to redistribute the burden of current unemployment to those countries least able to cope with the problem. . . . Less economically advanced countries appear to be bearing a disproportionate share of the current unemployment problem.'

(OECD 1979:8)

Prior to the sudden recruitment bans it was estimated that there were

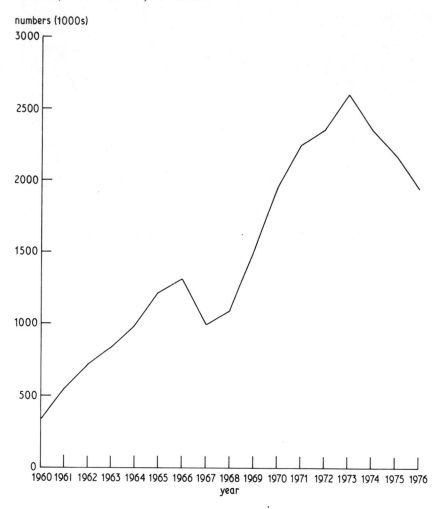

Figure 7.3 Migrant workers employed in West Germany (1960–76)

Source: Rist (1978:62)

about 7.5 million official migrant workers in Western Europe (Böhning 1974:15; OECD 1979:17), a figure which does not include migrants' dependents. Neither does this figure include clandestine migrants (see Moulier Boutang *et al.* 1986), although political decisions can transform their illegal status into a legal one (e.g. Singer-Kerel 1983; but see Couper and Santamaria 1984). Since the recruitment ban there has been no substantial decrease in the size of the migrant population, not least because there was no large-scale forced expulsion of migrant workers. Rather two processes have overlapped, the consequence of which has been an increase in the total foreign population resident in Western Europe (Penninx 1984a: 13–17; see also Slater 1979: 4, 8; Kubat 1984).

On the one hand there have been large, mainly voluntary, return flows of migrants to Spain, Greece, Italy, and Yugoslavia in the mid- and late 1970s, the total number of returnees being around two million (King 1984: 157–58; for West Germany see Booth 1984: 25). These have been stimulated by, *inter alia*, the worsening economic situation and racist violence in Western Europe and by a combination of limited economic development and the collapse of military, rightwing governments in the European periphery (e.g. Van Gendt 1977: 11–17; King 1984: 158–60). On the other hand there has been no comparable return flow of migrants to the southern Mediterranean and Turkey, but rather an increase in the entry of dependents, a process that has been underway for a longer period for migrants from the northern Mediterranean countries.

In certain countries there has been a small increase in the number of migrants recruited for paid work (for West Germany see Döhse 1982: 1). These overall patterns mask important differences in political policy concerning the extension of temporary status to migrants and over family reunification (Kayser 1977; Penninx 1984a: 21–4), differences which have effects on return rates (Van Amersfoort *et al.* 1984). Taken together the result of these two processes has been an increase in the overall size of the resident population of foreign origin in Western Europe. Collectively migrant workers and their dependents now constitute a total population of some 15 million persons in Western Europe (Castles *et al.* 1984: 87, 90–1).

When the migration began it was envisaged in most social formations as a temporary movement of people who would return to their place of origin. This expectation had apparent legal substance where migration was organized on a contract basis. The legal framework for temporary residence while selling labour power for a wage held out the prospect, first, that there would be an ongoing circulation of individuals and, second, that in periods of cyclical depression, unemployment could be exported by reducing the number of contracts available. Additionally the temporary migration of single persons implied a limited infrastructural provision for the reproduction of labour power. Single people with no family dependents, residing on a temporary basis, could be persuaded to accept low quality accommodation and would make few or no demands on education, health and social security expenditure. In this very specific sense contract migrant labour was viewed as a form of cheap labour in so far as labour production and reproduction costs were lower than for the indigenous working class (Gorz 1970; Meillassoux 1981: 124–26).

In the case of Netherlands, Switzerland, and West Germany (Mayer 1965: 124–25; Castles *et al.* 1984: 70, 75; Hammar 1985: 63, 178–79, 210) it was state policy that contract migrant workers would not settle permanently in these social formations. In this respect France is

154 Capitalism and Unfree Labour

exceptional because the state has legalized migrants as permanent settlers for demographic reasons (Kennedy-Brenner 1979:17; United Nations 1979b:23). Britain is also exceptional for the reasons previously stated. The intentions of the state and capital were paralleled by the subjective intentions of many of the migrants, most of whom viewed their migration as a temporary departure, during which they would earn sufficient money to improve their economic and social circumstances upon return (Kayser 1971:201–2; Hoffman-Nowotny 1978:101; Böhning 1984:67).

However, despite these intentions and expectations there has been a shift from mass labour migration characterized by rotation, to permanent settlement via a phase of family reunification (Castles *et al.* 1984:11–15; see also Böhning 1972), a process that has characterized certain earlier international migrations (e.g. McDonald and McDonald 1964). Thus although voluntary rotation continued throughout the 1960s and 1970s, the predominant tendency was a shift towards permanent settlement of a large number of migrants.

The transition was the consequence of three processes (Miles 1986). First, the migrants discovered that their earning target (Böhning 1984: 67) could not be realized as quickly as they had anticipated, and as their length of stay increased, they wished to be joined by, or to form, family units. This carried the prospect of increased earnings as family members entered wage labour, although it also increased reproduction costs and extended their commitments to the social formation to which they had come (e.g. school attendance by children). For many the consequence was to further increase the length of stay. Second, a policy of worker rotation entailed costs to capital because it meant that each new group of workers had to be recruited and then trained for the labour process. Where a stable and experienced, if not skilled, labour force was required, there were financial advantages in extending the contracts of workers already hired and dispensing with rotation. Third, as the demand for labour increased the states which contracted to supply migrants could demand and achieve better conditions for their citizens, including the right to family reunification and extended settlement. In turn, this improved the conditions for the reproduction of the migrant worker but also for the reproduction and increase in the total migrant population resident in Western Europe (e.g. Mayer 1965:125). The consequence is evident in statistics concerning migrants' length of stay. In West Germany in 1881, 15.3 per cent of all migrants had been resident for in excess of fifteen years and 56.9 per cent had been resident for eight years or more (Booth 1984:36–7, and Table 80).

Underlying these three specific reasons is the central determinant, the continuing demand for workers to fill particular positions in the economies of Western Europe. Hence although migration flows of persons recruited under contract to work have been very limited since 1973–74, a large proportion of those who came before the end of large-scale recruitment continue to play an important economic role and are, in effect 'permanent proletarians'.

Migrant workers in economic relations

Given that migrant workers were recruited to fill positions newly created or vacated by indigenous workers, and given that those positions were often characterized by some combination of low wages and unpleasant working conditions, it is not surprising to find that migrant workers continue to be concentrated in these same positions. Despite large increases in unemployment since the mid-1970s, indigenous labour has shown little willingness to replace the migrant worker in these positions, even when, as in West Germany, they have a legally defined priority access to the labour market (Döhse 1982:23–9). Consequently, and when the sectors of employment are an integral part of the capitalist economies, the presence of migrant workers is central to the reproduction of the capitalist mode of production. Although there have been certain changes in the position of migrant workers in economic relations, it remains the case that the labour power of migrant workers remains essential to the reproduction of the capitalist economies of Western Europe.

In the early 1970s the economic position of migrant workers had three features (Castles and Kosack 1973:112–15; Giner and Salcedo 1978: 98–101). First, migrant workers were heavily concentrated in certain industries or sectors, for example building, engineering, textiles and clothing, catering, and domestic service. Second, a large majority of migrants were manual workers, predominantly semi- and unskilled. Third, they were more likely to be unemployed, and to be unemployed for longer periods of time, when compared with indigenous workers. More detailed studies amplify this picture.

Data for France show that in 1968 94 per cent of migrant workers were employed in manual work, and 69 per cent were employed in semi- and unskilled manual work. In the early 1970s there were particular concentrations of migrant workers in mining, metal work and production, manufacture of building materials, production of rubber and asbestos, construction and public works, and sanitation (Freeman 1979:27, 29). For the Netherlands, over three-quarters of temporary work permits issued between 1969 and 1975 were for industrial occupations, whilst most of the remainder were issued for service occupations (WRR 1979:96; Marshall 1973:35–7, 88–93). A Dutch survey of employers in the mid-1970s found that 79 per cent of migrant workers were employed in manual production jobs, of whom 47 per cent were unskilled and 39 per cent were semi-skilled. It also found that 43 per cent of workers were on shift work (cited in WRR 1979:129–30). A more recent survey reported a continuing high concentration of migrant workers in industrial production (Penninx 1984b:23–7).

In Switzerland migrant workers were predominantly employed in agriculture, domestic service, hotels and restaurants in the 1950s, but increasingly migrants were recruited into industry and by the 1960s there were large concentrations in construction, metals and machinery, textiles and clothing (Mayer 1965: 129). In West Germany in 1974 61.9 per cent of migrants were employed in manufacturing, 11.9 per cent in construction, and 11.8 per cent in service industries (Rist 1978: 70). Throughout the 1960s and early 1970s well over half of Turkish workers in West Germany were employed in industry, while in excess of 15 per cent were employed in construction (Kubat 1979b: 250). More recent data for West Germany show that in 1978 just over 80 per cent of migrant workers had manual jobs, and that in 1981, 57 per cent of migrant workers were employed in manufacturing industry and 10 per cent in building. Within manufacturing there were high concentrations of migrants in plastics, metal industries, vehicle construction, manufacture of electrical goods, paper products, and textiles (Castles *et al.* 1984: 130, 132–32). Other studies show that migrant workers in West Germany are disproportionately represented amongst those engaged in shift work and on piece work (Döhse 1982: 42–5).

The position of migrant women in economic relations requires special attention (Phizacklea 1983a). The early phase of labour migration was characterized by the movement of single persons, the majority of whom were men (Kubat 1979b: 249; Booth 1984: 18). But the migration of women should not be ignored (Morokvasic 1983, 1984). For example in the case of Spanish emigration during the 1960s around 20 per cent of all emigrants were women (Trinidade 1979: 221). In the cases of Caribbean migration to Britain and Portuguese migration to Western Europe the proportion of women has been significantly higher (Smith 1977: 28–9; Trinidade 1979: 230). Concerning Turkish migration to West Germany, employers in the manufacturing and iron and metal industries turned to the recruitment of female workers after the 1966–67 recession (Abadan-Unat 1977: 31–5; Eraydin 1981: 248), a process that has occurred elsewhere in Western Europe (United Nations 1979a: 129–30). These women migrated in their own right to become wage labourers, although in the Turkish case, female migrants were usually regarded as paving the way for the later migration of male relatives.

In addition the phase of family reunification has led to the arrival of large numbers of women. A number of factors determine whether or not this latter group of women enter wage labour, including the level of demand in different economic sectors, legal restrictions, patriarchal control within family units, and racial discrimination (e.g. Stone 1983). Consequently, the proportion of migrant women amongst the total migrant workforce varies from country to country (United Nations 1979a: 136–37), but is rarely minimal (see *Figure 7.4* for West Germany). Such statistics obscure the extent to which entry into wage labour varies according to national origin (Phizacklea 1983b: 102–3; Booth 1984: 26–7) and underestimate the total number of women involved in wage labour because of the extent of unregistered work (Phizacklea 1983b: 102).

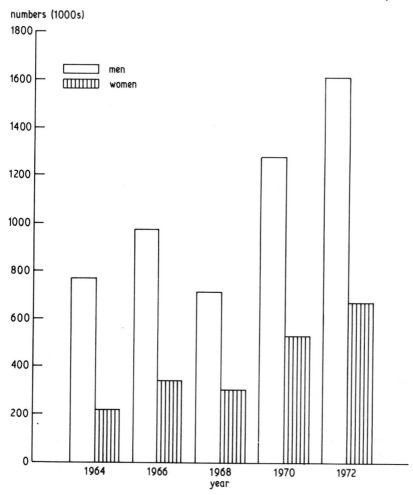

numbers (1000s)

Figure 7.4 Foreign men and women in labour force (West Germany, 1964–72)

Source: Bundesantalt für Arbeit (1979)

Given the crisis of Western European capitalism in the early 1970s there is reason to consider whether this overall picture has changed in any significant way. Castles and colleagues (1984) found for West Germany, first, that there has been a small increase in the proportion of migrants (mainly women) employed in the service sector (see also Rist 1978:70) and, second, that there had been some promotion from unskilled to semi-skilled work for both men and women (Castles *et al.* 1984:129, 136–38; see also Salt and Clout 1976:86–7; Reimann and

Reimann 1979:78). Third, although about half a million migrant workers left the labour force between 1973 and 1978, an increasing proportion of migrants who have been made redundant since then have remained in West Germany where permitted by law (Döhse 1982:27–8), registered as unemployed (Castles *et al.* 1984:143–49). But only a minority have been affected in this way, the vast majority of migrant workers remaining in paid labour in manual work. Of the 2,040,700 migrant workers employed in West Germany in March 1980 over 1.1 million were employed in manufacturing industry and 209,800 were employed in construction (Döhse 1982:43; see Castles *et al.* 1984:127).

An analysis of the position of migrant workers in France following the economic crisis of 1973–74 showed that the proportion of migrant workers in the labour force did decline, but only by a small amount, and that although there were absolute and proportionate reductions in the numbers of migrant workers in certain sectors of production there were also absolute and proportionate increases in other sectors, including growth sectors (Singer-Kerel 1980). The conclusion is that the continuing exploitation of the labour power of migrant workers is vital to the reproduction of the capitalist relations of production (cf. Hiemenz and Schatz 1979:88–9).

Although the majority of migrants are either wage labourers, unpaid household workers (or both), or a component part of the floating reserve army of labour, there is a small minority of petit-bourgeois entrepreneurs who are dominated by capital in a different way. The size of this class is difficult to determine because of the paucity of data (Boissevain 1984: 33–6). The British data suggest that the numbers are small, although increasing (Smith 1977:92–3; Reeves and Ward 1984:127; Brown 1984: 165–66). Generalizing from this data to the rest of Western Europe is hazardous because the *de jure* legal position of the majority of migrants to Britain is different to the majority of migrants to the rest of Western Europe. In West Germany, for example, residents who lack German nationality are prevented by law from becoming self-employed.

The reasons for the development of this migrant petit-bourgeoisie are only partly clear. In Britain the experience of discrimination in the labour market and workplace has encouraged a move into self-employment (Nowikowski, 1984:163), but it is also the case that many migrants were initially motivated by petit-bourgeois aspirations and retained an interest in property ownership. In addition a small proportion of migrants originally set out with the intention of continuing or initiating petit-bourgeois or even fully capitalist enterprises. One can cite as an example of the former Italian migrants to the Netherlands and other parts of Western Europe who migrated as icecream sellers (Bovenkerk *et al.* 1983), and of the latter, Indian migrants to Britain who intended to extend their organization of textile manufacture from India (Nowikowski 1984:154, 156, 160–61).

The marginality of the migrant entrepreneur is not only numerical. The very nature of the capitalist mode of production, with its structural tendency towards the concentration of capital, limits the scope for the entry of small units of capital. One obvious opening for a potential migrant entrepreneur is the provision of commodities and services to migrant communities and hence the extent of retailing and cafe owner-ship (Smith 1977: 92–3). But however important, both economically and culturally, such activities might be to these communities, this petit-bourgeois entrepreneurship is marginal to the capitalist economies as a whole. In Britain, where a small but significant proportion of Asian migrants have moved into the retail sector (e.g. Brown 1984: 166), the typical experience is for the shopkeeper to earn less than could be gained from the sale of labour power for a wage (Adlrich *et al.* 1984: 191, 209). Moreover in all the sectors of petit-bourgeois activity, male entrepreneurship is invariably dependent upon the exploitation of the labour power of kin, and especially of female relatives (Hoel 1982; Phizacklea 1983b: 109–110; Mitter 1986).

In the early 1980s the position of the majority of male and female migrants in economic relations was that of a manual wage labourer. A minority had been forced to join the reserve army of labour and an even smaller minority had moved into a petit-bourgeois position. Of those in wage labour, a proportion remained vulnerable to unemployment (and even forced return migration where the individual does not qualify for long-term residence) where they are employed in sectors of manufac-turing undergoing further rationalization. But a larger proportion are employed in key sectors of the economy and constitute, at the level of economic relations, a relatively permanent part of the European proletariat.

Migrant labour and political relations

We have seen that the large-scale migration into Western Europe since 1945 has been stimulated by a labour shortage in particular economic sectors. Those who came to fill those vacant positions elected to do so (although usually in the context of relative material disadvantage) and were recruited as wage labourers. They sell their labour power for a wage and so, *formally*, are free workers. But the position that migrant workers occupy in economic relations cannot be isolated from their position in political relations, and it is as a result of this interdepen-dence that we can designate a large proportion of these migrants as *unfree wage labour*.

We must first return to an earlier distinction between migrants who originated from colonies and ex-colonies and those who originated from proximate social formations in the Mediterranean region. I describe the former as *colonial migrants*. They entered Western Europe with the legal right to seek work and to settle permanently as a result of their status as citizens of the colonial nation-state. These migrants workers are excluded from the subsequent discussion. I describe the latter as *contract migrants*. These emigrants were, in law, citizens of the proximate social formations, and therefore 'aliens' as far as the state of the social formation where they sold their labour power was concerned. The state in the social formation of recruitment therefore had to devise a legal and administrative mechanism which would allow the entry and residence of persons defined as 'foreigners' (e.g. Kubat 1979a) and which would regulate their activities once having migrated (Carchedi 1979).

By entering spatially the Western European social formations contract migrants entered simultaneously a web of state-defined and regulated rights and restrictions which affected their right to remain and to reproduce themselves and their families. The result has been the creation of a distinct legal category for contract migrant workers, one which not only affects their rights of participation in civil society, but also their ability to dispose of their labour power as a commodity. The particular characteristics and effects of this distinct legal category have varied from one country to another.

This distinct legal status is not so much a pertinent political effect on economic relations as a determinant of the specific character of economic relations. Contract migrants are, therefore, formally free wage labourers who are, in reality, substantively unfree because of the restrictions placed on their ability to commodify their labour power. This unfreedom in the realm of the commodification of labour power is overdetermined by restrictions on participation within civil society. Moreover, where contract migrants have become in effect permanent settlers, and have begun to reproduce themselves following family creation/reunification, the condition of unfreedom can under certain circumstances be reproduced. I now illustrate this argument by reference to the examples of migration to the Netherlands and West Germany. In both cases I shall be referring to the legal status of migrant workers as it was in the early 1980s, and thus not taking into account more recent changes (such as the decision to allow migrant workers to vote in local elections in the Netherlands).

Migration to the Netherlands since 1945 presents us with a complex picture (Bovenkerk 1979; WRR 1979; Van Amersfoort 1982). Decoloniz-ation in the Dutch East Indies led to the arrival in the Netherlands of up to 300,000 people with Dutch citizenship, along with a section of the Royal Netherlands East-Indies Army and dependents (collectively known as Moluccans). There has also been migration from the Dutch Caribbean which has not been caused directly by labour demand in the Netherlands (Marshall 1973: 33–4). It is only when we consider migration to the Netherlands from southern Europe and the Mediter-ranean that we deal with contract migrant workers (Bovenkerk 1979: 126).

The recruitment of labour from the periphery of Western Europe began tentatively after the short slump in 1958. Dutch employers initiated the recruitment directly, with only limited state intervention until cases of gross exploitation became public, forcing the government to establish a system of regulation. Formal agreements were reached with Italy (1960), Spain (1961), Portugal (1963), Turkey (1964), Greece (1966), Morocco (1969), Tunisia, and Yugoslavia (both in 1970). But employers continued to recruit independently of the state and between 1961 and 1966 over half of the workers recruited did not pass through the state's administrative machinery. In the second half of the decade, the state intervened to gain a virtual monopoly over recruitment.

Thus under the terms of the Aliens Act of 1965 and the Employment of Foreign Workers Act of 1978 (Smolders 1982; Entzinger 1985) any employer wishing to recruit workers from outside the Netherlands had to obtain state approval and the intending migrant worker had to meet certain criteria of eligibility (concerning age, ability to do certain work, absence of police record, health) in order to sign a contract. The migrant worker also required a work permit and a residence permit, although these were issued relatively automatically by the state where recruitment had been approved officially.

Initially the worker was issued with a temporary work permit which recorded the employer's name and the type of work which the holder was permitted to do, and which had to be renewed annually. However after three consecutive years of employment the worker became entitled to a permanent work permit valid for all types of work. Similarly the residence permit was issued for one year and renewable, and after five years of continuous residence the holder was granted the right of permanent residence and became eligible to apply for Dutch nationality. However, an application for the issue or renewal of a residence permit could be rejected if the applicant was no longer working (but not where this was no fault of the applicant) or where it could be shown that his or her presence was contrary to public interest. The residence permit had priority over the work permit in so far as a work permit could not be issued to a person without a residence permit, while a work permit would be cancelled where an application for the renewal of a residence permit was rejected.

The migrant worker recruited under these provisions had the right to be joined by family members after twelve months' residence and work in the Netherlands, and on the condition that the worker was guaranteed employment over the subsequent twelve months and had access to adequate accommodation for the family. Family members admitted under these conditions had the right to sell their labour power on the labour market without restriction. Concerning political participation, the migrant worker had the right of association but not to vote or to stand for election. Additionally the migrant worker was prohibited from behaving in a manner prejudicial to the security of the Dutch state or to public order.

Post-1945 migration to West Germany presents a less complex picture because it did not include colonial migrants. The demand for a flexible and expanding supply of labour for the decade after 1945 was met, first, from the massive influx of Germans (about 10 million people in total) into what was to become West Germany and, second, from the continuing flow of political refugees who left East Germany between 1949 and 1961 (estimated to total 2.5 million people) (Hennings 1982: 477, 480). Then in 1955 an agreement was signed with the Italian government to permit the recruitment of Italian labour on a contract basis for agriculture and the construction industry, a practice that was extended by agreements with the states of Greece and Spain (1960), Turkey (1961 and 1964), Morocco (1963), Portugal (1964), Tunisia (1965), and Yugoslavia (1968). It was under the terms of such agreements, and of the Aliens Act (1965), the Labour Promotion Act (1969), and the Work Permit Decree (1971), that the bulk of the migration into West Germany occurred during the 1960s and the early 1970s (Rist 1978: 61–2; Castles *et al.* 1984; Esser and Korte 1985).

As a result the West German state established recruiting offices to screen and select workers in these countries. Having been selected, the individual signed a contract valid for one year with an employer and was transported to West Germany and provided with accommodation, both at the employer's expense. In West Germany the worker was issued with a residence and a work permit. Residence permits were issued for one year in the first instance, and thereafter could be renewed for two-year periods. These permits usually required the individual to live in a particular area. There were two additional categories of residence permit (of unlimited duration and for permanent residence) which were dependent upon the applicant having five and eight years' continuous residence respectively, and meeting a range of additional and strict conditions (including possession of a special work permit, language tests, and occupation of decent housing). Unlimited duration and permanent residence permits could be withdrawn subsequently for reasons concerning the 'national interest'.

Work permits were issued initially for one year, but after a stay of three years, a work permit could be issued for a duration of two or more years. Work permits were issued for employment with a named employer in a specified occupation within a particular administrative region. When an application to extend a work permit was made, or when a migrant worker who had lost a job applied for a new permit, the Federal Labour Department first ascertained whether the job could be filled by a German worker. There was also provision to issue a special work permit to migrant workers resident in Germany for eight years and employed continuously for five years or having a spouse of German nationality. This permit was valid for five years, for any occupation and for any employer. Work permits could only be issued to migrant workers who had been granted the right to live in West Germany and expired at the same time as a residence permit. The Aliens Act, 1965, provided for the deportation of an alien for any of eleven reasons, all of which were open to wide interpretation (Rist 1978: 136–37; Mehrländer 1979: 149–50; Hönekopp and Ullman 1982: 116–21; Döhse 1982: 23–4, 30–1; Esser and Korte 1985: 184–88).

There were strict rules governing the entry into West Germany of the spouse and children of migrant workers. Residence permits for family members were issued only after the migrant has been working in West Germany for at least three years and if he or she could demonstrate access to satisfactory accommodation. The rights of family members after entry into West Germany were also severely curtailed. Work permits were issued to spouses only after five years' residence and to children after two years' residence (Hönekopp and Ullman 1982:124). Additional restrictions on the issue of residence and work permits to workers and to their families were contained in procedures adopted in 1975 to limit the residence of foreign workers in areas where 12 per cent of the total population were foreigners. These were later abolished in 1977 (Rist 1978:78–80; Hönekopp and Ullman 1982:123).

There were equally strict controls over political activity. Legislation stipulated that the contract migrant worker had only those constitutional rights which are not reserved explicitly for German citizens. Hence the migrant worker was denied the freedoms of assembly, association, movement, and to choose and exercise his or her occupation. A migrant was also denied the right to vote and participate in any elections. Additionally any other political activity could be prohibited if it was considered to prejudice the interests of the state or the development of political consensus. Foreign workers could join political parties but could not participate in the selection and presentation of candidates for election and were prevented from functioning as delegates. They could join trade unions, participate in legal strike action, and vote for works councils (Rist 1978:142–48; Reimann and Reimann 1979:67; Hönekopp and Ullman 1982:134–38).

There have been differences in the legal status of migrant workers in the Netherlands and West Germany through the 1970s and in the early 1980s, the regulations in West Germany having been more restrictive than in the Netherlands. Further specific differences emerge when one considers the legal status of migrant workers in other Western European social formations (e.g. Thomas 1982a; Commission of the European Communities 1984). For example in Switzerland in 1968 migrant workers were prevented from changing their employers, occupations, or areas of residence for five years (a restriction that was subsequently reduced to one year for changes in employment and two years for changes in occupation and area of residence). Moreover a contract migrant worker required state permission to take another job within the same occupation or to change occupation (Hoffman-Nowotny 1978:86, 1985:218).

But there were also important similarities. One of the most significant concerns the restrictions imposed by the contract, and the power of the state, to limit the migrant worker's access to the labour market (that is, to prevent migrant workers from selling their labour power as they wish, either directly or indirectly, where restrictions are placed on their place of residence). In other words by becoming a contract, migrant worker the individual alienated control to a varying degree over the commodification of his/her labour power to the cosignatory of the contract (the employer) and to the state of the social formation where his/her labour power was exploited.

Formally there are now two distinct politico-legal statuses following the partial transition from rotation to permanent settlement. First there are those migrant workers who have a work permit which limits their employment to a particular employer and/or occupation and a temporary residence permit. Such powers are a defining feature of a contract, migrant labour system based on the principle of rotation or temporary residence because it is assumed that the worker's sale of labour power is limited both temporally and to the economic sector facing labour shortage. The state therefore *necessarily* retains control over the residence of the migrant worker and his or her ability to commodify labour power. Second, there are those migrant workers who have a work permit which entitles them to sell their labour power in any labour market, and to any employer they are able, and to a permanent residence permit.

In the former case, the degree of unfreedom is considerable because the state retains considerable powers which limit directly the individual's ability to commodify labour power. In the latter case, the individual occupies a politico-legal status which approximates the condition of free, wage labour because the individual is free to dispose of labour power as a commodity subject to the circumstances of the labour market. But an element of unfreedom remains in so far as the individual's continuing residence in the social formation, and therefore the individual's ability to commodify labour power in that social formation, remains dependent upon the will of the state. Moreover as in the former case, the migrant worker is deprived of various rights of political participation.

For example in West Germany and in Switzerland in the early 1980s the majority of migrant workers were subject to state controls over to whom they might sell their labour power, no matter how long they had been resident. Having been recruited to do semi- or unskilled work, the worker was not free to sell his or her labour power in the labour market in order to move into some other kind of work. Formally, labour power was a commodity exchanged for wages, but the state (and not the market) remained the immediate arbiter over where and when it could be sold, and therefore over the upper limit to the wages that the worker could gain from such a sale. In the case of wives and children of migrant workers the state prohibited them from selling their labour power for specified periods. The work and residence permit system, combined with the regulation that a migrant worker may only be considered for a job vacancy when it is known that no German citizen is available to fill it, therefore gave (and still gives) the state considerable powers to determine whether or not, and how, migrant workers' labour power might be utilized. The Dutch state had similar powers in the early 1980s, although only over migrant workers who had worked continuously in the Netherlands for less than five years.

These restrictions on the commodification of labour power are the defining feature of contract, migrant labour as unfree (wage) labour. But the unfreedom is overdetermined by a denial of the rights of political participation and representation. This denial not only prevents full participation in the political process but also, by a deprivation of the right to vote, obstructs the formation of an interest group which elected representatives might wish to, or be forced to, negotiate for. Consequently the contract migrant worker, although subject to a much greater degree of political constraint by the state relative to the indigenous working class, has fewer legally sanctioned rights to challenge that constraint.

This political unfreedom within the bourgeois democratic process is then further overdetermined by the power of the state to deprive the migrant worker of permission to remain a resident of the social formation wherein labour power is commodified. This is a significant disincentive to engage in any form of activism formally denied to the migrant worker because the state retains wide powers of deportation, even over migrant workers who have achieved long-term residence permits and the right of family reunification, where a migrant is found guilty of a criminal offence or to have engaged in activity contrary to the 'national interest'. The non-specific nature of this power of deportation potentially encompasses a wide range of activities, and not only those outside the bourgeois political process. It creates an overall climate of insecurity, inducing the migrant worker to refrain from political activism for fear that the state might cite such activity as a reason for deportation (Döhse 1982: 66). Such general powers tend to create a wider degree of political acquiescence and to further hinder the development of solidarity.

However, they do not eliminate political activism. Certain forms of activity are allowed, often in conjunction with authorities representing the social formation from which the migrant originates (e.g. Schmitter 1980; Miller 1981), and usually in the realm of trade union activism (e.g. Minet 1978). In addition, migrant workers have organized collectively and have joined with other workers in struggle under specific circum-stances, and therefore they should not be regarded as a completely passive political force (Miller 1981). Nevertheless the specificity of their politico-legal situation does serve to discourage political activism on the same scale as that of the indigenous working class and to diminish their effectivity as a distinct political force which others might represent.

The political insecurity of migrant workers is highlighted by state policies for repatriation. Repatriation proposals have taken different forms and, as yet, there have not been mass expulsions of migrant workers and their families. In Switzerland agitation against the presence of migrant workers has led to referendums on the issues of the size of the migrant population and of forced expulsion since the mid-1960s, but no expulsion policy has yet been implemented (Hoffman-Nowotny and Killias 1979; 55–8; Hoffman-Nowotny 1985:230–31). Where attempts have been made to reduce the size of the migrant worker population, these have usually taken the form of the offer of cash inducements to return to the country of origin. There are a number of instances.

In the Netherlands in 1974 the government proposed a reintroduction of the rotation principle whereby migrant workers would commit themselves to a stay of two years, after which they would return to the country of origin, receiving a payment of Fl.5,000 upon departure. There was widespread opposition to this proposal and it was never implemented (Bovenkerk 1979:120–30; Entzinger 1985:66–7). In France in 1977, a scheme was implemented which applied to all migrant workers who had been employed in France for a minimum of five years and which involved the payment of a cash sum and the cost of air fares in return for a commitment from the worker and family to relinquish any right to live and work in France (King 1984:159). And in 1980 a special agreement was signed between the French and Algerian governments to encourage return migration by means of loans and vocational training (Thomas 1982b; Verbunt 1985). Further initiatives were made in 1984 following redundancies of migrant workers at car assembly plants in France (*The Times* 1984; Anon 1984:12; Howe 1984). In West Germany a law passed in 1983 offered migrant workers who returned 'home' between 1 October 1983 and 30 September 1984 a payment of DM10,000, additional sums of money for dependents, and earlier repayment of social security contributions (*The Times* 1985).

Two features of the position of contract, migrant workers in Western Europe are revealed by these developments. First, the fact that only a small proportion of migrant workers have been affected by them is an indication of the continuing economic significance of migrants' labour power to the reproduction of the capitalist mode of production. Second, the fact that such schemes can be proposed and implemented is a measure of the insecurity of migrants' residence within Western Europe.

Conclusion

The scale of the labour migration and the size of the migrant worker population within Western Europe in the 1980s, even after a decade or more of capitalist crisis, mean that the contract labour system cannot be regarded as peripheral to the reproduction of the capitalist mode of production. Thus the fact that the contract migrant system embodies a form of unfree wage labour is highly significant, indicating that the historical reproduction of the capitalist mode of production is not synonymous with the progressive elimination of all forms of unfree labour in favour of free labour. Rather it indicates that there are circumstances in which forms of unfree labour are reintroduced and reproduced to ensure the reproduction of the capitalist mode of production.

In this instance the precondition for labour migration was a shortage of labour within the capitalist economies of Western Europe which could only be 'solved' by recruitment from within the various social formations by increasing wages to attract workers from other economic sectors. Such a solution would have obstructed the capital accumulation process, and so another source of labour power from outside these social formations was sought. There were however economic and political reasons to admit only on a temporary basis the people who would supply the labour power into the social formations of Western Europe, and so politico-legal mechanisms of recruitment and control were implemented in order to mediate their access to the labour market. Hence although these migrant workers received a cash wage, their status as a wage labourer was only formal because both the state and the contract of recruitment prevented them from freely disposing of their labour power on the labour market. These circumstances were over-determined by the role of the state in the social formation from which the migrants were recruited in so far as it regarded its citizens as sources of internal economic development as a result of their migration.

Part 3

Anomaly or necessity?

'Men make their own history, but they do not make it just as they please; they do not make it under circumstances chosen by themselves, but under circumstances directly encountered, given and transmitted from the past. The tradition of all the dead generations weighs like a nightmare on the brain of the living.'

(Marx 1968c: 96)

8

On relations of production

Introduction

I have argued in Part 1 that the concept of *unfree labour* refers to relations of production where labour power is distributed, exploited, and retained by politico-legal mechanisms and/or by physical compulsion. It is therefore synonymous either with the absence of a labour market or with circumstances where politico-legal measures limit the exchange of labour power within a labour market (i.e. with only the formal appearance of a labour market). Implicit in this definition is a contrast with *free labour* which refers to relations of production where labour power is exploited and retained primarily by means of economic compulsion, the mediating institution being the labour market, to which buyers and sellers of labour power remain free to return at their will. Consequently the distinction between free and unfree labour is one which turns on the presence or absence of a commodification of labour power; unfree labour is non-commodified or only formally commodified, while free labour exists where the individual retains access to his/her labour power as private property and can freely dispose of it within a labour market. The historical studies in Part 2 have examined in a largely descriptive manner a number of different forms of unfree labour and here I summarize and justify this description analytically. The order of presentation is not intended to suggest a process of linear progression. Thereafter I examine further central features of unfree relations of production.

Forms of unfree labour

First, there is *slave labour* which predominated in the Caribbean and at the Cape colony throughout the eighteenth and early nineteenth centuries. Relations approximating to those of slave labour were also evident in some Australian colonies for parts of the nineteenth century. In these instances of slave labour (and recognizing that slave labour took different forms in other social formations and historical periods), the human being was not only divorced from the means of production, but also became a commodity. It was the human being, not labour power, who became an exchange value which entered market networks (cf. Padgug 1976: 4; Mintz 1978: 90–1). Consequently relations between producer and non-producer were determined by the fact of possession. By this means the non-producer became entitled to determine the use of the labour power of the person enslaved as well as the disposal of the total production of that person's labour power. In the absence of a wage, the producer was dependent upon the non-producer to provide directly the means of subsistence and reproduction, or the means by which he/she could produce them independently. For the labourer, there was no chance to determine whom he/she could produce for, and formally, the right to determine the utilization of his/her labour power had passed to the non-producer as a result of ownership.

Second, there is *convict labour* which was the predominant form of labour exploitation in the Australian colonies in the late eighteenth and early nineteenth centuries (and was also utilized in Canada in the nineteenth century (Pentland 1981: 13–21)) and which exhibited features similar to thoses of slave labour (Dunn 1975: 33–5; McMichael 1984: 148–49). As a result of conviction for criminal activity the individual was deprived of the right to individual autonomy in most spheres of economic and political life, and the state was responsible for the convict's material reproduction where the punishment was imprisonment and/or transportation. Although the convict was not a commodity available for sale or purchase, the powers that accrued to the non-producer as a result of the purchase of human beings as commodities were, in the case of convict labour, gained by the state. The convict, like the slave, was dependent upon others to directly determine the disposal of his/her labour power and to determine much else about his/her daily existence. These powers invested in state officials were transferred when convicts were assigned to private individuals for whom they would provide labour power and who thereby became responsible for the convicts' material reproduction.

Hence a relation of direct domination was established between producer and non-producer. For the convict, like the slave, provision of the means for material reproduction was the responsibility of the non-producer, but the latter intended to obtain those means by utilizing the convict's labour power. Production and reproduction were therefore unmediated by either a labour market or money. There was neither a formal nor a real commodification of labour power. The most important difference between convict and slave labour was that the period of unfreedom was explicitly limited in time in the case of convict labour (except where a sentence was for life). This constituted an inherent contradiction because the relations of production based on convict labour were therefore slowly undermined by the 'release' of labourers from conditions of forced labour (Dunn 1975:36), with the consequence that the relations of production could be sustained only by a continual flow of new convicts.

Third, there is *labour tenancy* which was widespread in the South African colonies and later in South Africa. This relation of production was closer to serfdom than to slave labour in that the labourer was bound to the non-producer by force and/or politico-legal means, and not by direct ownership of the person as a thing. In addition the labourer retained a significant degree of economic independence by remaining responsible for the production of the means of reproduction, and by owning the tools necessary for production. The labour tenant was not, therefore, completely dispossessed of the means of production as was the case with slave and convict labour. But the relations of production were shaped by the establishment of private property rights in land and by a legal prohibition on land ownership by the labourers who therefore could gain access to the land as a means of production only by providing labour power directly to the landowner. The right to use the land was thereby exchanged directly for the right to command and utilize labour power. This exchange was not mediated by money until the twentieth century when a more formal contractual element was also slowly introduced to structure the relation between labour and non-labourer (De Kiewiet 1941:202–5; Morris 1980:204–6).

As far as the labourer was concerned the formation of this relation of production was involuntary, but in two different senses. European settlement and the establishment of private property rights in land often destroyed the ability of African populations to reproduce their 'traditional' mode of production and they were therefore compelled by economic forces to enter into relations of direct dependence. But additionally direct force was often also used to establish conditions of servitude, and the reproduction of those relations were usually guaranteed by legal means.

Fourth, there is *contractual servitude* (which includes certain kinds of apprenticeship) which was evident in the South African and the Australian colonies during the nineteenth century. Evidence concerning this relation of production is sparse in the case of South Africa, although more is known about the use of contractual servitude to exploit Aboriginal labour power in Australia. Contractual servitude approximated to both nineteenth-century indentured labour and contract migrant labour but differed from these two relations of production in so far as the contract was not used to facilitate the migration of labourers into one social formation from another. The central feature of this form of unfree labour (as with indenture and contract migrant labour) lay with the contract itself which bound by legal means the labourer to the non-labourer for varying periods of time (up to five years) and which thereby obstructed the commodification of labour power. By alienating labour power to another person for a specified period the labourer no longer possessed his/her labour power as an object of private property, and during that period had no access to a labour market. The relations of production established by and in the contract were reinforced by politico-legal means because breaches of contract were defined as criminal offences.

In South Africa the method by which the labourer gained the means of subsistence and reproduction is not clear, although it is known that the contractual nature of servitude applied where the labourer was paid a wage in exchange for the use of his/her labour power. Thus even where wage relations appeared in the South African colonies in the nineteenth century, they were largely formal because of the contractual constraint on the labourer's ability to dispose of labour power as a commodity. The extent of formal wage labour (and therefore the use of money to obtain the means of subsistence) is not known and so one can only speculate about the extent of non-wage relations where the labourer under contract was provided directly with the means of subsistence and reproduction. In the latter circumstances the degree of direct domination was substantially increased. In the Australian colonies small cash payments were made to Aboriginal labourers in return for the use of their labour power in certain circumstances, but these were usually supplemented by the provision of food items, and/or tobacco and alcohol, in addition to their own hunting and gathering. Where no cash wage was paid, and this was common, only food and other items for subsistence were provided in exchange for the use of labour power. Where rights to land occupation were also granted, this relation of production shaded into a situation approximating to labour tenancy.

Fifth, there is *indentured labour*. In this form of unfree labour, the non-producer had a monopoly of the means of production and recruited and retained labour power by means of a formal, legal contract. Under the terms of this contract, the producer alienated the use and product of his/her labour power to the non-producer for a specified period of time and the non-producer assumed responsibility for the provision of the means of subsistence and reproduction, supplemented in certain circumstances by the payment of a small cash wage. The producer was therefore structurally constrained by politico-legal means from disposing freely of labour power as a commodity. For the duration of the contract, the producer could not be a seller seeking a buyer for his/her labour power and so could not be one of the necessary constituent agents in the formation of a labour market. Indentured labour was therefore a form of temporarily limited servitude (Pentland 1981: 8): the legal contract ensured that the non-producer had full access to the producer's labour power for a stipulated period, either unmediated or only partially mediated by money. There was no market for labour power and either it was not bought and sold for money or, where it was, the wage was insufficient to cover all the costs of reproduction.

Consequently there was no real commodification of labour power.

Indentured labour approximated to slave labour in so far as the labourer was deprived of all direct access to the means of production and was bound to the non-producer. But there were important differences. Under relations of indenture the labourer was bound only for a specified period. Moreover there was a greater (but not a necessary or absolute) element of choice on the part of the producer to enter a contract of indenture. Historically various forms of deception and compulsion have been common methods of inducement to enter a contract, although it is also the case that a proportion of indentured labourers have chosen freely (although often in a context of considerable economic deprivation) to enter these relations in the belief that they might realize some benefit from so doing. This distinction is evident in the fact that the recruitment system involved a network of agents who were formally committed to gaining the consent of the prospective indentured labourer, and in the fact that the state made certain efforts to eliminate compulsion and deception when it was shown to be on a widespread scale.

Two forms of indentured labour have been discussed. The first was that utilized in the Caribbean in the seventeenth and eighteenth centuries, and the second was that form widely utilized during the nineteenth century following the abolition of slave labour in the British Empire. There were two important differences between these instances of indentured labour. The first concerned the formal appearance of a wage in the case of the indenture system of the nineteenth century. But this did not constitute a full commodification of labour power because the wage was never sufficiently large for the individual producer to purchase the means of reproduction, and the labourer remained largely dependent upon the means supplied directly by the non-producer. The cash wage was used primarily to meet financial commitments in, or to purchase commodities which could enter the process of 'gift exchange' in, the social formation of origin. The earlier form of indenture did not involve any financial transaction between non-producer and producer because the producer was supplied directly with the means of reproduction by the former. At the end of the period of indenture, either land or a quantity of sugar was granted to the producer, but there was rarely any cash payment.

The second major difference between the two systems concerned the degree of state support used to sustain and enforce the contract system. Compared with the seventeenth century, the nineteenth century system of indenture was characterized by a more systematic regulation by the state. Legal regulation of recruitment and of the relations of production was more extensive, and so the state served more directly as a contract enforcement agency, reinforcing the relations of direct domination of non-producer over producer. Moreover during the nineteenth century the state played a more important role in establishing the indentured labour system and the accompanying migration.

Sixth, there is *contract labour*. Like indentured labour this involved a legal contract between producer and non-producer for a stipulated period of time, during which the producer was required to make labour power available to the non-producer who monopolized the means of production. It differed from indentured labour in so far as the contract *required* the non-producer to pay a money wage to the producer which was used by the labourer to purchase a large part, if not all, of the means of reproduction. There was, then, a commodification of labour power in the sense that the producer elected to exchange labour power for a wage. But it was a commodification limited by the form of recruitment (as was the case with contractual servitude and indentured labour). The contract committed the producer to providing labour power to a particular non-producer for a specified period, during which the freedom to seek another purchaser of labour power was constrained.

The instances of contract labour that I have examined have a further common characteristic in that the contract system was devised and used to recruit labourers from one spatial location and to exploit their labour power in another for the period of the contract, after which the producer was usually (although not exclusively) required to return to the place of origin (or enter another contract). We can refer to this as *contract migrant labour*. This migratory system was premised on the particular politico-legal status of the migratory labourer, a status by which the labourer had no right to freely enter and reside in the territory to sell labour power. The contract therefore became a facilitating mechanism for two reasons: first, it granted the labourer the legal right to enter the social formation for the purpose of selling labour power to a named non-producer for a wage. Second, it granted the right of residence for a specified time period. But the coincidence of the two reasons over-determined the condition of unfreedom because the producer was not free to dispose of labour power to any other non-producer within that territory within which residence was permitted.

I have discussed contract migrant labour in two contexts, South Africa and Western Europe, where the particular circumstances of unfreedom differ in important respects. In Part 2 I discuss the original constitution of the contract migrant labour system in South Africa alongside the emergence of the capitalist mode of production, rather than its manner of current operation, while in the case of Western Europe I discussed the emergence of contract migrant labour in social formations centrally structured by the capitalist mode of production. There are important differences between these two instances of contract migrant labour.

First, the system of contract migrant labour in South Africa was constructed directly on the foundation of an extant system of contractual servitude, central aspects of which were reproduced. As a result the inferior politico-legal situation of the African population was over-determined by additional legislation which laid down that breach of contract constituted a criminal rather than a civil offence. Although the state within Western Europe established a legal structure for labour recruitment, directly participated in the process of recruitment, and regulated the entry and continued residence of the contracted labourers, the legal relations between producer and non-producer remained a matter of civil law. The state in Western Europe did not incorporate aspects of extant precapitalist legal relations of production to reinforce the politico-legal subjugation of the labourer by the non-producer in the labour process.

Second, within South Africa the position of the African population in the labour market has been further regulated and restricted by legal measures which have prevented their employment in certain kinds of job. These measures were initially intended to restrict the use of African labour power to semi- and unskilled manual work, although the categories of permitted employment have been subsequently extended. Hence although the African population had the formal right to dispose of labour power as a commodity, politico-legal measures have prevented Africans from selling that labour power to whomever they wish, subject principally to market conditions. In Western Europe politico-legal restrictions have not been used to formally exclude migrant workers from employment in particular sectors of the economy or in certain categories of job. The migrant worker in Europe, once under contract, could not return to the labour market for the duration of the contract (and neither could the African worker recruited under contract), but there have been no formal politico-legal measures designed to limit the sectors of the economy or the level of job for which a contract might be signed. In so far as the contract migrant worker has been confined to particular sectors of the economy and to particular types of job (as indeed they have), this has been determined largely by economic factors and/or 'informal' processes of exclusion.

Forms of unfree labour compared

These various forms of unfree labour represent varying degrees of approximation towards the condition of free labour. In the case of slave, convict, and the eighteenth-century form of indentured labour, the non-producer monopolized the means of production and there was no formal or real commodification of labour power. The relations of production by which surplus extraction was achieved were an expression of direct domination in that the total produce of the labourer's labour power belonged to the landowner and the labourer was directly dependent upon the landowner to provide the means of subsistence and reproduction. In the case of slave and convict labour, recruitment was involuntary and forced. This was less consistently true of the eighteenth-century form of indentured labour.

In cases of contractual servitude, the nineteenth-century form of indentured labour and of contract migrant labour, there was a closer approximation towards the condition of wage labour. The non-producer

178 Capitalism and Unfree Labour

had a monopoly of the means of production and, at least in part, exchanged cash for the use of labour power, although in the case of contractual servitude and indentured labour the money paid was insufficient to meet the costs of reproduction, food, and accommodation being provided directly by the non-producer. Moreover, nineteenth-century indentured labour and contractual servitude were transitional between direct forms of servitude and free wage labour. They were constituted in situations where free wage labour was emergent, but where there was a shortage of labour and where, for varying reasons, non-producers wished to retain extra-economic controls over labour power in certain sectors and yet retain some flexibility in the recruitment and disposal of labour power. Thus indentured labour, for example, was compatible with the reorganization of plantation production in the latter half of the nineteenth century in the Caribbean when large sums of money were invested in sugar production and the production process was significantly reorganized in order to introduce central factory processing (Courtenay 1965:45; Beckford 1972:102-4). However the contract system, the use of state power to enforce the contract and, where the wage paid was insufficient to meet reproduction costs, the continued dependence of the labourer upon the direct provision of the means of reproduction in the form of use values, combined to constitute real conditions of unfreedom.

With contract migrant labour there is a formal exchange of labour power for a wage, and so the unfreedom of the contract migrant worker is created and reproduced by restrictions on the exercise of the right to dispose of labour power. Indeed, the labourer commodifies labour power under contract, but the state establishes the politico-legal criteria which prohibit the labourer from entering the labour market at his/her will and/or from offering labour power for sale in certain sectors of the labour market. A formal (and real) labour market therefore exists, and surplus extraction takes the form of surplus value, but there is an uneven commodification of the labour power of those who wish or who are forced to participate in the labour market. I have earlier defined this as *unfree wage labour* in recognition of the formal appearance of wage labour, although constrained by direct politico-legal relations of domination. From the perspective of the employer, annual or biannual contracts permit a degree of flexibility in the recruitment and expulsion of labour power.

In principle the contractual element in all these three systems implied a recruitment system based upon individual free choice. In the case of indentured labour, there was a long history of various forms of compulsion, whereas in the case of contract migrant labour, economic compulsion has been the prime determinant, although this has been assisted by direct politico-legal intervention by the state (especially in South Africa). But the primary significance of the contract to the designation of relations of production as unfree lies not only with whether or not the contract was freely entered into by both parties, but also with its effects upon the labourer's use and control over labour power. We have seen that all contract systems not only alienate the labourer's labour power to another for a specified period but also alienate the labourer's right to dispose of labour power as a commodity for a specified period. Thus the labourer, once under contract, cannot freely enter a labour market to commodify labour power. Hence relations of direct domination between labourer and non-labourer are established and maintained by politico-legal means.

Labour tenancy was closer to serfdom than to wage labour in so far as, first, surplus extraction took the form of the labourer producing directly for the non-labourer, and, second, for a long period of time the labourer retained partial access to the means of production and could directly produce the means of reproduction. However, during the twentieth century a formal contractual element and the partial appearance of a wage element meant a closer approximation to wage labour and allowed the characterization of labour tenancy in that later form as a transitional relation of production in the sense previously discussed.

These various forms of unfree labour differ on another measure, the degree of temporality or permanence of the relations of unfreedom for the individual placed in them. Slave labour and labour tenancy were both generally characterized by permanence in so far as the labourer was bound for life. The other forms of unfree labour were all characterized by temporality. In the case of convict labour the individual was bound involuntarily by relations of unfreedom for the period of conviction. As in the other instances the contractual element permitted the individual formally to elect to enter relations of unfreedom for a negotiated period. Although in reality this formal freedom was often significantly constrained, if not non-existent, the individual was cognizant of a time when he or she would be released from the relations of unfreedom. In these circumstances the condition of unfreedom was a position in production relations which was preceded and superceded by a position in another set of relations of production. This mobility from one set of production relations to another was usually mediated by migration.

All these relations between producers and non-producers were class relations (cf. Genovese 1969: 6–7, 1975: 3). But in the absence of either a formal or real commodification of labour power (and retaining Marx's conception of the essential, defining characteristics of the capitalist mode of production), these various relations of production cannot be considered to be capitalist. This, then, is a major point of disagreement with Wallerstein who regards all instances of labour exploitation where the objective was commodity production as only different forms of capitalist exploitation. Not all the historical instances of unfree labour considered in Part 2 were associated with commodity production, but even where they were, I deny that commodity production is, in itself, a defining feature of capitalism. Only where commodity production is *generalized*, and so where labour power itself is commodified, can one refer to capitalist relations of production. This condition is not met in the relations of production surveyed above.

Moreover, and first, in the absence of the commodification of labour power, or where labour power is exchanged for some combination of cash and the direct provision of the means of reproduction, commodity circulation as a whole is restricted, limiting the absolute size of the market for all commodity exchange. Second, the character of direct domination involved in creating and reproducing these relations of production is dependent upon and sustains a distinct set of political and ideological relations, so that the character not only of the relations of production but also of other central features of the social formation take a specific form where these relations of production predominate.

More specifically, it follows that I reject the argument that plantation production, using slave labour, was a capitalist form of agricultural production. This has many adherents, including Gray (1941:302), Patterson (1979:53–9), and Elkins (1968:43, 47). Other writers, such as Mintz, appear to adhere to this view in certain of their writings (e.g. 1969:33, 1974:72, 74), yet reject it in others (e.g. 1978, 1985:57–61). Genovese asserts that Caribbean planters were capitalists but that planters in the southern United States were not, and that in the latter circumstance a slave mode of production dominated (e.g. Fox-Genovese and Genovese 1983:16–23). This distinction seems to contradict his claim that the master/slave relation necessarily shapes other constitutive relations (Fox-Genovese and Genovese 1983:151). Moreover, similar positions are taken by both Marxist and non-Marxist writers, as when Patterson (1979:54) cites the work of Fogel and Engerman (1974; cf. Engerman 1978) to advance his argument that the use of slave labour was a variant of capitalism.

In the historical examples of slave labour considered in Part 2, only in the case of the British Caribbean was slave labour used for large-scale commodity production. Moreover these plantations were dependent upon a flow of wealth and commodities from Britain, and so on both dimensions they can be considered to be participants in the growing world economic system of production and exchange. Nevertheless the manner in which labour power was recruited, retained, and exploited in the British Caribbean in the eighteenth century was different from, for example, the recruitment, retention, and exploitation of wage labour in Britain. Furthermore, I have shown in Chapter 4 that the overall organization of plantation sugar production had a specific character, notably its domination by the interests of merchant capital and the absence of any process approximating to accumulation, which was related to the form taken by the relations of production. In sum, a distinct set of institutions and processes of direct domination ensured the reproduction of slave production, as Genovese has shown in the case of the southern United States (1966:16).

In the remainder of this chapter, and drawing on the historical evidence of Part 2, I focus on further and more specific aspects of the relations of production which accompany and sustain unfree labour. First, I highlight the central significance of the role of the state in the formation and reproduction of unfree labour, and second, I trace the role of racism in the formation and legitimation of unfree labour. My argument is that these are not instances of the 'secondary' determination of political and ideological factors (which 'react back upon' the 'economic structure or base') but are constitutent elements of unfree labour. The state and racism are, therefore, integral relations of (unfree) production.

The state and unfree labour

The state is that institutional complex (government, courts, army, administration, etc.) which organizes social relations within a social formation to ensure the reproduction of a particular mode, or articulation of modes, of production. It therefore organizes a particular ensemble of class relations. In the first instance it appears as a 'purely' politico-legal structure but the manner and effects of its intervention mean that it is, in its functioning, a relation of production. This is because the state attempts, *inter alia*, to secure, by direct force and/or in law, the particular conditions considered necessary at any time (and thus, is the site of political struggle because what those conditions might be is the object of debate and dispute) to determine the relations between producers and non-producers and to determine that those relations are reproduced and/or reformed in particular ways. Thus the state is not simply a political institution which 'intervenes in' the economy. Rather, in the light of arguments in Chapter 1, it is an ensemble of structures and practices which directly constitutes the relations of production. Its very existence is essential to the formation and maintenance of the relations of production that it constitutes, and therefore it is a relation of production in its own right.

Where the relations of production are unfree, the role of the state as a relation of production is essentially and directly pivotal to their constitution and reproduction. If labour power is recruited, retained, and exploited directly by politico-legal means, then the intercession of the state between producer and non-producer, by orchestrating and legitimating the politico-legal conditions of their interdependence, is unmediated. Therefore as a relation of production the state confronts the labourer as an unmasked agent of exploitation. It is otherwise where labour power is recruited by means of a market and retained principally by the underlying condition of dispossession. In such circumstances the state remains an essential relation of production, but its intercession between producer and non-producer is indirect, for its task is to orchestrate the reproduction of the conditions of existence of the market mechanism which determines the exchange of labour power for wages. I go on to illustrate this unmediated role of the state as a relation of production by reference to the historical material presented in Part 2.

That material has focused on certain periods of English (later British) colonization, and upon the migration of labour into Western Europe since 1945, and this necessitates an examination of the role of the state in two different contexts. First, I consider the role of the state in the process of colonization (within which the constitution and reproduction of unfree relations of production was a central element) during which the capitalist mode of production was emergent in Britain, and articulated with various non-capitalist modes of production in the colonial social formations (see Chapter 9). In these circumstances economic and political connections were established, using force and violence where necessary, between spatially separated social formations, each with its own relations and forces of production and therefore with its own class structure, all organized in a hierarchy of domination. Within the colonized social formations a state was simultaneously emergent, and interrelated with the state in Britain, an articulation which was often expressive of conflicting economic and political interests in the two spatial locations.

Second, I consider the role of the state in constituting a form of unfree labour within social formations dominated by the capitalist mode of production. The performance of that role involved an articulation with other state formations, those within the social formations from which contract migrant labour was recruited, and/or with other modes of production. But in contrast to the colonial situations, direct force and violence have not been a central feature in the recruitment and retention of labour power.

In the colonial contexts discussed in Part 2, the state served as a relation of production in the following senses. First, as I have shown in some detail, it *constituted* in law the relations of production. Legislation set out the conditions under which labour power could be exploited and the various obligations of the non-producer to the producer, particularly with respect to the reproduction of the producer. In this respect, there is a structural complimentarity between the slave codes of the eighteenth century, the legislation and administrative interventions of the late eighteenth and early nineteenth centuries governing the use of convict labour, the laws governing the various indentured labour systems of the nineteenth century, and the various proclamations and acts which constituted contractual servitude and labour tenancy in the same century in South Africa and Australia. In other words, slave labour, indentured labour, labour tenancy, contractual servitude, and convict labour were never relations of production privately constituted by a relation of domination between producer and non-producer but were constituted and reproduced by, and were therefore dependent upon the existence of, the state.

Second, and following from the first, the state *enforced* the relations of production. Relations of unfreedom included being legally bound to provide labour power for a specified non-producer who monopolized some or all of the means of production, with the result that producers who refused to work or who absconded were in breach of contract. In the examples considered in Part 2, breaches of contract were almost exclusively defined as criminal rather than civil offences (i.e. offences against the state), with the consequence that the state was directly involved in contract enforcement. In the case of indentured labour in the nineteenth century, action which constituted a breach of contract was defined very broadly to include a failure to reach certain work norms, with the result that the state intervened to enforce production targets. Moreover, in order to prevent producers absconding and in an attempt to apprehend those who did, the state established controls over the spatial mobility of labourers in the Caribbean, Australia, and South Africa by, *inter alia*, a pass system which state officials were responsible for enforcing.

Third, the state *arbitrated* the relations of production in order to ensure their reproduction. Relations of direct domination, both in labour recruitment and in the labour process, encouraged violence of various kinds by the non-producer, often contrary to the legally constituted relations of production. Particularly during the nineteenth century after the abolition of slave labour, the reproduction of unfree relations of production was questioned by political forces in Britain, who used evidence of violence in their arguments against indentured labour and other forms of servitude. Moreover, evidence of violence and other forms of ill-treatment was cited by the agents responsible for organizing a supply of recruits as reasons for withdrawing the supply and, where recruitment involved a significant degree of voluntarism, served to discourage entry into relations of servitude. For these reasons the British state intervened to both regulate recruitment and labour exploitation by the appointment of officials with specific duties of investigation and, in certain circumstances, to change the law regulating the relations of production in an attempt to eliminate excessive abuse. Humanitarian motives were evident in determining this process of arbitration, but equally, if not more, important was the need to maintain a continuing supply of recruits.

Fourth, the state directly *exploited* unfree labour in the case of convict labour in the early phase of Australian colonization. In the late eighteenth and early nineteenth centuries the state directly organized a labour process utilizing convict labour in order to produce the means of subsistence and to construct a physical infrastructure for the colony in the form of buildings and roads. The state was also directly responsible for the reproduction of the labourers.

Fifth, the state was a leading force in the *recruitment* of people who entered unfree relations of production. State intervention took a number of forms. First, in the late seventeenth century, it created monopoly chartered companies to procure and supply human beings to be enslaved in the Caribbean. Second, in the Australian and South African colonies, it organized indigenous populations into political and economic units with the objective of creating labour reserves.

Third, in the South African colonies in the late nineteenth and early twentieth centuries, the state imposed taxation with the objective of forcing Africans to enter unfree wage labour in order to earn a cash wage to meet that obligation. Fourth, the British state, by maintaining and extending the boundaries of the Empire, contained and conserved within its sphere of political and military influence populations which could be recruited as unfree labour.

Sixth, and the *sine qua non*, the state established and maintained the political conditions for production by the *suppression of resistance*. In all the colonial situations analysed in Part 2, the indigenous populations engaged in various forms of resistance in response to the colonizers' disruption and/or destruction of their traditional modes of reproduction, and to the colonizers' attempts to incorporate them into the relations of production that they established to produce subsistence and to develop commodity production. Moreover where the labourers incorporated into unfree relations of production were recruited from outside the colonized regions, other problems of 'law and order' occurred, and again the state was involved in the suppression of resistance. This objective was achieved by the use of various forms of force, and by genocide in the Caribbean and in Australia.

In several respects the state as a relation of production has played a similar role in the creation and reproduction of unfree labour in the social formations of post-1945 Western Europe where the contract migrant labour system is the direct product of state intervention and organization. In these social formations the state has *constituted* in law, *enforced*, and *arbitrated* the unfree relations of production, has organized the *recruitment* of people to occupy the positions of unfreedom, and has *suppressed* resistance. But these instances warrant separate discussion in so far as, first, the form of unfree labour has been constituted *within* social formations where the capitalist mode of production has been emergent or dominant. This has established particular constraints on the specific character of unfree labour and of state intervention. Second, the political context is distinct because the reality of nation-state formation prevents an extension of commodity production and of labour recruitment by means of colonization.

The Western European social formations constitute distinct political units (nation-states), each with its own boundary and criteria of membership (citizenship). The historicity of this proces demonstrates that the nation-state is not a naturally occurring, universal phenomenon, but is interdependent with the uneven development of capitalism (Nairn 1981:334–48; Gellner 1983:62). This is reinforced by the historicity of nationalism, an ideology which specifically constructs a myth of origin and selects signifiers of common cultural inheritance in order to create and sustain a sense of imagined community (Anderson 1983:14–16; also Hobsbawm and Ranger 1983; Wright 1985). By virtue of having citizenship of one nation-state, the individual gains access to certain rights and responsibilities within it, and is denied access to rights and responsibilities in all others. This has an important economic dimension in so far as the development of the welfare state at the centre has socialized certain costs of reproduction, with the result that membership of the nation-state carries with it rights of access to certain resources and payment of monetary benefits.

The consequence is that human beings are immobilized in a particular nation-state by these political and ideological circumstances. In other words the existence of the nation-state and of nationalism are *impediments* to the free movement of people across those boundaries (a fact highlighted by specific initiatives to remove those obstacles, as in the case of the European Economic Community). Yet so many of the other processes of the capitalist mode of production (e.g. capital export) operate with only partial regard to these boundaries and restrictions. With the virtual exhaustion of the reserve army of labour within the nation-states of Western Europe, state intervention was therefore essential to 'release' labourers from the 'restrictions' of citizenship.

Consequently the unfreedom of the contract migrant worker is not solely determined by the desire of capital to recruit a super-exploitable workforce to fill gaps in the working class (e.g. Gorz 1970; Meillassoux 1981: 124–26). The unfreedom of the contract migrant worker is also rooted in the *contradiction* between the uneven expansion of the capitalist mode of production, that expansion being concentrated in specific spatial locations, and the political division of the capitalist world economy into nation-states. This political division is a structural reality with its own effects, and the state, as a relation of production, has to *mediate* the consequent contradictions. In the early phase of the migrant labour system the state in the Western European formations constituted the contract labour system and reified national status in order to legitimate and retain the economic benefits that accrue from utilizing the wage labour of workers whose costs of production and reproduction are borne, at least partially, by another nation-state on the periphery of the world system. With the shift from rotation to permanent settlement, many of these economic advantages no longer pertain and it is envisaged that capital export will replace labour migration (Bourguignon *et al.* 1977: 13–14; Hiemenz and Schatz 1979: 6–11; Frobel *et al.* 1980).

As a process the migrant's transition from a position in the relatively surplus population to wage labourer was nothing new in historical terms. It was no more than a continuation of a central dimension of the reproduction of the capitalist mode of production. But there were novel aspects to the process because those recruited to fill vacant positions in the Western European economies did so defined in law as *foreigners* or *aliens*, as people who do not belong. And this legal category has been utilized to deny the migrant worker a legal right of permanent residence and of political participation, which are corollaries of the conditions of unfree labour. This is doubly determined. Not only does the state within the recruiting nation-state define the migrant worker as a foreigner, but so does the state within the sending nation-state.

In the latter instance, the state defines its own citizens as exploitable units of labour power but seeks to obtain economic and political advantages for the capitalist class by the export of labour. A precondition for the realization of these objectives is the reproduction of the political and ideological conditions for the migrant workers' return, and therefore the exporting state actively seeks to sustain the national identity of its migrants and to represent their interests while they remain in Western Europe (Miller 1981:31–42). Moreover, the political reality of distinct national units creates and sustains distinct political identities amongst both the migrants and the population amongst whom they work and live. All these political and ideological conditions, and the manner of their orchestration by the state, constitute essential relations of production in the case of contract migrant labour.

This is also true in a more specific sense in the case of the migrant labour system within South Africa where the legal status of the labourer as an 'alien' or 'non-citizen' has a distinct origin. As we have seen, within South Africa the state established a system of segregation and later a system of apartheid within its own territory (Wolpe 1972; Legassick 1974a) so that the African population was deprived of a large number of bourgeois rights, including the commodification of labour power, within most of South Africa. That this population is formally a population of 'non-citizens' within a large part of South Africa (that is, the African population is denied the right of political representation as well as the right to freely dispose of labour power as a commodity) is therefore a consequence of strategic political decisions by the South African ruling class. The structure of direct domination and the unfree relations of production constitute a particular strategy of both labour recruitment and political exclusion organized by the state *within* the social formation.

Thus in the case of contract migrant labour in Western Europe the category of 'non-citizen' had a longer-established reality grounded in a process of nation-state formation within and outside Western Europe over preceding centuries, whereas *within* South Africa, given its initial constitution as a single social formation, equivalent mechanisms of differentiation had to be 'artificially' created and maintained. Once those mechanisms had been established by the state, the pass system became essential to the regulation of the spatial mobility of the African population and to ensure that the African population remained 'permanently' resident in the reserves, or later the 'homelands'. Herein lies a political specificity of the South African case of capitalist development.

Racism as a relation of production

In the preceding section I have argued that the state, as an institutional political complex, plays an essential role as a relation of production in

the constitution and reproduction of unfree labour. The absence of a
labour market, or the failure of a labour market to procure and
distribute labour power, is the precondition for state intervention to
conduct these tasks which are fundamental to the possibility of
production. In the light of the arguments in Chapter 1, I go on to argue
that the ideology of racism is also, to varying degrees, a central relation
of production in the instances of unfree labour considered in Part 2.
This follows from the fact that labour power is inseparable from the
human being who provides it. Whether labour power is procured as a
commodity in exchange for a wage, or by a direct relation of domination,
the non-producer necessarily enters into a social relationship with other
human beings in order to exploit labour power. And whatever the
means employed it is always the case that labour power resides within
the labourer who must therefore be induced to expend it on behalf of
the non-labourer.

The acquisition and retention of labour power therefore necessitates
judgements about the characteristics and capacity of the human beings
to deliver it in the context of a potential range of constraints and
inducements. Such judgements involve the signification of real or
imagined characteristics of the labourer and the development of an
explanatory system linking those characteristics with the capacity to
provide labour power. They are made in situations where people are
immediately available for incorporation into relations of production,
but also where there are immediate shortages of labour and therefore
where labourers have to be recruited from other social formations. In
the former case, decisions have to be made about who, from the people
available, should be incorporated into production, while in the latter
case, decisions have to be made about which of the potential sources of
labour power should be drawn upon.

In addition to judgements about the real or imagined *capacity* of the
people who might constitute the labour force, decisions have to be
taken about the practicality of recruiting from one source rather than
another. In other words, it requires an evaluation of the *structural
conditions* of recruitment or acquisition. For example decisions have to
be taken concerning the likely inducements or degree of compulsion,
and the political and material consequences, required to recruit and
retain various potential sources of labour power in particular relations
of production in particular historical circumstances. An assessment
about capacity has implications for the assessment of structural
conditions, and *vice versa*.

Judgements about capacity and suitability can be made on a wide
variety of criteria, involving the signification of different characteristics.
Signification is therefore a necessary and inevitable feature of the
process of labour recruitment and retention, while racism is a
historically contingent mechanism of signification. Thus where a labour
force is selected by reference to negatively evaluated, real or imagined
biological, or any other allegedly inherent, criteria (as a result of which

a 'race' label is directly or indirectly signified), and where the people are in some other respect attributed with negatively evaluated characteristics (Miles 1982:78–9), then racism becomes a relation which constitutes the process of production. It is therefore a social relation of production, an ideological intervention which inheres in the productive process (see also Miles 1988). Moreover, racism also has the potential to legitimate a particular ensemble of relations of production and a signified group, to justify the assignation of particular people to a particular position in the productive process. Other ideologies can be employed to achieve these consequences, including nationalism, an ideology which also asserts a natural division of the world's population into discrete groups and the existence of inclusive/exclusive criteria of belonging, and which, consequently, articulates with racism in particular historical contexts (Miles 1987).

I therefore reject the traditional Marxist problematic for the analysis of racism, that which seeks in a functionalist manner to explain the *origin* of racism (*qua* ideology) as a *product* of capitalist development (e.g. Cox 1970:322; Nikolinakos 1973b:365–67; for a critique, see Miles 1980, 1982:81–7). In analysing racism as a relation of production I am not concerned with the *origin* of racism, but with its effectivity in particular historical and material circumstances, an effectivity which may or may not have consequences which are conducive to particular economic and political interests. Moreover I wish to advance beyond the interpretation of racism as a 'superstructural' phenomenon, an interpretation which asserts that racism is an ideology created by capitalists to legitimate exploitation and is therefore functional to capital. The historical evidence demonstrates that the *origin* of racism cannot be explained as being the product of a capitalist conspiracy (Miles 1982:97–101).

Hence I conceive racism (which has additional, secondary conditions of existence and reproduction) as a potential ideological element of signification by which to *select* and to *legitimate* the selection of, a particular population, whose labour power will be exploited in a particular set of unfree production relations. Once used in this manner, it may become a structural feature of the means used to recruit and retain labour power. However, because the economic and political conditions determining the relations of production and the populations available for recruitment change over time, both the reproduction and the content of racism are subject to change. In other words, as a relation of production, racism is characterized by changes in its ideological content and its object. Moreover, as we shall see in Chapter 9, once racism becomes a relation of production, it has contradictory consequences.

These relations and processes are evident in the colonization and exploitation of labour power in the Australian colonies in the nineteenth century. The colonizers from Britain racialized both their own attributed characteristics and those of the indigenous population and the other populations who migrated to the Australian colonies in the nineteenth century. They generally defined themselves as belonging to the 'higher civilized races', and believed themselves to be superior to the 'inferior races' in the colonial context. Indeed, one of their claimed 'racial' characteristics was a superior ability for colonization, a characteristic which revealed not only their racism but also their sexism. Thus:

> 'Physically proficient men, white and preferably British were regarded as the best colonisers whose forceful nature, competitiveness and even occasional resort to brutality against inferiors were regarded as virtues to be applauded.'
>
> (Evans *et al.* 1975: 10)

Colonization was defined as a 'natural' characteristic of the 'Anglo-Saxon race':

> 'If it is a divine law that the Anglo-Saxon people must double themselves every half-century, it must be a divine law that they are to emigrate and form for themselves new homes in waste lands. But every spot suitable for man's sustenance is held by some sort of human occupant; and, therefore, the Anglo-Saxon cannot choose but intrude upon the haunts of other races. . . . In obedience to natural laws over which they had no control, seeing that they would not and could not brain their infants as the Australians did, the Anglo-Saxons sought these lands, and settled side by side with the natives.'
>
> (cited in Reynolds 1972: 100)

Their characterization of 'the natives' was less 'positive'.

In the case of the Aboriginal population, it was originally believed by the early settlers, as I have already shown, that they were a 'backward race' which had the potential to be 'civilized' in order to carry out manual work of various kinds for the colonists (Hasluck 1970: 58–9). Governor Macquarie wrote in 1814:

> 'Those Natives, Who resort to the Cultivated Districts of this Settlement, Altho' prone like other Savages to great Indolence and Indifference as to their future Means of Subsistence, Yet in General, are of free, open and favourable Dispositions . . . and its seems only to require the fostering Hand of Time, gentle Means and Conciliatory Manners, to bring these poor Unenlightened People into an important Degree of Civilisation.'
>
> (cited in Reynolds 1972: 109–10)

Their attributed backwardness was said to be evident in their failure to cultivate the land, an interpretation which justified both land expropriation and attempts to 'retrain' them as labourers, the latter being sanctified by missionary activity which attempted conversion to the Christian religion (Hartwig 1978: 133–34).

The failure of these schemes, and the guerrilla-style resistance of the Aboriginal populations, prompted a revised signification which interpreted the subsequent decline of population as evidence of inherent biological inferiority. The Aboriginal population was racialized and identified as the inevitable loser in an unequal natural struggle between the 'races' for survival (Rowley 1970: 101; Loos 1982: 24). Thus in the *Cooktown Herald* in January 1874, it was argued:

'When savages are pitted against civilisation, they must go to the wall; it is the fate of their race. Much as we deplore the necessity of such a state of things, it is absolutely necessary in order that the onward march of civilization may not be arrested.'

(cited in Fitzgerald 1982:143)

Scientific racism provided a justification for the immediate settler experience of the military subjugation of the Aboriginal population (Evans *et al.* 1975:67) as follows:

'The Aboriginal cranium appears to be large, although in reality the brain is not so. The uncommon thickness of the skull and in the integuments surrounding it, accounts for this; and the strength of the Aboriginal head-piece in resisting the most powerful blows of their waddy is well known. . . . The great preponderancy of brain in the New Hollander, as in all savage nations, lies in the posterior parts of the head – the seat of the passions, and inferior sentiments; the moral and intellectual portions, with few exceptions, are very deficient.'

(cited in Reynolds 1972:114)

Christianity was combined with this scientific racism to explain the substantial destruction of the material and cultural foundation of Aboriginal reproduction in terms which placed the ultimate responsibility in the sanctified realms of 'Divine Providence' (see Reynolds 1972:Chapter 7; Fitzgerald 1982:204, 210).

But the 'doomed race' theory was inconsistent with attempts to incorporate Aboriginal labour power into the productive process initiated by settlers in circumstances where there was no other source of labour power. In those circumstances, as I have shown, various strategies were demanded of, and implemented by, the state which resulted in the formation of reserves and an official attitude of paternalism (Fitzgerald 1982:211; Loos 1982:182). The ideological concomitant of this shift is illustrated by this extract from an Editorial in a Sydney newspaper of February 1880:

'That the race is inevitably doomed to extinction has also become a conviction, and many practical people hesitate before aiding what they look upon as a futile enterprise. But, allowing that extinction awaits the aborigines, it does not follow that there is justification for permitting them to perish like dogs. It is at least possible to make extinction as painless as possible, and to compensate to later generations in some degree for the outrages and wrongs suffered by their forefathers.'

(cited in Curthoys 1982:46–7)

Thus the inevitable outcome of the Darwinian struggle between the 'races' was postponed into the indeterminate future, and in the meantime measures were taken in an attempt to prolong and humanize the death throes in order to ensure the incorporation of Aboriginal labour power by means of contractual servitude. As important as these shifts were in the content of racism, of greater significance is the fact that there was a concurrence of racialization and incorporation into unfree relations of production. In other words, unfree relations of production were constituted, and the labourers were incorporated into them, partly by means of racism. Racism, therefore, became an ideological relation of production. Racism was not an ideology which 'reacted back upon' economic relations but was itself an economic relation.

This may be illustrated further in two other instances in the history of nineteenth-century colonization of Australia. Both demonstrate the role of racism in racializing potential sources of labour power, and creating a hierarchy of desirability. First, as we have seen in Chapter 5, the extension of sheep farming in the 1830s and 1840s expanded the demand for labour power at a time when the use of convict labour was in decline, and various initiatives were taken to recruit labour from outside the Australian continent because Europeans and Asians were both regarded as being of superior 'race' in comparison with the Aboriginal population (Rowley 1970: 120–21). Yet Asians were also regarded as an inferior 'race' when compared with the British 'race'. Clark summarized the interpretation of the *Sydney Morning Herald* as follows:

> 'The colonists, they write, would never think of importing foreigners, much less savages and heathens, if their demands could be adequately supplied from their own countrymen. They would have no wish to people their sheep-walk with strange races. The mere idea of their doing so was repugnant to all their national predilections. Much rather would they see Australia replenished and subdued by the unmixed, undeteriorated progeny of their own Anglo-Saxon fathers.'
>
> (1973: 369);

Both the local and the British state considered the question of importing Indian labour, in the course of which concern was expressed about maintaining 'racial purity' along with a belief that the formation of an 'alien', 'pagan', and 'servile' population would lower the standard of living and would discourage migration from Britain (Willard 1967: 4–7; Clark 1969: 100). But racist ideas did not resolve the problem of labour shortage, and a small number of Indian labourers were brought into New South Wales, their presence and exploitation legitimated by claims that contact with 'civilization' would encourage conversion to Christianity (Clark 1969: 99).

Second, the problem of labour shortage was even more severe in the extension of colonization and the development of commodity production into Queensland, and the accompanying ideological debate was equally intense. Various solutions were considered, in the course of which different groups were racialized and their attributed 'racial' characteristics were compared. The possibility of using labour power of British origin was considered but ruled out on the grounds that the 'white race' was unable to work in tropical conditions (Willard 1967: 135, 178). One planter who began the recruitment from the Pacific Islands claimed:

'I think I deserve the thanks of the community for the introduction of that kind of labour which is suited to our wants and which may save us from the inhumanity of driving to the exposed labour of field work the least tropically hardy European women and children; for I suppose the most thorough advocate for European labour will admit that in cotton clearing and picking, they, as well as the men, must take part in the labour.'

(cited in Docker 1970:14)

Chinese and Aboriginal labour was also considered, but was excluded partly because these 'races' were regarded as being inherently lazy (Fitzgerald 1982:245). The racialization of the Pacific islanders was more consistent with a potential for their exploitation on plantations. They were defined as 'uncivilized children', but biologically capable of providing manual labour in tropical conditions (Evans *et al.* 1975:163, 176). Given their supposed condition, their exploitation in the 'inhumane' conditions of plantation agriculture was legitimated on the grounds that it would civilize them (Docker 1970:11).

These debates became integral to the development of Australian nationalism. During the 1890s the pressures favouring the formation of a Commonwealth of Australia increased in strength and a key objective of those supporting this objective was an immigration policy which would ban the entry of 'inferior races'. The main focus of this agitation was migrants from Asia, and specifically Chinese labourers attracted by gold discoveries (Crawford 1923; Farley 1968:261). Huttenback has concluded:

'A survey of the period from the mid-nineteenth century to 1910 shows the slow evolution of a policy that started out as nothing more than a set of colonial laws basically designed to keep Chinese off the Australian goldfields into a racial philosophy that enjoyed many of the trappings of a state religion.'

(1976:315)

By the end of the century the economic interests of Queensland sugar farmers were pitted against the widespread racist agitation for a 'White Australia' policy (see Dallas 1955; Nairn 1956; Willard 1967; Yarwood 1962, 1964; Palfreeman 1971), which, once enacted in 1901, would not allow any exception. Consequently almost all of the Pacific island indentured labourers were 'repatriated'. Racism, by then a component part of nationalism, excluded all 'inferior races' from production relations in Australia.

Differences in historical context and development ensure that the particularity of these processes in the nineteenth-century Australian colonies are not evident elsewhere. But it is possible to trace similar processes whereby racism served as a relation of production in the other examples cited in Part 2. In the case of the Caribbean I have argued elsewhere that racism was not the initial justification for the selection of the African as a source of labour power and their enslavement, but was an emergent ideology, although with roots deep in European culture (Jordan 1968: 4–11), which paralleled the extension of the slave mode of production (Miles 1982: 97–117). In so far as justifications for the initial enslavement of Africans were sought and offered, it was their 'heathenness' which was cited (Davis 1966: 88–9, 108–9, 165–6; Rice 1975: 21), and arguments about inherent inferiority developed only during the eighteenth century (Williams 1970: 204; 208–16). By the late eighteenth century, there was an unquestioned belief that slavery and the African's 'blackness' were synonymous, and the generalization that only Africans were capable of providing labour power in tropical conditions was pervasive (Barker 1978: 60–1, 198).

Thus legitimation of the exploitation of African labour power in conditions of unfreedom drew upon racism, although this was not the sole argument, for many pro-slavery writers suggested that slave labour presented the African with more favourable opportunities for 'advancement' than those available in the 'savage wilderness' of Africa (Barker 1978: 198). This racist signification of the population of African origin was reinforced after the abolition of slavery when those freed from slave relations of production proved unwilling to provide labour power. The Governor of Guiana wrote of this population in 1849: 'A careless indolent semi-barbarous race, unprofitable to their rulers and helpless to themselves, and fast subsiding into a state of mere animal ease' (cited in Cumpston 1953: 149).

Racism imposed a hierarchy of acceptability on the potential sources of labour power, within which the Afro-Caribbean population was ranked at the bottom and Asians were accorded an intermediate position. But the ideological influence cannot be divorced from the political and economic context. The destruction of the Indian textile industry, and the consequent unemployment in the respective areas of India created a political and economic problem for the British colonial state, one that was overdetermined by the legitimation of colonial intervention which asserted that the objective was to advance the 'backward races'. Within this context the emigration under relations of indenture of dispossessed Indians was accompanied by an image of docility of the Asian 'races' which supposedly fitted them to resolve labour shortages in the Caribbean and many other parts of the colonial empire, including southern Africa. For example in Natal (which had been annexed on the grounds that the 'natives' would be civilized [Thomson 1952: 5]), the emergent planter class, when seeking a source of labour power to develop plantation commodity production for export, 'explained' the reluctance of the African population to provide labour power by claiming that it was 'naturally indolent' (Van der Horst 1971: 46). This trait was not thought to characterize the Indian workers recruited under indenture.

The effectivity of racism in selecting a labour force and legitimating the exploitation of its labour power in unfree relations of production has been particularly prominent in the history of South Africa. During the early nineteenth century the farmers of Dutch origin who migrated áway from the Cape believed that their own 'race' did not suit them to manual labour (De Kiewiet 1941:216), and that those who did provide labour power under relations of unfreedom were 'racially' distinct:

> 'The Voortrekkers were dependent on the use of servants of African, or Asian, or mixed descent, and assumed them to be of a different sub-species. They even referred to them in different terms – as *skepsels* (creatures) rather than *mense* (people).'
>
> (Wilson and Thompson 1969:366)

A self-identity of being a 'superior race' meant that groups defined as distinct 'races' were simultaneously defined as inferior, and this ideology became enshrined in the Constitution of the Union of South Africa which

> 'represented the triumph of the frontier, and into the hands of the frontier was delivered the future of the native peoples. It was the conviction of the frontier that the foundations of society were race and the privileges of race.'
>
> (De Kiewiet 1941:151)

Consequently a group signified as being 'of different race' was to be allocated to a position in the relations of production consistent with its attributed 'racial characteristics'. As a result the relations of production were themselves racialized, racism constituting and orchestrating them in a particular historical (and cultural) form. Thus Chinese labour recruited under indenture in the first decade of the twentieth centry was considered suitable because of its alleged docility (Richardson 1977:90).

In Western Europe since 1945 the legacy of fascism has been one of the factors which has obstructed the open expression of scientific racism and has changed its content. Nevertheless throughout Western Europe the presence of migrant workers has been problematized, although the ideological categories vary. In West Germany the problem is defined as one of *foreigners* while in France the categories employed are those of *étranger* or *immigré* (Castles 1984:190–212; Grillo 1985:51–83). These ideological categories define migrant workers and their families as separate from, and even a threat to, the imagined community that is the nation. The quality of foreignness implies an inability to belong to the imagined community which is said to be manifested in distinct cultural practices and in the migrants' phenotypical features. In turn, these signified characteristics become symbols of their supposed 'natural' inability to belong. This is a dialectical process because such claims simultaneously reinforce the legitimacy of the criteria which supposedly creates the sense of a common bond which is essential to nationalism.

To take one example, West Germany, academics have argued publicly that the German national character and culture is being overwhelmed by the 'foreign' presence, an argument which has received legitimacy in the national press. For example 'ever since the period of the historic migrations of peoples, the interchange between Slav, Romanic, Germanic and also Celtic peoples has become a habit. A tacit we-feeling has arisen in one and the same European culture. But excluded from this are the Turk-peoples, and also the Palestinians, North Africans and others from totally alien cultures. They, and only they, are the 'foreigner problem' in the Federal Republic.'

(cited in Castles *et al.* 1984:206)

Politicians and state officials have also played a prominent role in creating and legitimizing the idea of a 'foreigner problem' and identifying the population of Turkish origin as the archetypal instance (Wilpert 1983:138). These assertions are formally nationalist in content, but they may also enclose and reproduce racism (see Miles 1987b). For the purpose of this argument the main point is that these assertions overdetermine the politico-legal category of 'foreigner' and 'alien' which legitimates the migrants' position in unfree relations of production.

Conclusion

If classes are constituted as a result of the articulation of economic, political, and ideological relations (e.g. Poulantzas 1978:13–35) and if, as I have argued above, unfree relations of production are constituted to ensure the exploitation of labour power and the extraction of a surplus product by means of political and ideological practices (in the form of state intervention and ideological signification), then it follows that the people located in the varying relations of unfree labour constitute distinct classes or (in the case of unfree wage labour) a distinct fraction of the proletariat. In other words, under unfree relations of production not only is the mode of surplus extraction distinctive (in various ways), but that mode of exploitation is specifically constituted by means of state practices and ideological signification. These state practices and processes of signification are therefore as much a constitutive part of the relations of production as the mode of surplus appropriation. Thus those people who have occupied the positions of unfree labour discussed in this chapter (slave labour, convict labour, indentured labour, contractual servitude, labour tenancy, and contract migrant labour) have constituted distinct classes or class fractions. However, Poulantzas's distinction between the *sites* and the *agents* of class relations serves to emphasize the fact that the people who have occupied certain sites of unfreedom have done so only temporarily, their migration being not only spatial but also a migration between different class *sites*.

9

Unfree labour:
an anomalous necessity

Introduction

I am now in a position to propose an answer to the central question
posed in Part 1. There I indicated silences in Marx's writing concerning
unfree labour, and thereafter demonstrated the limitations of the work
of Wallerstein who, claiming to work within the Marxist tradition, has
attempted to explain the historical continuity and reproduction of forms
of unfree labour. In Part 2 I analysed historically the conditions for the
emergence and development of different forms of unfree labour over
four centuries in certain parts of the world, and it is in the light of this
evidence that I theorize the persistence and reproduction of forms of
unfree labour alongside the development of the capitalist mode of
production.

This theorization is not offered as an exhaustive, general theory. I do
not claim that it explains all historical instances of unfree labour. In so
far as the generalizations are derived from particular case studies they
are necessarily limited in scope. Nevertheless this is not an empiricist
analysis, and the generalizations are also derived from a theoretical
analysis of the essential characteristics of the capitalist mode of
production. Consequently I do suggest that the central conclusions of
this chapter have an explanatory power which extends beyond the case
studies of Part 2 to other instances where free and unfree relations of
production coexist and articulate. The extent of their explanatory power
remains an open question.

Unfree labour as an anomalous necessity

In order to retain and explore the explanatory power of Marx's
conception of capitalism as a mode of production characterized by the

(dominant) presence of wage labour, I presume that the spread of the capitalist mode of production involves, *inter alia*, the transformation of non-wage into wage relations of production, and hence the formation of a labour market. Historically this has occurred in the context of the development of a trading network under the control of merchant capital. This development was determined by the extension of extant political conflicts and by the search for new sources of state revenue within social formations dominated by the feudal mode of production. Thus

> 'the historic overseas expansion began under the aegis of the great landed monarchies – began, that is, under feudal auspices as a desperate if heroic effort to shore up a crisis-ridden feudal mode of production'.
>
> (Fox-Genovese and Genovese 1983:10)

In the sixteenth century the feudal ruling class welcomed not only the luxury imports procured by the merchant class but also the customs revenue and banking facilities that they provided. The state concentrated trade in the hands of a relatively small number of merchants so that the rise of the merchant class was synonymous with state-regulated monopoly (Hill 1969:74–5; De Vries 1976:133–34). As a result by the early seventeenth century there was in existence a loosely articulated world economic system, organized under the hegemony of merchant capital (De Vries 1976:113–15).

This was the context for the emergence of the capitalist mode of production in England, and later throughout Western Europe. Although capitalist relations of production were generalized first within this single social formation, this process cannot be isolated from wider 'international' relations. An explanation for the transition from feudalism to capitalism must therefore be able to take account of that network of production, consumption, and exchange which linked together an increasing number of spatially separated social formations during and after the sixteenth century. But this world economic system was an emergent form rather than an extant reality in the mid-seventeenth century as Wallerstein and others suggest. It was dominated initially by merchant capital and therefore it cannot be defined as capitalist in the sense understood by Marx (see Chapters 1 and 2). But it was and has remained a world economic system which has mediated between different modes of production in different spatial locations. It has come to be dominated by the capitalist mode of production as that mode has come to predominate in an increasing number of the constituent social formations and as an increasing proportion of commodities in circulation have originated from within the capitalist mode.

Within this context forms of unfree labour can be explained as both *anomalous* and *necessary* to the reproduction and spread of the capitalist mode of production within, and to an increasing number of, social formations. They are *anomalous* when viewed in relation to the tendency for the emergence and increasing dominance of free wage labour, and yet they are *necessarily* introduced and reproduced because historical conditions obstruct the universalization of wage relations of production. The commodification of labour power and the formation of labour markets do not 'naturally' exist or arise, but depend upon certain (pre)conditions, the presence of which are historically variable, and upon human agency. It is because of this dialectic between material circumstances and human agency that one must regard the existence and reproduction of the capitalist mode of production as being the product of human beings, but human beings constrained by those material circumstances.

Thus the emergence and development of the capitalist mode of production has been and is dependent upon the realization of a particular set of historical conditions, with the result that the formation and reproduction of capital/wage labour relations of production can be hindered or blocked by the character of the particular historical combination of economic and political relations existing within any social formation. In sum, historically, unfree relations of production have accompanied the emergence and reproduction of the capitalist mode of production partly because economic and political conditions do not permit its unproblematic expansion, even though an increasing amount of commodity production is pulled into its sphere of influence.

This argument will be elaborated and expanded by the use of concepts (two of which were discussed in Part 1) which grasp key aspects of the historical development of the capitalist mode of production. First, there is the concept of *primitive accumulation* which refers to the process whereby the relations essential to the capitalist mode of production are formed. In other words, the formation of the capitalist mode of production presupposes the historical existence of non-wage and unfree relations of production, relations which are the foundation for, but which are transformed by, the capitalist mode of production.

Second, there is the concept of the *commodification* of *labour power* which is derived from the concept of *primitive accumulation* and which draws attention to the historical conditions under which a labour market is formed and reproduced (cf. Pentland 1981:25). The conditions for the formation of a labour market include, first, the presence of a sufficient number of people, relative to the development of the productive forces and to the demand for labour power, for competition to occur between them, the competition being sufficient to reduce wages below the point where capital accumulation is possible; and second, the potential for their partial or complete separation on a permanent basis from the means of production in sufficient numbers. The potential for dispossession is determined by a number of factors, including the relative power of the state and the particular composition of economic, political, and ideological relations which constitute the extant mode of production. These conditions for the commodification of labour power are not universally present. Where they are absent, labour power cannot be made available and distributed by a purely economic mechanism and some form of politico-legal intervention and/or compulsion becomes necessary. Historically, these conditions have often been absent in colonial contexts, as a result of which the development of the capitalist mode of production has been obstructed.

Additionally, within the capitalist mode of production the conditions for the reproduction of a labour market may be disrupted or subverted. Under certain circumstances labour markets may cease adequately to realize their objective, as for example where a labour market proves unable to 'deliver' labour power at a price which permits the creation and appropriation of surplus value. This can occur where, first, the quantity of labour power in circulation is reduced, leading to increased competition for it, and consequently, an increase in wages which may then threaten the accumulation process; and second, it can occur where the labour market cannot 'deliver' labour power of the required quality (i.e. level of skill and experience). Such circumstances arise in the context of the 'normal' reproduction of the capitalist mode of production.

The third concept is that of *articulation of modes of production*. The process of capital accumulation and the accompanying increases in productivity have implications for the supply and production of commodities, including labour power. Capitalist production increases both the velocity and quantity of commodity production and circulation, and this in turn requires an increase in the supply of labour power as well as raw materials for commodity production. There should, therefore, be an increase in the size of the market within which commodities are sold. The development of the capitalist mode of production therefore necessarily extends the parameters of the world market, drawing in commodities (including labour power) produced in non-capitalist modes of production. Thus we confront the historical conditions governing the relationship between capitalist and non-capitalist modes of production, and hence the interdependence of free and unfree relations of production. The existence of the world market has been the mediating institution for this articulation. This has been particularly evident in the case of the development in colonial contexts (where the relations of production have taken an unfree form) of exchange values for export to a social formation dominated by a capitalist mode of production. In addition, the reproduction of non-capitalist modes of production can also be intended to produce labour power for exploitation within a capitalist mode of production.

I now use these concepts of *primitive accumulation, commodification of labour power*, and *articulation of modes of production* to specify those historical circumstances where unfree labour exists and is reproduced as an anomalous necessity.

Colonization, primitive accumulation, and unfree labour

In the instances of the British colonization of Australia and South Africa the historical evidence demonstrates that capitalist interests were of little significance in initiating settlement. As a result these parts of the world were incorporated into the expanding world economic system initially in a secondary and peripheral role. Productive activity was confined largely to subsistence production under various forms of non-capitalist relations of production. Consequently in both historical instances one can trace the emergence of capitalist relations of production only after the act and initial process of colonization, during which unfree relations of production predominated for reasons to be discussed in the following section. In other words, there was a prior period of primitive accumulation, a period during which non-capitalist relations of production were dominant but during which capitalist relations of production were constituted.

The historical details of Marx's account of primitive accumulation in England are of little relevance to an analysis of the Australian and South African colonies, concerned as it is with, *inter alia*, the expropriation of a peasantry by means of land enclosures (Lazonick 1974; see also Mantoux 1961: 141–85). European colonists did not settle in social formations dominated by long-established feudal relations of production and so close parallels with England should not be sought in these colonial instances (Denoon 1983: 124). Historically, there is no single path leading to the emergence of the capitalist mode of production. Hence the 'transition debate' reviewed in Chapter 3 cannot be limited to instances where the capitalist mode of production is preceded by, and emerges from, the feudal mode of production.

But Marx's reference to a period necessarily preceding the dominance of the capitalist mode of production in a social formation, a period when capitalist social relations are created, is of analytical significance. This has been recognized in the case of Australia (Buckley 1975; Dunn 1975) but not in the case of South Africa, about which the Marxist debate has tended to focus upon the rationality or otherwise of systematic racist exclusion and/or the 'functions' of the migrant labour system (e.g. Wolpe 1972; Legassick 1974a). I argue that the period of primitive accumulation in the case of New South Wales occurred between the 1790s and the 1840s (later for the other Australian colonies because colonization was itself an uneven process) while, in the South African colonies, it occurred between the mid-nineteenth century and the period immediately after the Natives Land Act (1913).

During these periods different forms of unfree labour predominated. In New South Wales it was convict labour, while in Cape colony and the three other South African colonies, labour tenancy, contractual servitude, and indentured labour all played a part. But what was common to both cases was the introduction and/or consolidation of the conception and practice of private property to deal with the distribution and use of land, so that access to and control over the land was increasingly monopolized, not by Europeans but by a particular class of European origin. This necessitated a struggle not only with the indigenous populations, as a result of which they were eventually wholly or partially dispossessed of the means of production in areas of European settlement, but also with other migrants of European origin in order to ensure that they did not all establish themselves as independent producers.

In the Australian colony of New South Wales the state officials charged with organizing the convict colony were granted sufficient political power to subsequently establish themselves as a landowning and/or merchant class. And a source of labour power, in the form of convicts, was readily available and was utilized under the assignment system. Again it could be so utilized because the military personnel, who constituted the local state, had sufficient power to establish the necessary legal conditions. Thus the exploitation of convict labour constituted an important source for the initial accumulation of wealth in the hands of a small minority of landowners.

How long these relations predominated is a matter of dispute (Buckley 1975: 36; Dunn 1975: 33–5), although the historical evidence suggests that it was nearer the middle of the nineteenth century rather than the beginning. The claim that free wage labour predominated as early as 1805 ignores, on the author's own admission, both female convict labour and male convicts not assigned to private producers (Buckley 1975: 26) while the numbers of free migrants arriving in the Australian colonies remained very small until the 1830s (De Lepervanche 1975: 72). By the 1840s the means of production in New South Wales were certainly concentrated in the hands of a small class of landowners and merchants, and labour power began to emerge as the main means of labour exploitation, the class being composed of both ex-convicts and free migrants of European origin. These relations of production did not then predominate in all parts of the Australian colonies and neither were they automatically extended to all other areas of settlement. But their initial emergence was contiguous with the development of wool production for the international market as well as commodity production to supply the internal market.

The case of the South African colonies is more complex because British colonization followed approximately 150 years of control by the Dutch East India Company and of relations of production based on slavery (and labour tenancy in the case of free settlers who maintained an independent presence). But little productive activity was for sale on a market. Following the establishment of British control over the colony there was a limited migration from Britain of people wishing to organize production for the world market. They constituted a dynamic element, extending private property rights of land ownership. But in common with the rest of the British Empire the abolition of the slave trade and then slave labour itself led only to the introduction of other forms of unfree labour (contractual servitude and indentured labour). This was because the British colonists, like the Dutch who preceded them, did not gain a monopoly of land ownership and because a large proportion of the African population retained direct access to land as a means of production. Thus when sugar production was established in Natal, it was not African labour that was recruited but indentured labour from India.

This property-owning class with interests in agricultural production for exchange was joined by a property-owning class with interests in mining in the late nineteenth century. Both were sustained by investment from Europe rather than from within the colonies and, in the case of mining, competition quickly led to monopolistic or near-monopolistic production. This new fraction emerged alongside a longer established fraction of landowners of Dutch origin who organized agricultural subsistence production, with whom it was in competition for access to labour power. But if the concentration of the means of mining production in a few hands (a key component of the process of primitive accumulation) was relatively quickly and easily achieved, the formation of a property-less proletariat within the South African colonies was not. The previous economic marginalization of large sections of the African population now had to be reversed, but this was not easily achieved, exposing the limits to human intervention to create a labour market. The extent of the difficulties was evident with the import of skilled labour from Europe and by the recruitment of semi- and unskilled labour under indenture from Portuguese Mozambique and from China. It was only with the Natives Land Act, 1913, that a systematic strategy for labour recruitment, retention, and exploitation from within South Africa was initiated.

Thus, in both the Australian and the South African colonies primitive accumulation resulted from, but was not consonant with, European colonization. In both sets of colonies private property relations were initially introduced to determine the disposal and control of the land as a means of production by a section of the European colonizing population, and this differentiated them as a class. It was with the later attempt to initiate large-scale commodity production for exchange on the world market that the second crucial transformation occurred. In the case of the Australian colonies this was begun using convict labour but these unfree relations gave way, although not exclusively, to free wage labour as migration flows from Europe bringing property-less persons increased from the 1830s and after transportation was abolished. The Aboriginal population was largely marginal to this process, partly because of its resistance to European colonization and partly because of the partial disintegration of its 'traditional' mode of production.

The process of creating a labouring population with only its labour power to sell was much more problematic in the South African colonies because, in the absence of large migration flows of property-less labourers from Europe, and of systematic and widespread dispossession of the African populations, and as a result of resistance by the African population to incorporation in emergent forms of commodity production, the formation within the colonies of a permanent class of labourers selling their labour power was obstructed. Thus relations of servitude were adopted by the emergent mining bourgeoisie to recruit labour from outside the South African colonies and to establish relations of production which were characterized by only a formal wage element (i.e. relations of indenture) prior to the 1913 Natives Land Act. Only in the case of skilled labour did a labour market almost immediately emerge, and international migration was the mediating mechanism, transferring already proletarianized 'agents' from Britain to the South African colonies.

Colonization and unfree labour

We have seen in the preceding section that the course and consequences of the process of primitive accumulation are historically contingent. I now consider the circumstances under which the process of primitive accumulation can be obstructed so that capitalist relations of production are either not constituted or are constituted in a 'deviant' form. First, I examine conditions of colonization which were not conducive to the formation of capitalist relations of production so that primitive accumulation did not occur. Second, I show how features of the colonial situation shaped the process of primitive accumulation, to the extent that its progress was simultaneously hindered and given a peculiar character, one consequence of which was the reproduction of unfree relations of production alongside the formation of a labour market and the commodification of unfree labour.

The first set of conditions is revealed in the colonization of the Caribbean in the seventeenth century where English settlement was followed by the incorporation of the region into circuits of production and exchange based in Europe in order to supply exchange values (i.e. tobacco, later sugar). This incorporation involved the introduction of new systems of commodity production rather than the establishment of exchange relations with indigenous populations engaged in the production of use-values which were then transformed into commodities which circulated in European markets. In order for commodity production to occur relations of production had to be created and means of production had to be accumulated. The agricultural origin of the commodity ensured that land was a primary means of production, and so the relations governing access to and use of land were of central importance. Equally important were the issues of who would provide labour power and under what conditions. In the colonial context access to and the use of both land and labour power were dependent in part upon whether or not an indigenous population was present and, if it was, upon the outcome of the economic and political transaction between it and the European settlers. We have seen that in the Caribbean the indigenous population was largely exterminated.

Consequently commodity production was only possible by recruiting a labour force from outside the Caribbean and transporting it to the region, and by establishing politico-legal means to bind migrants to landowners to prevent the migrants from establishing themselves as independent producers. Given the sparsely populated land, and its free availability, independent subsistence production remained an option for a free migrant. Unmediated coercion was overdetermined by the consequences of the first circumstance, from which it followed that those organizing commodity production were also responsible for meeting the costs of bringing a labouring population to the Caribbean. Landowners wished to retain the use of that labour power, at least until the labourer had produced sufficient to meet the costs of recruitment, an outcome that could be achieved only by relations of direct domination. Thus indentured labour was introduced, to be succeeded by slave labour.

Nieboer argued that the extensive use of slave labour was only possible in situations of 'open resources', that is where the means of subsistence were available to all. Slave labour has been absent when a section of the population has been able to concentrate the ownership and control of the means of production in its own hands, a situation he defined as one of 'closed resources' (1971:384–85, 418–19). This argument requires re-formulation (cf. Domar 1970:21; Evans 1970:861–63; Engerman 1973:58–9; Mintz 1977:257). First, the ability of a class to monopolize the means of production depends upon the interrelationship between the extent of the state's resources to enforce objectives and the spatial and politico-economic character of the territory within which it claims authority and sovereignty. The significance of this point will be elaborated shortly. Second, the historical evidence presented in Chapter 4 demonstrates that slave and serf labour were not the only forms of unfree labour that could be utilized in the circumstances that Nieboer describes (see also Mintz 1977:260). The earliest period of English colonization of the Caribbean was dominated by the use of indentured labour to obtain and retain a source of labour power from Europe. Thus Nieboer's situation of 'open resources' is not conducive to the commodification of labour power and therefore predisposes the introduction of politico-legal measures of coercion to ensure the exploitation of labour power, but there are a number of different forms that such measures may take. The particular form that unfree relations of production take therefore depends on the additional factors discussed in Chapter 4.

The historical example of the Caribbean confirms that the following general conditions are necessary to allow the emergence and development of capitalist relations of production. First, there has to be a population of sufficient size to both constitute a labour force after dispossession and guarantee competition between sellers of labour power in order to ensure that labour power is not exchanged for wages which are sufficiently high to preclude accumulation. Second, the politically dominant class has also to have established monopoly control over the means of production. This requires the active intervention of the state, using force and legal measures. None of these conditions was realized during British colonization of the Caribbean in the seventeenth and early eighteenth centuries. There was neither a population of sufficient size to constitute a labour force nor a class within all the islands able to monopolize the means of production, and nor did the state have the means of enforcement relative to the circumstances. In sum, the historical circumstances obviated the commodification of labour power in the Caribbean until the nineteenth century.

The second set of conditions was evident in the nineteenth century in the Australian, southern African, and Caribbean colonies. In the Australian and South African colonies British colonization also proceeded in the context of 'open resources'. Large areas of land were available for permanent settlement, although in many locations this could only proceed if the indigenous population was denied 'traditional' patterns of land usage, with the result that settlement expanded only after, or parallel with, resistance and the military subjugation of those populations. Additionally in parts of the Caribbean (specifically in Jamaica, Trinidad, and British Guiana) a situation of 'open resources' recurred after the abolition of slave labour.

In all of these places the development of commodity production was inhibited by a shortage of labour. Moreover, a major obstacle to the formation of a labour market was the option of an independent existence on the land, either for subsistence or for production for exchange. This was the case for both the 'indigenous populations' and for migrant settlers from Britain. And where access to land ownership was obstructed for migrant settlers, the numbers of people freed of the means of production remained small in relation to the demand. But the resolution of the problem took a different form when compared with the Caribbean in the seventeenth and eighteenth centuries. Rather than preventing a process of primitive accumulation, these conditions ensured that it had an uneven character in that unfree relations of production were reproduced alongside the emergence of wage labour. This was because the wider economic and political context was distinct in the following respects.

First, the option of slave labour was no longer available. Second, within the world economy the political and economic influence of merchant capital had considerably weakened (Hobsbawm 1969: 227–32; Kay 1975: 99). It had become increasingly subordinate to industrial capital whose interests lay more with increasing the productivity of labour in order to reduce the value of each commodity and increase the scale and velocity of exchange within the market. Consequently the concern of industrial capital was predominantly with the most efficient utilization and exploitation of labour power as the means to increased profitability and accumulation. Third, this development within Britain had repercussions in the colonial arena where commodity production for exchange was either established (in the Caribbean) or in the process of development (in the Australian and South African colonies). In the context of increasing international competitiveness measured by the mechanization of production and pressure to increase the productivity of labour, the efficiency of the recruitment, retention, and exploitation of labour power in these colonial locations was of considerable significance (a concern that was evident in the reorganization of sugar production in the second half of the nineteenth century).

Fourth, in the case of the Australian and South African colonies (but not in the Caribbean), a migration of settlers from Britain was taking place (partly sustained by state assistance), although the scale of the migration was insufficient to meet the demand for labour. Finally, there were significant sums of wealth available in Britain for investment, and during the second half of the nineteenth century, a significant proportion was directed to the colonies (Hobsbawm 1969:147–48; Barratt Brown 1974:138–44, 170–200). For example, in the case of Australia, large sums of money were directed into pastoralism and communications (especially railways) (Jenks 1963:231), and during the last quarter of the century into industrial and manufacturing industry (Butlin 1964:2, 29–33, 194, 201–10; Denoon 1983:153).

The overall consequence was a process of primitive accumulation, a hesitant and uneven emergence of capitalist relations of production. In the preceding section I have argued that this was happening in the Australian and the South African colonies, but a similar transition was also occurring in the Caribbean (Post 1978:24–35). In each of these instances, although in somewhat different ways, it was a transition which was shaped crucially by what was, for the property-owning class organizing production, a shortage of labour in a context of 'open resources'. Hence, we must consider the way in which the process of primitive accumulation was hindered by those circumstances because it was this latter constraint that led to the reproduction of unfree relations of production.

In the context of expanding commodity production and continuing labour shorage there was a particular logic to the extensive utilization of indentured labour in the Caribbean and Australian and South African colonies in the nineteenth and early twentieth centuries. The indenture system was simultaneously a method of adding to the labour supply and of suppressing labour costs by denying the new migrant workers free access to an emergent labour market where they could otherwise have 'exploited' market forces by selling their labour power to the highest bidder. In other words, the conditions of the emergent labour market were such that it would only supply labour at a cost that obviated the realization of a surplus. Indentured labour therefore allowed the class which controlled the means of production to obtain a supply of labour without recourse to the emergent labour market while the contractual nature of recruitment ensured that the labourers were unable to participate in that labour market for the duration of the contract. They were bound to the non-labourer, and yet were not an item of private property that had to be maintained for life but only for the duration of the contract. Additionally, the state enforced the terms of the contract by making breach of contract a criminal offence while the non-labourer could exploit the contract system to increase the rate of exploitation. Finally, given that recruitment from outside the colonial social formation involved additional expenses, the contract system provided a guarantee that the worker could be retained for at least the minimum time necessary to allow the accumulation of sufficient surplus product to meet those expenses. There were, in other words, certain historically contingent economic advantages arising from the system of indentured labour which encouraged its utilization in the context of labour shortage.

The indentured labour system of the nineteenth century was a transitional form of labour recruitment, retention, and exploitation. It occupied an intermediate position between slave and wage labour (see Chapter 8). It appeared as a form of wage labour but the contractual nature of the system ensured a sufficient degree of servitude and direct domination to allow the non-labourer to exercise considerable control over the labourer, and yet the latter was eventually 'freed' from the contract and either re-indentured or replaced. Moreover, indentured labour was combined with large financial investments in the mechanization of the productive process in order to increase the productivity of labour. Thus although the characterization of nineteenth-century indentured labour as the 'new slavery' (Tinker 1974) is apt in so far as it was another historical instance of unfree labour, it does underplay the significance of its combination with means of production which had a higher technical component and its degree of approximation to wage labour, and hence my preference to characterize it as a transitional form.

But, as we have seen in Part 2, the indentured labour system was not the only form of labour recruitment and retention utilized in the colonial context. The indentured labour system depended upon politico-legal mechanisms to recruit and retain labour in a context of 'open resources' and labour shortage, but an economic mechanism was also used by the state to deprive migrants of access to the means of production. We have seen that for writers such as Wakefield, the 'art of colonization' in the nineteenth century was to turn land into a commodity, but at a price which ensured that only a minority of people could afford to buy it (Wakefield 1869; but see Merivale 1928; 382–448). It was envisaged that the majority of settlers would be unable to establish themselves as self-supporting subsistence producers and that they would be obliged therefore to sell their labour power for a wage, with which they could then purchase the means of subsistence. The objective was to encourage the formation of a labour market and the real commodification of labour power. It was therefore an integral element of primitive accumulation, intended to create a situation of 'closed resources'.

These two strategies were used to differentially incorporate people into production relations. Politico-legal mechanisms of incorporation and retention were combined with a process of racialization. The migrants from India and the South Pacific and the indigenous populations in the Australian and South African colonies were incorporated into various forms of servitude and contract labour, as a result of which control over their labour power was alienated to others, and they were signified by racism. But European settlers were incorporated into emergent commodity production either as property-owners or as free sellers of labour power, their subsistence and reproduction dependent upon the operation of a labour market. They too were racialized, but their racist theories placed them in a privileged position which was economic and ideological. Thus, racism (as an ideological relation of production) differentiated populations that were simultaneously differentially allocated to emergent free and unfree relations of production. Racism did not 'react back' upon economic relations but was an ideological form which was integral to the constitution of economic relations.

It follows that a situation of 'open resources' is a necessary, but not a sufficient, condition for the formation and reproduction of unfree relations of production (cf. Domar 1970:21). Put another way, the major weakness of Nieboer's argument is that it divorces material circumstances from human agency and from the particular balance of economic and political forces. A non-labouring class had at least two options in these conditions of colonization. It could use politico-legal means to recruit and bind labourers, a process which did not, in itself, necessarily transform the situation of 'open resources' into one of 'closed resources'. Or it could act in ways to remove the option of an independent existence and so create conditions where economic compulsion forced the labourer to offer labour power as a commodity for sale. This meant monopolizing the means of production under its own control, an objective difficult to achieve in colonial situations when state power was extremely circumscribed and where there were large areas of land which were not individually owned and permanently settled (cf. Mintz 1977:257). Hence the early history of these colonies includes the continual extension of the boundaries of settlement beyond the control of the colonial state and widespread 'squatting'. The effective power of the state is therefore a crucial independent variable in the determination of unfree relations of production, as is the balance of class struggle in so far as it determines the mode and consequences of state intervention. This reinforces the earlier argument that the state is an essential relation of production in the formation and reproduction of unfree relations of production.

Both options were pursued simultaneously in the Australian and South African colonies in the nineteenth century. In the former case the commodification of land was intended to limit access to the means of production for those who elected to migrate with the intention of permanent settlement, but because this migration flow was not on a sufficient scale, and because of the inability of the colonial state to prohibit squatting, the size of the labour market was restricted and was insufficient to meet demand as commodity production expanded from the 1830s and 1840s. Thus fractions of the property-owning class in Western Australia and Queensland elected to resolve the problem of labour shortage by using unfree relations of production to exploit either Aboriginal labour power or Pacific island labour recruited and imported under contract.

In South Africa during the early part of the nineteenth century there was only limited demand for labour because production was largely for subsistence. In the absence of any widespread process of dispossession of the indigenous population some form of unfree labour was the only option available to the propety-owning class of Dutch and British origin. This remained the case when commodity production did expand. Although this expansion was accompanied by a limited free migration from Britain, the migrants' access to the means of production was obstructed by existing widespread settlement and by the commodification of land. Thus this free migration and parallel formation of a labour market was accompanied by the migration under indenture and contract of labourers from India, Mozambique, and China.

The situation in the Caribbean in the nineteenth century was distinct because commodity production for exchange and private property relations were already well established and because the relations of production previously established were abolished by the British state. In addition the Caribbean was no longer viewed as an arena for colonization. The feature in common with the Australian and South African colonies was found only in Trinidad, Jamaica, and British Guiana where a situation of 'open resources' provided opportunities for those freed from slavery to engage in independent subsistence and commodity production as peasant producers. This obstructed the formation of a labour market which would provide labour power at a price that would permit the realization of a surplus and so sugar producers were forced to recruit a supply of labour from outside the Caribbean and to bind it by legal means to the plantations.

There was another significant dimension to colonization in the case of Australia and South Africa. The utilization of unfree labour was bound up not only with the limited and partial progress of the process of primitive accumulation but also with the process of nation-state formation. We have seen that because the internal labour supply and migration flows from Britain were inadequate, additional supplies were sought in other parts of the world. But the issues involved in this recruitment were not exclusively economic. Indentured labour (and other forms of unfree labour) did have certain cost and control advantages over wage labour and a fraction of the property-owning class did develop interests in the retention and expansion of these relations of production. But these economic issues were inseparable from the political and ideological implications of the different ways of resolving the labour shortage. The additional migration flow could have been designed to increase the number of settlers or it could have been organized to ensure only temporary residence. The former strategy raised questions about the cultural character of the imagined national community that was being created in these colonial social formations, a dimension that was intimately connected with racist debates about the capacity of different populations for 'civilization'. Consequently political and ideological factors were implicated in the process of resolving labour shortages in these two colonizing situations.

In sum, I have argued in this section that unfree relations of production emerge in situations of colonization where a labour market either could not be formed or could not adequately satisfy the demand for labour that accompanied an initial expansion of commodity production in the context of primitive accumulation. A similar problem can develop in the context of the 'normal' production of the capitalist mode of production.

Capital accumulation and unfree labour

I therefore move from the analysis of primitive accumulation where the wage labour/capital relation is emergent to the analysis of a situation where the capitalist mode of production is dominant. In such circumstances, by definition, the wage labour/capital relation of production is the primary relation of production and labour power is allocated by means of the market mechanism. My argument is that under certain historical circumstances the operation of this market mechanism can partially break down and politico-legal means of labour recruitment will be utilized, temporarily but necessarily, to recruit and retain labour power. In order to understand the circumstances in which this occurs it is necessary to understand the relationship between capital accumulation (Marx 1976: 762–802) and labour migration.

Once capitalist production is established the source of accumulation lies in the extraction of surplus value which is used to increase the quantity of the means of production (constant capital) and labour power (variable capital). If all other factors remain the same, capital accumulation would mean equivalent increases in constant and variable capital (Marx 1976: 763). In other words, the concentration of capital would be accompanied by a continually growing demand for labour power, and Marx notes that when these conditions have occurred, the result has been rising wages. But other factors are not constant, as was indicated in a preliminary manner in Chapters 1 and 3.

The composition of capital, the interrelation between constant and variable capital, is not static because competition leads to increased productivity in order to reduce the cost of the commodity produced. This is best achieved by combining the same or a lesser quantity of labour power with an increased quantity of means of production (that is by increasing constant capital relative to variable capital) (Marx

1976: 773). In other words, as capital becomes more concentrated, less labour power is required to activate a given quantity of means of production. Additionally, capital becomes more centralized by means of mergers, following which production is reorganized to take advantage of new machines and technologies with the aim of increasing productivity. This can lead to a reduction in the demand for labour. Thus

'On the one hand . . . the additional capital formed in the course of further accumulation attracts fewer and fewer workers in proportion to its magnitude. On the other hand, the old capital periodically reproduced with a new composition repels more and more of the workers formly employed by it.'
(Marx 1976: 780–81)

To this point it appears that the changing composition of capital results in a continuous reduction in the size of the working class. This is not so. First, the concentration of capital, although reducing the relative quantity of variable capital, does not necessarily prevent an increase in its absolute quantity (Marx 1976: 774–75). The concentration of capital may therefore be accompanied by an absolute increase in the demand for labour, and therefore by an increase in the size of the working class. Second, a reduction in variable capital may lead to an increase in the number of workers employed where the introduction of new machinery leads to the elimination of highly paid skilled labour and its replacement by lower cost semi- and unskilled labour (Marx 1976: 788). Third, the concentration (i.e. increasing quantity) and centralization (i.e. concentration in fewer hands) of capital can occur at different rates in different sectors of production (Marx 1976: 782–83). In certain sectors the concentration of capital may be accompanied by an increasing demand for labour while simultaneously, in others, the centralization of capital may be accompanied by the expulsion of skilled labour and its replacement with semi-skilled labour. The consequence is an increased quantity of accumulated capital, an increase in constant capital over variable capital, and an increase in the total number of wage labourers. The precise interrelationship between these different elements is a matter for historical investigation.

So the capital accumulation process has two tendencies which

'constantly cut across one another; (firstly,) to employ as little labour as possible, in order to produce the same or a greater quantity of commodities, in order to produce the same or a greater net produce, surplus value, net revenue; secondly, to employ the largest possible number of workers (although as few as possible in proportion to the quantity of commodities produced by them), because – at a given level of productivity – the mass of surplus value and of surplus-product grows with the amount of labour employed. The one tendency throws the labourers on to the streets and makes a part of the population redundant, the other absorbs them again and extends wage slavery absolutely, so that the lot of the worker is always fluctuating but he never escapes from it.'
(Marx 1969: 573; see also 1973: 399)

The coincidence of these two processes creates and requires the existence of a relatively surplus population which serves to regulate the general movement of wages (Marx 1976: 781–94, 899). This reserve army of labour (for recent discussion of this concept, see Anthias, 1980; Sommerville 1982; Lever-Tracy 1983; Miles 1986b) supplies labour power where sections of capital are expanding production, obviating a competitive struggle to attract an otherwise limited labour force by means of escalating wages, and receives labour power in periods of capital recomposition when new machinery and techniques of production are introduced. These are normal processes of capitalist production which are accentuated in periods of crisis when large numbers of workers are expelled to join the reserve army of labour.

Historically the processes of capital concentration and centralization have been associated with the migration of labour, both internally within social formations and from one social formation to another. Migration is therefore an integral feature of the development and expansion of the capitalist mode of production (Standing 1981: 192; Miles and Phizacklea 1984: 142–52). For example, what Marx referred to as the *latent surplus population* was the source of recruitment for the first factory proletariat in Britian which was composed largely of rural, agricultural workers who were underemployed and badly paid in the countryside and who migrated to the towns in response to the demand for labour (e.g. Redford 1964). But for such a migration to occur the population has also to be 'released' from immobilization on the land (cf. Standing 1981), a process which Marx identified, for example, in Britain in land enclosure, as we have already seen.

In sum, the expansion of the working class is an inherent tendency of the capitalist mode of production, although dependent on certain historical conditions. We have seen in Chapter 7 that such conditions were present during the 1950s and 1960s in Western Europe, where the expansionary cycle of accumulation increased the demand for labour to the point where it could no longer be met within the political boundaries of each social formation and so, in order to avoid increases in wages, labour was recruited from other social formations. The existence of the nation-state, the political unit within which labour power is reproduced and politically organized, was therefore a potential obstruction to the further accumulation of capital. By establishing systems of labour recruitment from outside those political boundaries, the capitalist class and the state were therefore further internationalizing the process of labour recruitment.

The predominant (but not the only) solution was the use of the contract migrant labour system which had certain historically contingent advantages. First, because the accumulation process is cyclical, migrant workers were granted only temporary admission, allowing for their removal when the demand for labour lessened. In turn this required that the state mediate their access to the labour market, thereby establishing relations of direct domination. Second, by externalizing some of the production and reproduction costs of labour power there were historically contingent economic advantages for both state and capital when recruiting temporary workers under contract from other social formations (e.g. Gorz 1970; but see Burawoy 1976). Finally, to varying degrees it was believed that the temporary admission of migrant workers would not challenge the assumed cultural homogeneity of the social formation, the sense of singular identity which lay at the centre of the imagined community (see Chapter 8).

These unfree relations of production did not displace the capitalist relations of production. The formal commodification of labour power that they embodied was compatible with the wider dominance of wage labour, and in so far as the system was successful in the recruitment of labour, the capitalist accumulation process was able to continue largely unhindered until the early 1970s. These unfree relations of production were therefore established and reproduced by the state and capital in order to ensure the reproduction of the capitalist mode of production in a context where there was a conjunctural contradiction between economic and political relations, that is between the continuing concentration and centralization of capital and the reproduction of the nation-state as the context for the material reproduction of labour power and for its political organization and representation.

In one sense the problem was identical to the colonial contexts discussed above, where a shortage of labour could not be resolved by recruitment from within the social formation. It differed in the crucial sense that the predominant relations of production were capitalist, and for political reasons the form of labour recruitment and reproduction had to conform in appearance to the norm of wage labour, although a relation of direct politico-legal domination was established over the labourer. Contract migrant labour was therefore also anomalous, yet necessary. But it was also inherently contradictory, and those contradictions coincided with a much more deep-seated crisis in the capitalist mode of production in the 1970s, leading to the suppression, but not elimination, of the contract migrant labour system during the latter half of the 1970s.

Unfree labour and the articulation of modes of production

In this section I argue that under certain historical circumstances the conditions which induce the emergence of forms of unfree labour are reproduced, thereby sustaining those relations of production. Where economic and political interests become enmeshed and invested in their reproduction, and where they come to sustain a specific pattern of economic processes and a specific set of political and ideological relations, a distinct mode of production may be reproduced. Included amongst the conditions for this reproduction may be practices and interests which originated in another mode of production and, under such conditions, there will be an articulation of modes of production. An articulation of modes of production may therefore become the basis for the reproduction of unfree relations of production and for their coexistence with capitalist relations of production.

This is most obviously the case where forms of unfree labour have been reproduced over long periods of time, notably slave labour in the Caribbean, and slave labour, labour tenancy, and contract migrant labour in South Africa. In both the Caribbean and South Africa the use of unfree labour has constituted the major means of labour recruitment and exploitation and, for certain periods of time, has sustained commodity production for the world market on a large scale. What were the historical conditions which ensured the reproduction of these various forms of unfree labour in the Caribbean and South Africa?

As we have seen (in Chapter 4 and above), in the Caribbean the absence of an indigenous population of sufficient size to constitute a labour force necessitated a migratory system to establish a labouring population which was retained by unfree relations of production. The slave relations of production that followed the decline of indentured labour were reproduced, in part, because both the commodity produced and the labourers required to produce it became integral parts of an exchange network dominated by the interests of merchant capital. Moreover, the political and ideological relations were so pervasively and thoroughly shaped by the task of reproducing the slave relations of production that they did not leave space for the emergence of any alternative relations of production. The conception of ownership of human beings as private property as the means to the creation of a surplus, the fear of the consequence of terminating direct relations of domination, and racist imagery of the Afro-Caribbean labourer, all served to deny the possibility of a transition to some alternative mode of production. As Goveia has argued, referring to the late eighteenth century:

> 'By that time . . . the West Indies could no longer afford to regard slavery simply as the economic expedient for supplying labour which it had been originally. The slave system had become more than an economic enterprise which could be abandoned when it ceased to be profitable. It had become the very basis of organised society throughout the British West Indies, and therefore it was believed to be an indispensable element in maintaining the existing social structure and in preserving law and order in the community.
> (Goveia 1965:329)

Indeed the ability of the slave mode of production to reproduce itself, even while in crisis, is revealed by the fact that it was abolished by the British state against the wishes of the plantation owners.

The slave mode of production in the Caribbean supplied a commodity to the world market from the end of the seventeenth century until the third decade of the nineteenth century and hence its existence and reproduction cannot be divorced from the linkages with the social formations of Western Europe, and with the transformations occurring within them (cf. Genovese 1966: 19, 23). One point of articulation with the emergent capitalist mode of production in Britain was the flow of commodities to the Caribbean (e.g. clothing, tools, machinery), without which the production of sugar could not have continued. In other words, the slave mode of production constituted a market for commodities produced in Britain under emergent, free wage relations of production (cf. Hobsbawm 1969: 50–1). But second, sugar (in common with other plantation products) became a commodity for working class consumption in Britain, constituting a low-cost food substitute, and later becoming a vital ingredient in the preparation of other foodstuffs which were produced as commodities (Mintz 1985: 143–50). Thus sugar not only sustained further commodity production, but also contributed to the reproduction of the British working class.

A third point of articulation concerned the utilization of the surplus arising from plantation production. Plantation sugar production realized a surplus product (Williams 1964: 25; Craton 1974: 136), although no one plantation or island remained profitable throughout the long history of sugar production (Ragatz 1971: 124–25). It has been argued that there was an overall trend of declining profitability throughout the Caribbean (Ragatz 1971), and that this was a crucial determinant of the abolition of the British slave trade and, later, slave labour itself (Williams 1970: 280–327), although others have disputed this (e.g. Aufhauser 1974; Ward 1978). Similarly there is disagreement over the extent to which the surplus that was returned to Britain served as a principal source of investment for the development of industrial commodity production (e.g. Pares 1937: 130; Williams 1964: 51–78, 98; Campbell 1964, 1967; Anstey 1968; Sheridan 1969; Hill 1969: 237; Engerman 1972; Barratt Brown 1974: 82; Devine 1974, 1976, 1978; McDonald 1979), although few would claim that none of the surplus contributed to the accumulation of industrial capital in Britain.

In summary these were the main points of articulation between the slave mode of production in the Caribbean and the emergent capitalist mode of production in Britain. There was, therefore, a mutual but hierarchical interdependence between the unfree relations of production established in the Caribbean and free relations of production that were being extended in Britain. The articulation, and therefore the unfree relations of production in the Caribbean, were sustained as long as there were economic advantages to the dominant class in Britain and in the Caribbean.

The situation in South Africa was different and more complex, not least because there was an indigenous population which was sufficiently large to make genocide difficult and which was potentially available as a source of labour power. The reproduction of unfree relations of production during the period of colonization and subsequent development of the capitalist mode of production is analysed most usefully in two phases. First, there was the period from the mid-seventeenth century to the mid-nineteenth century (i.e. the period prior to primitive accumulation) which was dominated by slave labour and labour tenancy (and after the abolition of slavery, by contractual servitude).

During this period there was little or no commodity production for the world market. These unfree relations of production existed alongside relations of production (also oriented primarily to subsistence) which ensured the reproduction of the African populations. The material and cultural existence of the latter had been considerably disrupted by the middle of the nineteenth century, and a significant minority had been incorporated into unfree relations of direct domination established by Dutch and British colonizers who became the landowning class in certain areas. Nevertheless a large proportion of the African population remained outside the relations established by the European colonizers and maintained an economically independent existence based on some form of domestic mode of production.

This was a complex articulation of precapitalist modes of production with only the most marginal connection with either the world market or with the capitalist mode of production in Europe. Moreover it was an unstable articulation because of conflict between European settlers and the indigenous African populations over access to, and the use of, land as European settlement extended its boundaries, and between the different groups of European settlers over the legitimacy of slave labour, amongst other things. But unfree relations of production established by the European settlers were retained and reproduced because direct domination was the primary mechanism to recruit and exploit labour in a colonial situation where a large part of the indigenous population retained direct access to the means of production. In such circumstances the commodification of labour power was impossible.

The transformative factor was the development of commodity production in the last third of the nineteenth century during which capitalist relations of production began to emerge. The second phase of articulation of modes of production occurred after this period of primitive accumulation, and the specific character of this articulation was shaped by the particularity of the process of primitive accumulation which occurred in a context where unfree labour was deeply embedded and sustained by racialization. This resulted in assumptions that the African population was biologically suited only to menial, unskilled labour. Moreover the African population resisted incorporation into production relations established by the colonizing, property-owning class. Consequently the process of freeing a section of the African population from the means of production was not easily achieved, as attempts to introduce a hut tax demonstrated. In other words, class struggle (between property-owners of European origin and that section of the African population who retained access to land) was a historical contingency which obstructed the commodification of labour power. Furthermore the demand for labour for mining was limited and did not require the incorporation of the majority of the African population into emergent forms of production, with the result that some means for the material reproduction of the 'surplus' African population had to be maintained. We have seen in Chapter 6 the contradictions that arose from strategy of marginalization of the African population which allowed its reproduction by independent access to land.

Yet the demand for a labour force was immediate. Moreover the process of primitive accumulation and the resulting commodification of labour power had, for the emergent capitalist class, to produce not simply labour power, but labour power within a particular price range and in sufficient quantity. In Chapter 6 we have seen that in the South African colonies the initial demand was for a limited quantity of labour power for the mines at low price. This could be achieved by a combination of partial dispossession and the contract system, so long as the state was prepared to bear the costs of organizing and enforcing the system. Moreover there was a historical legacy of unfree relations of production which could be adopted and modified.

Thus extant forms of legal coercion (such as the Masters and Servants Act) were given a renewed significance by the state, in combination with a process of partial separation from the means of production (i.e. partial proletarianization) also directed by the state in an attempt to establish capitalist relations of production, and the consequence was a form of unfree wage labour for the African populations, alongside free wage labour for the European labourer. Hence the wage form was formally introduced for the African, but market mechanisms alone were not allowed to increase the supply of African labour power by wage increases. In the absence of politico-legal intervention labour shortages would have led to sharp increases in the price paid for labour power. Yet once established these unfree relations of production were extended to incorporate more African labour power as the demand for labour within the growing capitalist mode of production increased.

The contract migrant labour system was a central feature of the relations of production that emerged from the process of primitive accumulation and was pivotal to the articulation of modes of production within the South African formation (e.g. Wolpe 1972; Meillassoux 1980; cf. Berg 1965: 174). This form of unfree wage labour was premissed on the maintenance of the established African domestic mode of production within which labourers were brought up (produced) and maintained (reproduced) in order to reduce the immediate labour costs of the mining companies (while extending the role of the state, and therefore the costs of state intervention). Thus labour power was produced in one mode of production and exploited in another. But before it could be exploited, Africans had to be forced to migrate and this required a process of dispossession. This dimension of primitive accumulation was achieved by the creation of the reserve system by the state, as we have seen above. Historically there was nothing unusual about the fact of state intervention in so far as coercion has been a common means of creating a labour market and a population with only its labour power for sale.

Nevertheless this articulation of modes of production took a distinctive form and was a specific means of capitalist development within a social formation. Rather than completely dispossessing the vast majority of the population of the means of production, the emergent capitalist class effected a strategy of partial dispossession (and hence partial commodification of labour power, and semi-proletarianization). It was partial in a dual sense. Only a section of the African population was required to sell labour power (leaving a larger proportion with independent access to the means of production and therefore to subsistence), and that section was not permanently proletarianized but migrated between two distrinct class positions. This was combined with the introduction of a variety of politico-legal constraints on the freedom of the labourer to dispose of his/her labour power, in order to restrict the ability of the African to respond to changing market circumstances, preventing the price mechanism from determining the supply of labour power. Thus labour power was commodified, but commodification was partially negated by the politico-legal constraints on the freedom of the African to dispose of labour power as a commodity.

The specificity of this articulation of modes within South Africa should be contextualized. The strategic utilization, and even retention and reproduction, of non-capitalist modes of production to produce and reproduce labour power has occurred for short periods in other historical circumstances surveyed in Part 2. First, instances of indentured labour in the nineteenth century in various parts of the world economic system depended on a similar articulation of modes of production, although the modes were spatially distant and did not articulate within the same social formation. The indentured labour system in the nineteenth century was invariably, although not exclusively, designed to recruit single, male workers who would return to their place of origin at the termination of their contract and who would receive subsistence only for themselves (and this was not paid fully or even largely in cash). The indenture system was therefore premised on the reproduction of the mode of production from which the indentured labourer originated and to which he would return. That mode of production bore the costs of production of that labourer and would bear the subsequent reproduction costs. And it was premissed on ensuring that the labourer lost the freedom to sell his labour power as a commodity for the duration of the contract which permitted temporary residence within the social formation where the labour shortage was located.

Second, within the Australian continent in the nineteenth century there were state initiatives in certain colonies to establish a reserve system which approxiated to that set up in South Africa in 1913. Similarly, the intention was to conserve the 'traditional' (but disrupted) mode of production of the Aboriginal population within a convenient spatial location within the same social formation and to devise inducements to pull sufficient numbers of the Aboriginal population into wage labour when required. Recruitment was often facilitated by means of a contract which bound the labourer to the non-labourer for a specified period. The scale and overall importance of this initiative was, compared with the South African colonies, minor because of the numerically and proportionately smaller Aboriginal population (compared with the African populations) and because of the more widespread use of the labour of European settlers. It was only in circumstances where there were particular difficulties in recruiting labour that a policy developed for the establishment of reserves in the Australian colonies. Thus the reserve policy in the Australian colonies (and the articulation of modes of production that it was dependent upon) was more marginal than in the South African colonies.

Third, the contract migrant labour system established in parts of Western Europe had similarities with the South African case in so far as labour was recruited from and returned to peasant subsistence or commodity producing sectors of another social formation. In such circumstances labour was recruited from a non-capitalist mode of production which, it was assumed, would continue to reproduce itself (and perhaps transform itself) so that the temporarily contracted migrant could return to it. Indeed, in certain circumstances the reproduction of this mode of production became increasingly dependent on cash remittances which were sent back by contracted wage labourers. But there were also important differences between the two systems. Not all contracted migrant workers in Western Europe were peasant agricultural producers and the modes of production which were in articulation were spatially distant, located in different social formations. Moreover the Western European system of contract labour migration was intended to resolve conjunctural problem of labour shortage and not to constitute a basis for the development of a capitalist mode of production.

In all these instances there was an articulation of modes of production which sustained a supply of labour power produced in a non-capitalist mode of production to an emergent or established capitalist mode of production. This, then, was an articulation, mediated by migration, which (as in the case of the Caribbean in the eighteenth century, although for different reasons) required the conservation, rather than the destruction, of non-capitalist modes of production. The apparent predominance of the interests of capital in this articulation often leads to analyses which describe contract migrant labour as both a functional system and a method of providing cheap labour (e.g. Standing 1981: 194–201). It is certainly the case that where the production and reproduction of labour power is located in a non-capitalist mode of production, the exploiter of that labour power may avoid paying a wage sufficient to maintain a family and to meet other reproduction costs. But undue emphasis on this, or an emphasis which ignores the historical conditions and the contradictory dimensions of the articulation, leads to a static, functionalist interpretation.

The creation and maintenance of the different labour supply systems previously listed all entailed costs which would not have arisen if the labour force was permanently settled and urbanized. For example for the employer, rotation of labourers increases training costs and may depress the productivity of labour where some element of skill and experience increases efficiency over time. It also increases recruitment costs. Moreover the centrality and extent of state intervention to establish and reproduce the migrant labour system also involves considerable administrative and enforcement costs (as for example in enforcing contracts and the pass system, and administering the process of recruitment) (e.g. Wilson 1972a: 137–38; Burawoy 1976). Furthermore, in so far as it does cheapen the cost of labour power, it increases the potential for conflict between unfree labourers and those enmeshed in labour relations of production because the latter become vulnerable to displacement on grounds of cost.

I have described the consequences of this in the South African and Australian colonies. When the mining companies in South Africa effected this strategy in order to reduce labour costs, the inevitable economic resistance of the European workers was articulated ideologically in the same terms that were used to signify the incorporation of Africans in positions of unfreedom. Because racism was a relation of production which inserted the African into a specific position in commodity production, racism was the ideological means used by free wage labourers of European origin to retain the African labourer in that position in order to protect their privileged position. In Queensland it was the fear of displacement which led to a conflict with a similar ideological component. Thus migrant labour systems, grounded in unfree relations of production, create distinct and contradictory economic and political interests which sustain conflicts which may disrupt production and which require mediation and suppression.

As a method of creating and retaining a labour force these various labour supply systems based on an articulation of modes of production are more accurately understood as being necessarily contradictory rather than functional. Analysis of those contradictions encourages a search for the factors of historical contingency and therefore for the effectivity of human agency. For example, Wolpe has shown in the case of South Africa that the migrant labour system depended upon the ability of the reserves to successfully reproduce a potential labour force and that this is obstructed by declining agricultural productivity in the non-capitalist mode of production (1972). Elsewhere (Miles 1986a), I have identified the historical contingencies of the migrant labour system in Western Europe, arguing that it produced 'cheap' labour only while the system prevented the migration of dependents.

In sum, unfree labour may coexist with free labour as a result of an articulation of modes of production either within or between social formations. The continued existence of forms of unfree labour may therefore be explained, in part, in terms of the historically contingent economic advantages realized by the dominant class within the dominant mode of production. However those beneficial consequences may be grounded in historical necessity where free labour cannot be reproduced at a price which would permit capital accumulation, i.e. where historical conditions obstruct the full commodification of labour power. Moreover the reproduction of unfree labour in parallel with free labour gives rise to contradictory consequences which require negotiation.

Conclusion

Although human beings have the capacity to act in ways which transform the material world (Marx 1968b: 28–9), the scope for such transformative activity is always constrained by the character of the particular material circumstances in which they live (Marx 1968c: 96). This is clearly evident in the case of that most transformative of activities, the act of revolution, where the effectivity of human agency interacts with the constraining role of particular material and social circumstances. Living within capitalist social formations, revolutionary transformation is usually analysed in terms of the overthrow of the capitalist mode of production and the transition to socialism, but we should not ignore the historical fact that the transition from feudalism to capitalism was an equally significant revolutionary transformation (Marx and Engels 1968c: 36–40), in which there was also a dialectic between human agency and material constraint.

It is important to dwell upon the significance of this dialectic when considering the subsequent development of the capitalist mode of production in order to avoid writing a history in which the 'logic of capital' is portrayed as invincible, as if 'capitalism' is a steamroller which sweeps aside instantly and effortlessly all obstacles to its expansion. The capitalist mode of production is a particularly dynamic and self-expanding system, but there are limits and obstacles to that development as has been illustrated by the history of the maintenance and reproduction of forms of unfree labour alongside the transition to and reproduction of the capitalist mode of production. That history demonstrates that those forms of unfree labour have been and are an anomalous necessity, revealing circumstances where either capitalist relations of production cannot develop or where their development is obstructed.

In the context of colonization and the extension of commodity production, a number of factors stand out as obstacles to the development of capitalist relations of production. First, the availability of land for settlement and independent subsistence and commodity production obstructs the formation of a class of free labourers with only their labour power for sale. In such circumstances the relative power of the state is a determinant factor. Second, the character of the mode of production of the indigenous population affects the nature of the outcome of the intrusion of commodity production and of its disintegrative effects. Third, class struggle, including the struggles of the indigenous populations, may be an obstacle to the formation of capitalist relations of production where there is resistance to colonial settlement and to incorporation into consequent production relations. And in the context of the domination of the capitalist mode of production within a social formation the 'normal' operation of the labour market may be obstructed, preventing the supply of labour power in sufficient quantity and/or at a sufficient price to permit the continuation of capital accumulation. All of these circumstances require the use of direct domination (either sanctioned and legitimated or directly utilized by the state), to recruit and retain labourers, who will provide labour power, by the utilization of politico-legal constraint and, if necessary, by the conservation of non-capitalist modes of production.

This contrasts sharply with the argument advanced by Wallerstein, who interprets unfree labour as only one form of capitalist exploitation of labour power within a capitalist world system firmly established by the middle of the seventeenth century. For Wallerstein these forms of production relation exist because they are appropriate to the position of the social formation in which they occur in the capitalist world economy. It is an argument that is characterized by more than a hint of 'capital logic' and functionalism.

Alternatively, and drawing upon concepts derived from Marx's analysis, I argue that the existence and reproduction of different forms of unfree labour persistently identifies the historical limits to the development of the capitalist mode of production within the social formations which constitute the emergent world economic system. Forms of unfree labour exist and are reproduced because the conditions for capitalist relations of production are neither universally nor automatically present, but depend upon a combination of specific material preconditions and active human intervention. My explanation for the survival and reproduction of unfree relations of production in a world economic system increasingly dominated by the capitalist mode of production is, therefore, that under certain historical conditions:

> (1) forms of unfree labour (which may be extant or may be reconstituted) can be a constitutive element of the proces of primitive accumulation preceding the emergence of a capitalist mode of production;
> (2) forms of unfree labour can exist because the commodification of labour power is either obstructed or breaks down; and
> (3) forms of unfree labour can coexist with free labour where non-capitalist modes of production are sustained in some form of interrelation with the capitalist mode of production, either within or between different social formations.

In these historical circumstances, which may coexist in varying combinations, unfree labour is an anomalous necessity.

Conclusion

The reproduction of unfree relations of production indicates the limits of the development of the capitalist mode of production in social formations incorporated into the world economic system created by merchant capital during the sixteenth century. In the nexus of the relations of production and exchange arising from the emergence of the capitalist mode of production and the expansion of that world economic system, different peoples have been brought into contact with each other, but always in a hierarchy of material and political domination, of class relations. That contact was not of people in the abstract, but real human beings embedded in, and often resisting, particular social relations of production and reproduction, that is human beings constituted in, but sometimes attempting to overthrow, specific modes of production. The outcome of that contact has depended on the character of those modes of production, the patterns and consequences of human accommodation and resistance, and the material context in which contact was initially established. As a result of the various circumstances analysed above certain populations have been incorporated and retained in that nexus by means of various forms of compulsion, and therefore have provided labour power under unfree relations of production.

Consequently the historical emergence (i.e. transition to) and extension of the capitalist mode of production has been associated with the following processes. First it has depended upon large-scale migrations of people from one social formation to another, often great distances apart, and from one set of class relations to another. I have documented a significant number, including those from England to the Caribbean in the seventeenth century, from Africa to the Caribbean in the eighteenth century, from England to Australia and South Africa in the nineteenth century, from India and China to the Caribbean and South Africa in the nineteenth century, from the south Pacific to Australia in the nineteenth century, and from the Mediterranean and north Africa to Western Europe in the twentieth century. As I have demonstrated, these migrations all have their material determinants and have all contributed to considerable cultural diversity within social formations at different sites in the world economic system.

Second, it has been associated with the differential incorporation of indigenous populations, as well as migrant populations, into relations of production established by a class of migrant colonizers who have established a partial or complete monopoly of the means of production. I have analysed this process in Australia and South Africa where the modes of production of different populations have been variously destroyed or partially reproduced to ensure that at least a proportion of those populations have provided labour power in emergent modes of production consequent upon subsistence production and, especially, commodity production for the world market.

Third, this process of incorporation has taken place under varying economic, political, and ideological relations. Certain groups have been incorporated as free wage labourers while many others have been incorporated in unfree relations of production. Differential incorporation has been a measure of the historical conditions necessary to the formation or absence of a labour market within which labour power is commodified and distributed. The state has been integral to both forms of incorporation, and has been central to the latter as an agent of direct domination. In the examples considered, racism has also been a constitutive element in the formation and reproduction of both free and unfree relations of production which have therefore taken on a particular cultural form and given rise to particular classes and class fractions. Although historically contingent, these features are not deviations from some assumed 'normal' pattern of capitalist development. Rather they are integral aspects of the emergence and expansion of the capitalist mode of production to other social formations in the world economic system.

For this reason I question the validity of isolating and abstracting certain facets of the historical development of capitalism by creating 'race relations' studies and seeking to construct a theory of 'race (or ethnic) relations' (e.g. Rex 1970; 1973; 1980; 1986). I continue to argue that this interpretation is ideological. This is not only because such attempts necessitate attributing to ideological terms the status of scientific concepts (Miles 1982: 22–43), but also because they obscure the universal dimension of the material dynamic by which populations are incorporated into relations structured by the capitalist mode of production and its articulation with other modes of production. By this I mean that although the emergence and expansion of the capitalist mode of production (and its articulation with other modes of production) is historically contingent and therefore historically specific, there are features and processes which are necessarily a constituent part of that emergence and expansion, such as the formation of a class of free labourers as a dimension of the generalization of commodity production, the effectiveness of the process of capital accumulation, and the role of the state as a relation of production. These are simultaneously universal features of the capitalist mode of production and yet always appear in a historically specific form.

The history of Marxist analysis of racism has often given good cause for the development of a sociology of 'race relations'. This is partly because the mechanical 'base/superstructure' model has encouraged a functional analysis of racism, while vulgar materialism has often concluded that racism is a mere epiphenomenon. Moreover by virtue of concentrating attention on the development of capitalism at the centre the social relations characterizing that location have too often been regarded as the 'normal' development, against which differences are concluded to be 'deviations', for which *ad hoc* explanations are offered, if explanations are considered to be warranted at all.

I have contested certain aspects of this functionalism and mechanicism by conceptualizing racism as an ideological relation of production which has a necessarily contradictory character, by analysing migrant labour systems also as a necessarily contradictory economic form, and, most importantly of all, by seeking to identify and account for the specificity of class relations in historical circumstances which, although structured by the emergence of the capitalist mode of production, block that emergence or which give that emergence a particular character, circumstances which thereby give rise to and often lead to the reproduction of racialized, unfree relations of production.

Hence, contrary to the sociology of 'race (and ethnic) relations', I believe that an adequate explanation for unfree relations of production (which includes racism) is best sought in the context of a general theory of capitalist development (which must include an explanation for the absence, or uneven character, of capitalist development), rather than in the formation of an intellectual sub-discipline of 'race relations' which is necessarily ideological. Yet there is no single or uncontested Marxist theory of capitalist development, as we have seen in Part 1. But, for the reasons stated there, the approach that I offer begins with, although is not limited to, production relations and the reproduction of production relations and highlights the political and ideological (e.g. racist) relations of production in order to identify the means by which peoples have been differentially incorporated into production which contributes to the emergent world economic system.

Bibliography

Abadan-Unat, N. (1976) *Turkish Workers in Europe, 1960–75.* Leiden: Brill.
—— (1977) Implications of Migration on Emancipation and Pseudo-Emancipation of Turkish Women, *International Migration Review.* 11(1): 31–57.
Abbott, G. J. (1969) The Pastoral Industry, in G. J. Abbott and N. B. Nairn (eds) *Economic Growth of Australia 1788–1821.* Melbourne: Melbourne University Press.
Abrams, P. (1982) *Historical Sociology.* Shepton Mallet: Open University Books.
Adamson, A. H. (1972) *Sugar Without Slaves: The Political Economy of British Guiana, 1838–1904.* New Haven: Yale University Press.
Adler, S. (1981) *International Migration and Dependence.* Farnborough: Gower.
Aldrich, H., Jones, T. P., and McEvoy, D. (1984) Ethnic Advantage and Minority Business Development. In R. Ward and R. Jenkins (eds) *Ethnic Communities in Business: Strategies for Economic Survival.* Cambridge: Cambridge University Press.
Alessa, S. Y. (1981) *The Manpower Problem in Kuwait.* London: Kegan Paul International.
Al-Moosa, A. and McLachlan, K. (1985) *Immigrant Labour in Kuwait.* London: Croom Helm.
Anderson, B. (1983) *Imagined Communities: Reflections on the Origin and Spread of Nationalism.* London: Verso.,
Anderson, P. (1979) *Lineages of the Absolutist State.* London: Verso.
Andreski, A. (ed.) (1983) *Max Weber On Capitalism, Bureaucracy and Religion: A Selection of Texts.* London: Allen & Unwin.
Anon. (1984) Racism and Immigration in France. *Race and Immigration* 170: 8–15.
Anstey, R. T. (1968) Capitalism and Slavery: A Critique. *Economic History Review* 21: 307–20.
Anthias, F. (1980) Women and the Reserve Army of Labour. *Capital and Class* 18: 50–63.
Armstrong, J. C. (1979) The Slaves, 1652–1795. In R. Elphick and H. Giliomee (eds) *The Shaping of South African Society, 1652–1820.* Cape Town: Longman.
Armstrong, P., Glyn, A., and Harrison, J. (1984) *Capitalism Since World War II: The Making and Breakup of the Great Boom.* London: Fontana.
Armstrong, W. (1978) New Zealand: Imperialism, Class and Uneven Development. *Australia and New Zealand Journal of Sociology* 24: 297–303.
Armstrong, W. and McGhee, T. G. (1985) *Theatres of Accumulation: Studies in Latin American Urbanization.* London: Methuen.
Asad, T. and Wolpe, H. (1976) Concepts of Modes of Production. *Economy and Society* 5: 470–506.
Ashton, T. S. and Sykes, J. (1964) *The Coal Industry of the Eighteenth Century.* Manchester: Manchester University Press.

Aston, T. H. and Philpin, C. H. E. (1985) *The Brenner Debate: Agrarian Class Structure and Economic Development in Pre-Industrial Europe.* Cambridge: Cambridge University Press.

Aufhauser, R. K. (1974) Profitability of Slavery in the British Caribbean. *Journal of Interdisciplinary History* 5:45–67.

Bach, R. L. and Schraml, L. A. (1982) Migration, Crisis, and Theoretical Conflict. *International Migration Review* 16(2):320–41.

Baines, D. (1985) *Migration in a Mature Economy: Emigration and Internal Migration in England and Wales, 1861–1900.* Cambridge: Cambridge University Press.

Baker, D. G. (1983) *Race, Ethnicity and Power: A Comparative Study.* London: Routledge & Kegan Paul.

Banaji, J. (1977) Modes of Production in a Materialist Conception of History. *Capital and Class* 3:1–44.

Banerjee, D. (ed.); (1985) *Marxian Theory and the Third World.* Delhi: Sage.

Banton, M. (1967) *Race Relations.* London: Tavistock.

—— (1977) *The Idea of Race.* London: Tavistock.

—— (1983) *Racial and Ethnic Competition.* Cambridge: Cambridge University Press.

Barker, A. J. (1978) *The African Link: British Attitudes to the Negro in the Era of the Atlantic Slave Trade, 1550–1807.* London: Frank Cass.

Barratt Brown, M. (1974) *The Economics of Imperialism.* Harmondsworth: Penguin.

Baucic, I. (1972) *The Effects of Emigration from Yugoslavia and the Problems of Returning Emigrant Workers.* The Hague: Martinus Nijhoff.

Bean, R. N. and Thomas, R. P. (1979) The Adoption of Slave Labour in British America. In H. A. Gemery and J. S. Hogendorn (eds) *The Uncommon Market: Essays in the Economic History of the Atlantic Slave Trade.* New York: Academic Press.

Beckford, G. L. (1972) *Persistent Poverty: Underdevelopment in Plantation Economies of the Third World.* New York: Oxford University Press.

Beckles, H. (1981) Rebels and Reactionaries: The Political Responses of White Labourers to Planter-Class Hegemony in Seventeenth Century Barbados. *Journal of Caribbean History* 15:1–19.

Beinart, W. (1979) Joyini Inkomo: Cattle Advances and the Origins of Migrancy from Pondoland. *Journal of South African Studies* 5:199–219.

Bell, H. C. (1917) The West India Trade Before the American Revolution. *American Historical Review* 22:272–87.

Bennett, J. H. (1958) *Bondsmen and Bishops: Slavery and Apprenticeship on the Codrington Plantations of Barbados, 1710–1838.* Berkeley: University of California Press.

Bennholdt-Thomsen, V. (1981) Subsistence Production and Extended Production. In K. Young *et al.* (eds) *Of Marriage and the Market.* London: CSE Books.

Berg, E. J. (1965) The Economics of the Migrant Labour System. In H. Kuper (ed.) *Urbanisation and Migration in West Africa.* Berkeley: University of California Press.

Bernabé, F. (1982) The Labour Market and Unemployment. In A. Boltho (ed.) *The European Economy: Growth and Crisis.* London: Oxford University Press.

Bhana, S. and Pachai, B. (eds) (1984) *A Documentary History of Indian South Africans.* Cape Town: David Philip.

Birch, A. (1961) The Implementation of the White Australia Policy in the

Queensland Sugar Industry, 1901–12. *Australian Journal of Politics and History* 11(2): 198–210.

Birks, J. S. and Sinclair, C. A. (1980) *International Migration and Development in the Arab Region*. Geneva: International Labour Organisation.

Biskup, P. (1973) *Not Slaves, Not Citizens: the Aboriginal Problem in Western Australia 1898–1954*. St Lucia: University of Queensland Press.

Blainey, G. (1983) *The Tyranny of Distance*. Melbourne: Sun Books.

Boeseken, A. J. (1977) *Slaves and Free Blacks at the Cape, 1658–1700*. Cape Town: Tafelberg.

Böhning, W. R. (1972) *The Migration of Workers in the United Kingdom and the European Community*. London: Oxford University Press.

—— (1974) Immigration Policies of Western European Countries. *International Migration Review* 8(2): 155–63.

—— (1984) *Studies in International Labour Migration*. London: Macmillan.

Boissevain, J. (1984); Small Entrepreneurs in Contemporary Europe. In R. Ward and R. Jenkins (eds) *Ethnic Communities in Business: Strategies for Economic Survival*. Cambridge: Cambridge University Press.

Bolland, O. N. (1981) Systems of Domination After Slavery: The Control of Land and Labour in the British West Indies After 1838. *Comparative Studies in Society and History* 23(4): 591–619.

Booth, H. (1984) *Guestworkers or Immigrants? A Demographic Analysis of the Status of Migrants in West Germany*. Birmingham: ESRC Research Unit on Ethnic Relations.

Bourguignon, F., Gallais-Hamonno, G., and Fernet, B. (1977) *International Labour Migrations and Economic Choices: The European Case*. Paris: OECD.

Bouscaren, A. T. (1969) *European Economic Community Migrations*. The Hague: Martinus Nijhoff.

Bovenkerk, F. (1979) The Netherlands. In R. E. Krane (ed.) *International Labour Migration in Europe*. New York: Praeger.

Bovenkerk, F., Eijken, A., and Bovenkerk-Teerink, W. (1983) *Italiaans Ijs, De Wonderbaarlijke Historie Van Italiaanse Ijsbereiders in Nederland*. Meppel: Boom.

Bozzoli, B. (1981) *The Political Nature of a Ruling Class: Capital and Ideology in South Africa, 1890–1933*. London: Routledge & Kegan Paul.

Bradby, B. (1975) The Destruction of Natural Economy. *Economy and Society* 4(2): 125–61.

Braverman, H. (1974) *Labor and Monopoly Capital*. New York: Monthly Review Press.

Brenner, R. (1976) Agrarian Class Structure and Economic Development in Pre-Industrial Europe. *Past and Present* 70: 30–75.

—— (1977) The Origins of Capitalist Development: A Critique of Neo-Smithian Marxism. *New Left Review* 104: 25–92.

—— (1978) Dobb on the Transition From Feudalism to Capitalism. *Cambridge Journal of Economics* 2: 121–40.

Brereton, B. (1981) *A History of Modern Trinidad, 1783–1962*. Kingston: Heinemann.

Brewer, A. (1980) *Marxist Theories of Imperialism: A Critical Analysis*. London: Routledge & Kegan Paul.

—— (1984) *A Guide to Marx's* Capital. Cambridge: Cambridge University Press.

Brookes, D. (1975) *Race and Labour in London Transport*. London: Oxford University Press.

Brown, C. (1984) *Black and White Britain: The Third PSI Survey*. London: Heinemann.

Brubaker, R. (1984) *The Limits of Rationality: An Essay on the Social and Moral Thought of Max Weber*. London: Allen & Unwin.

Buckley, K. (1975) Primary Accumulation: The Genesis of Australian Capitalism. In E. L. Wheelright and K. Buckley (eds) *Essays in the Political Economy of Australian Capitalism* (vol. 1). Sydney: ANZ Book Company.

Bukharin, N. (1972) *Imperialism and World Economy*. London: Merlin Press.

Bundy, C. (1979) *The Rise and Fall of the South African Peasantry*. London: Heinemann.

Burawoy, M. (1976) The Functions and Reproduction of Migrant Labour: Comparative Material from Southern Africa and the United States. *American Journal of Sociology* 81(5): 1050–87.

Burn, W. L. (1937) *Emancipation and Apprenticeship in the British West Indies*. London: Jonathan Cape.

Burroughs, P. (1967) *Britain and Australia 1831–1855: a Study in Imperial Relations and Crown Lands Administration*. Oxford: Clarendon Press.

Butlin, N. G. (1964) *Investment in Australian Economic Development 1861–1900*. Cambridge: Cambridge University Press.

Campbell, R. H. (1964) An Economic History of Scotland in the Eighteenth Century. *Scottish Journal of Political Economy* 11: 17–24.

—— (1967) The Industrial Revolution: A Revision Article. *Scottish Historical Review* XLVI: 37–55.

Carchedi, G. (1979) Authority and Foreign Labour: Some Notes on a Late Capitalist Form of Accumulation and State Intervention. *Studies in Political Economy* 2: 37–74.

Carrothers, W. A. (1929) *Emigration from the British Isles With Special Reference to the Development of the Overseas Dominions*. London: P. S. King & Son.

Castles, S., Booth, H., and Wallace, T. (1984) *Here for Good: Western Europe's New Ethnic Minorities*. London: Pluto Press.

Castles, S. and Kosack, G. (1973) *Immigrant Workers and Class Structure in Western Europe*. London: Oxford University Press.

Clark, C. M. H. (1962) *A History of Australia, I: From the Earliest Times to the Age of Macquarie*. Melbourne: Melbourne University Press.

—— (1968) *A History of Australia, II: New South Wales and Van Dieman's Land 1822–1838*. Melbourne: Melbourne University Press.

—— (1969) *A Short History of Australia*. London: Heinemann.

—— (1973) *A History of Australia, III: The Beginning of an Australian Civilisation*. Melbourne: Melbourne University Press.

—— (1978) *A History of Australia, IV: The Earth Abideth for Ever 1851–1888*. Melbourne: Melbourne University Press.

Commission of the European Communities (1984) *Comparative Survey of the Conditions and Procedures for Admission of Third Country Workers for Employment in the Member States*. Brussels: Commission of the European Communities.

Connell, R. W. and Irving, T. H. (1980) *Class Structure in Australian History*. Melbourne: Longman Cheshire.

Coquery-Vidrovitch, C. (1985) The Political Economy of the African Peasantry and Modes of Production. In P. C. W. Gutkind and I. Wallerstein (eds) *Political Economy of Contemporary Africa*. Beverly Hills: Sage Publications.

Corrigan, P. (1977) Feudal Relics or Capitalist Monuments? Notes on the Sociology of Unfree Labour. *Sociology* 11(3): 435–63.

Corrigan, P. and Sayer, D. (1985) *The Great Arch: English State Formation as Cultural Revolution*. Oxford: Basil Blackwell.

Corrigan, P., Ramsay, H. and Sayer, D. (1980) The State as a Relation of Production. In P. Corrigan (ed.) *Capitalism, State Formation and Marxist Theory: Historical Investigations.* London: Quartet Books.

Corris, P. (1972) 'White Australia' in Action: the Repatriation of Pacific Islanders from Queensland. *Historical Studies* 15: 237–50.

—— (1973) *Passage, Port and Plantation: a History of Solomon Islands Labour Migration 1870–1914.* Melbourne: Melbourne University Press.

Couper, K. and Santamaria, V. (1984) An Elusive Concept: The Changing Definition of Illegal Immigrant in the Practice of Immigration Control in the United Kingdom. *International Migration Review* 18(3): 437–52.

Courtenay, P. P. (1965) *Plantation Agriculture.* London: G. Bell and Son.

Cox, O. C. (1970) *Caste, Class and Race.* New York: Monthly Review Press.

Craton, M. (1974) *Sinews of Empire: A Short History of British Slavery.* London: Temple Smith.

Craton, M. and Walvin, J. (1970) *A Jamaican Plantation: The History of Worthy Park.* Toronto: University of Toronto Press.

Crawford, P. C. (1923) *Chinese Coolie Emigration to Countries Within the British Empire.* London: P. S. King & Son.

Cross, G. R. (1983) *Immigrant Workers in Industrial France.* Philadelphia: Temple University Press.

Crowley, F. K. (ed.) (1974) *A New History of Australia.* Melbourne: Heinemann.

Crummey, D. and Stewart, C. C. (1981) *Modes of Production in Africa: The Pre-Colonial Era.* Beverly Hills: Sage Publications.

Cumpston, I. M. (1953) *Indians Overseas in British Territories, 1834–1854.* London: Oxford University Press.

Curthoys, A. (1982) Good Christians and Useful Workers: Aborigines, Church and State in NSW 1870–1883. In Sydney Labour History Group, *What Rough Beast? The State and Social Order in Australian History.* Sydney: Allen & Unwin.

Curtin, P. (1969) *The Atlantic Slave Trade: A Census.* Madison: University of Wisconsin Press.

Dallas, K. M. (1955) The Origins of 'White Australia'. *Australian Quarterly* 27: 43–52.

Davenport, T. R. H. and Hunt, K. S. (eds) (1974) *The Right to the Land.* Cape Town: David Philip.

Davidoff, L. (1974) Mastered for Life: Servant and Wife in Victorian and Edwardian England. *Journal of Social History* 7: 406–28.

Davies, K. G. (1957) *The Royal African Company.* London: Longmans, Green & Co.

—— (1974) *The North Atlantic World in the Seventeenth Century.* Minneapolis: University of Minnesota Press.

Davies, R. H. (1979) *Capital, State and White Labour in South Africa, 1900–1960.* Brighton: Harvester Press.

Davis, D. B. (1966) *The Problem of Slavery in Western Culture.* Ithaca: Cornell University Press.

De Kiewiet, C. W. (1941) *A History of South Africa.* Oxford: Clarendon Press.

De Lepervanche, M. (1975) Australian Immigrants, 1788–1940: Desired and Unwanted. In E. L. Wheelright and K. Buckley (eds) *Essays in the Political Economy of Australian Capitalism, Vol. 1.* Sydney: Australian and New Zealand Book Company.

—— (1984) *Indians in a White Australia.* Sydney: Allen & Unwin.

De Vries, J. (1976) *The Economy of Europe in an Age of Crisis, 1600–1750.* Cambridge: Cambridge University Press.

Debbant, H. and Declerck, J. (1982) The Status of Immigrant Workers in Belgium. In E.-J. Thomas (ed.) *Immigrant Workers in Europe: Their Legal Status.* Paris: UNESCO.

Deerr, N. (1949) *The History of Sugar* (vol. 1). London: Chapman & Hall.

—— (1950) *The History of Sugar* (vol. 2). London: Chapman & Hall.

Denoon, D. (1967) The Transvaal Labour Crisis, 1901–6. *Journal of African History* 7(3): 481–94.

—— (1983) *Settler Capitalism: the Dynamics of Dependent Development in the Southern Hemisphere.* Oxford: Clarendon Press.

—— (1984) The Political Economy of Labour Migration to Settler Societies: Australasia, Southern Africa and South America Between 1890 and 1914. In S. Marks and P. Richardson (eds) *International Labour Migration.* London: Temple Smith.

Desmond, C. (1971) *The Discarded People: An Account of African Resettlement in South Africa.* Harmondsworth: Penguin.

Devine, T. M. (1974) Sources of Capital for the Glasgow Tobacco Trade, c.1740–1780. *Business History* 16: 113–29.

—— (1976) The Colonial Trades and Industrial Investment in Scotland, c.1700–1815. *Economic History Review* 29(1): 1–13.

—— (1978) Colonial Commerce and the Scottish Economy, c.1730–1815. In L. M. Cullen and T. C. Smout (eds) *Comparative Aspects of Scottish and Irish Economic and Social History 1600–1900.* Edinburgh: John Donald.

Dignan, D. (1981) Europe's Melting Pot: A Century of Large-Scale Immigration into France. *Ethnic and Racial Studies* 4(2): 137–52.

Dobb, M. (1963) *Studies in the Development of Capitalism.* London: Routledge & Kegan Paul.

Docker, E. W. (1970) *The Blackbirders: the Recruiting of South Seas Labour for Queensland 1863–1907.* Sydney: Angus & Robertson.

Döhse, K. (1981) *Ausländische Arbeiter und bürgerlich Staat.* Konigstein: Hain.

—— (1982) *Foreign Workers in the Federal Republic of Germany.* Berlin: Wissenschaftszentrum.

Domar, E. D. (1970) The Causes of Slavery or Serfdom: A Hypothesis. *Journal of Economic History* 30: 18–32.

Doxey, G. V. (1961) *The Industrial Colour Bar in South Africa.* Cape Town: Oxford University Press.

Du Toit, D. (1981) *Capital and Labour in South Africa: Class Struggles in the 1970s.* London: Routledge & Kegan Paul.

Duckham, B. F. (1970) *A History of the Scottish Coal Industry: Volume 1, 1700–1815.* Newton Abbot: David & Charles.

Duffield, M. (1985) Rationalisation and the Politics of Segregation: Indian Foundry Workers in Britain's Foundry Industry, 1945–1962. *Immigrants and Minorities* 4(2): 142–72.

Duncan, R. (1967) *The Northern Territory Pastoral Industry, 1863–1910.* Melbourne: Melbourne University Press.

Dunn, M. (1975) Early Australia: Wage Labour or Slave Society. In E. L. Wheelright and K. Buckley (eds) *Essays in the Political Economy of Australian Capitalism* (vol. 1). Sydney: Australia and New Zealand Book Company.

Dunn, R. S. (1973) *Sugar and Slaves: The Rise of the Planter Class in the English West Indies 1624–1713.* London: Jonathan Cape.

DuPlessis, R. S. (1977) From Demesne to World System: A Critical Review of the Literature on the Transition from Feudalism to Capitalism. *Radical History Review* 3:3–41.

Dwight, A. (1976) The Use of Indian Labourers in New South Wales. *Journal of Royal Australian History Society* 62:114–35.

Elkin, A. P. (1951) Reaction and Interaction: a Food Gathering People and European Settlement in Australia. *American Anthropologist* 53:164–86.

Elkins, S. M. (1968) *Slavery: A Problem in American Institutional and Intellectual Life*. Chicago:University of Chicago Press.

Elphick, R. (1977) *Kraal and Castle: Khoikhoi and the Founding of White South Africa*. New Haven:Yale University Press.

—— (1979) The Khoisan to c.1770. In R. Elphick and H. Giliomee (eds) *The Shaping of South African Society, 1652–1820*. Cape Town:Longman.

Engerman, S. (1972) The Slave Trade and British Capital Formation in the Eighteenth century: A Comment on the Williams Thesis. *Business History Review* 46:430–43.

—— (1973) Some Considerations Relating to Property Rights in Man. *Journal of Economic History* 33:43–65.

—— (1978) Marxist Economic Studies of the Slave South. *Marxist Perspectives* 1:148–64.

Entzinger, H. (1985) The Netherlands. In T. Hammar (ed.) *European Immigration Policy: A Comparative Study*. Cambridge:Cambridge University Press.

Eraydin, A. (1981) Foreign Investment, International Labour Migration and the Turkish Economy. In F. E. I. Hamilton and G. R. J. Linge (eds) *Spatial Analysis: Industry and the Industrial Environment, Vol. II*. Chichester:Wiley.

Esser, H. and Korte, H. (1985) Federal Republic of Germany. In T. Hammar (ed.) *European Immigration Policy: A Comparative Study*. Cambridge:Cambridge University Press.

European Communities Commission (1975) *Freedom of Movement for Workers Within the Community*. Brussels:EEC.

Evans, R. (1970) Some Notes on Coerced Labour. *Journal of Economic History* 30:861–66.

Evans, R. (1984) 'Kings' in Brass Crescents: Defining Aboriginal Labour Patterns in Colonial Queensland. In K. Saunders (ed.) *Indentured Labour in the British Empire 1834–1920*. London:Croom Helm.

Evans, R., Saunders, K., and Cronin, K. (1975) *Exclusion, Exploitation and Extermination: Race Relations in Colonial Queensland*. Sydney:Australia and New Zealand Book Company.

FAO (1982) *Apartheid, Poverty and Malnutrition*. Rome:FAO Economic and Social Development Paper no. 24.

Farley, M. F. (1968) The Chinese Coolie Trade, 1845–1875. *Journal of Asian and African Studies* 3:257–70.

Feldstein, H. S. (1967) A Study of Transaction and Political Integration: Transnational Labour Flow Within the European Economic Community. *Journal of Common Market Studies* 6:24–55.

Fevre, R. (1984) *Cheap Labour and Racial Discrimination*. Aldershot:Gower.

Fieldhouse, D. K. (1969) British Colonial Policy. In G. J. Abbott and N. B. Nairn (eds) *Economic Growth of Australia 1788–1821*. Melbourne:Melbourne University Press.

Fine, B. and Harris, L. (1979) *Rereading* Capital. London:Macmillan.

First, R. (1983) *Black Gold: the Mozambican Miner, Proletarian and Peasant*. Brighton:Harvester Press.

Fitzgerald, R. (1982) *From the Dreaming to 1915: A History of Queensland*. St Lucia: University of Queensland Press.

Fletcher, B. (1976) *Colonial Australia Before 1850*. Melbourne: Nelson.

Fogel, R. W. and Engerman, S. L. (1974) *Time on the Cross: The Economics of American Negro Slavery*. Boston: Little Brown.

Foster-Carter, A. (1978) The Modes of Production Controversy. *New Left Review* 107: 47–77.

Fox-Genovese, E. and Genovese, E. D. (1983) *Fruits of Merchant Capital*. New York: Oxford University Press.

Frank, A. G. (1971) *Capitalism and Underdevelopment in Latin America*. Harmondsworth: Penguin.

—— (1978a) *Dependent Accumulation and Underdevelopment*. London: Macmillan.

—— (1978b) *World Accumulation, 1492–1789*. London: Macmillan.

Frankel, S. H. (1938) *Capital Investment in Africa: Its Course and Effects*. London: Oxford University Press.

Fredrickson, G. M. (1981) *White Supremacy: A Comparative Study in American and South African History*. New York: Oxford University Press.

Freeman, G. P. (1979); *Immigrant Labour and Racial Conflict in Industrial Societies: The French and British Experience, 1945–1975*. Princeton: Princeton University Press.

Freund, W. M. (1979) The Cape Under the Transitional Governments, 1795–1814. In R. Elphick and H. Giliomee (eds) *The Shaping of South African Society*. Cape Town: Longman.

Friedmann, H. (1978) World Market, State, and Family Farm: Social Bases of Household Production in the Era of Wage Labor. *Comparative Studies in Society and History* 20: 545–86.

Frobel, F., Heinrichs, J., and Kreye, O. (1980) *The New International Division of Labour*. Cambridge: Cambridge University Press.

Frost, A. (1980) *Convicts and Empire*. Melbourne: Oxford University Press.

Galenson, D. W. (1981a) *White Servitude in Colonial America: An Economic Analysis*. Cambridge: Cambridge University Press.

—— (1981b) The Market Evaluation of Human Capital: The Case of Indentured Servitude. *Journal of Political Economy* 89(3): 446–67.

Gellner, E. (1983) *Nations and Nationalism*. Oxford: Blackwell.

Genovese, E. D. (1966) *The Political Economy of Slavery*. London: MacGibbon & Kee.

—— (1969) *The World the Slaveholders Made*. New York: Pantheon Books.

—— (1975) *Roll, Jordan, Roll: The World the Slaves Made*. London: Deutsch.

George, C. H. (1980) The Origins of Capitalism: A Marxist Epitome and a Critique of Immanual Wallerstein's World-System. *Marxist Perspectives* Summer: 70–100.

George, H. (1984) *American Race Relations Theory: A Review of Four Models*. Lanham: University Press of America.

Giliomee, H. (1979) The Eastern Frontier, 1770–1812. In R. Elphick and H. Giliomee (eds) *The Shaping of South African Society, 1652–1820*. Cape Town: Longman.

Giliomee, H. and Elphick, R. (1979) The Structure of European Domination at the Cape, 1652–1820. In R. Elphick and H. Giliomee (eds) *The Shaping of South African Society, 1652–1820*. Cape Town: Longman.

Giliomee, H. and Schlemmer, L. (eds) (1985) *Up Against the Fences: Poverty, Passes and Privilege in South Africa*. Cape Town: David Philip.

Giner, S. and Salcedo, J. (1978) Migrant Workers in European Social Structures.

In S. Giner and M. S. Archer (eds) *Contemporary Europe: Social Structures and Cultural Patterns*. London: Routledge & Kegan Paul.

Gmelch, G. (1980) Return Migration. *Annual Review of Anthropology* 9: 135–59.

Gorz, A. (1970) Immigrant Labour. *New Left Review* 61: 28–31.

Goveia, E. V. (1965) *Slave Society in the British Leeward Islands at the End of the Eighteenth Century*. New Haven: Yale University Press.

Graves, A. (1983) Truck and Gifts: Melanesian Immigrants and the Trade Box System in Colonial Queensland. *Past and Present* 101: 87–101.

—— (1984) The Nature and Origins of Pacific Islands Labour Migration to Queensland, 1862–1906. In S. Marks and P. Richardson (eds) *International Labour Migration: Historical Perspectives*. London: Temple Smith.

Gray, L. C. (1941) *History of Agriculture in the Southern United States to 1860* (vol. 1) New York: Peter Smith.

Green, N. (1985) 'Filling the Void': Immigration to France Before World War I. In D. Hoerder (ed.) *Labour Migration in the Atlantic Economies in the Period of Industrialisation*. Westport, Conn.: Greenwood Press.

Green, W. A. (1984) The West Indies and Indentured Labour Migration – The Jamaican Experience. In K. Saunders (ed.) *Indentured Labour in the British Empire, 1834–1920*. London: Croom Helm.

Greenberg, S. B. (1980) *Race and State in Capitalist Development*. New Haven: Yale University Press.

Greenstein, L. J. (1973) Slave and Citizen: the South African Case. *Race* 25(1): 25–46.

Grillo, R. D. (1985) *Ideologies and Institutions in Urban France: The Representation of Immigrants*. Cambridge: Cambridge University Press.

Guelke, L. (1979) The White Settlers, 1652–1780. In R. Elphick and H. Giliomee (eds) *The Shaping of South African Society, 1652–1820*. Cape Town: Longman.

Gülalp, H. (1981) Frank and Wallerstein Revisited: A Contribution to Brenner's Critique. *Journal of Contemporary Asia* 11(2): 169–88.

Hall, D. (1959) *Free Jamaica, 1838–1865: An Economic History*. New Haven: Yale University Press.

—— (1962) Slaves and Slavery in the British West Indies. *Social and Economic Studies* 11(4): 305–18.

—— (1978) The Flight From the Estates Reconsidered: The British West Indies, 1838–42. *Journal of Caribbean History* 10: 7–24.

Hall, S. (1980) Race, Articulation and Societies Structured in Dominance. In UNESCO, *Sociological Theories: Race and Colonialism*. Paris: UNESCO.

Halliday, F. (1977) Migration and the Labour Force in the Oil Producing Countries of the Middle East. *Development and Change* 8: 263–92.

Hammar, T. (ed.) (1985) *European Immigration Policy: A Comparative Study*. Cambridge: Cambridge University Press.

Handlin, O. (1948) *Race and Nationality in American Life*. Boston: Little, Brown & Co.

Haraksingh, K. (1981) Control and Resistance Among Overseas Indian Workers: A Study of Labour on the Sugar Plantations of Trinidad, 1875–1917. *Journal of Caribbean History* 14: 1–17.

Haring, C. H. (1966) *The Buccaneers in the West Indies in the XVII Century*. Hamden: Archon Books.

Harlow, V. T. (1926) *A History of Barbados, 1625–1685*. Oxford: Clarendon Press.

Hartwig, M. (1978) Capitalism and Aborigines: The Theory of Internal

Colonialism and its Rivals. In E. L. Wheelright and K. Buckley (eds) *Essays in the Political Economy of Australian Capitalism* (vol. 3). Sydney: Australia and New Zealand Book Company.

Hasluck, A. (1959) *Unwilling Emigrants: A Study of the Convict Period in Western Australia*. Melbourne: Oxford University Press.

Hasluck, P. (1970) *Black Australians: A Survey of Native Policy in Western Australia 1829–1897*. Melbourne: Melbourne University Press.

Hecht, J. J. (1956) *The Domestic Servant Class in Eighteenth Century England*. London: Routledge & Kegan Paul.

Hennings, K. H. (1982) West Germany. In A. Boltho (ed.) *The European Economy: Growth and Crisis*. London: Oxford University Press.

Hiemenz, V. and Schatz, K. W. (1979) *Trade in Place of Migration*. Geneva: International Labour Office.

Higham, C. S. S. (1921) *The Development of the Leeward Islands Under the Restoration, 1660–1688*. Cambridge: Cambridge University Press.

Higman, B. W. (1976) *Slave Population and Economy in Jamaica, 1807–1834*. Cambridge: Cambridge University Press.

Hilferding, R. (1981) *Finance Capital: A Study of the Latest Phase of Capitalist Development*. London: Routledge & Kegan Paul.

Hill, C. (1969) *Reformation to Industrial Revolution*. Harmondsworth: Penguin.

Hilton, R., Sweezy, P., Dobb, M., Takahashi, K., Hilton, R., Hill, C., Lefebvre, H., Procacci, G., Hobsbawm, E., and Berrington, J. (1978) *The Transition from Feudalism to Capitalism*. London: Verso.

Hindess, B. and Hirst, P. (1975) *Precapitalist Modes of Production*. London: Routledge & Kegan Paul.

History Task Force (1979) *Labour Migration Under Capitalism: the Puerto Rican Experience*. New York: Monthly Review Press.

Hobart Houghton, D. (1976) *The South African Economy*. Cape Town: Oxford University Press.

Hobsbawm, E. J. (1964) *Karl Marx: Pre-capitalist Economic Formations*. London: Lawrence & Wishart.

—— (1965) The Crisis of the Seventeenth Century. In T. Ashton (ed.) *Crisis in Europe*. London: Routledge & Kegan Paul.

—— (1969) *Industry and Empire*. Harmondsworth: Penguin.

Hobsbawm, E. J. and Ranger, T. (eds) (1983) *The Invention of Tradition*. Cambridge: Cambridge University Press.

Hoel, B. (1982) Contemporary Clothing 'Sweatshops': Asian Female Labour and Collective Organisation. In J. West (ed.) *Work, Women and the Labour Market*. London: Routledge & Kegan Paul.

Hoerder, D. (ed.) (1985) *Labour Migration in the Atlantic Economies*. Westport: Greenwood Press.

Hoffman-Nowotny, H.-J. (1974) Immigrant Minorities in Switzerland: Sociological, Legal and Political Aspects. In M. Archer (ed.) *Current Research in Sociology*. The Hague: Mouton.

—— (1978) European Migration After World War II. In W. H. McNeill and R. S. Adams (eds) *Human Migration: Patterns and Policies*. Bloomington: Indiana University Press.

—— (1985) Switzerland. In T. Hammar (ed.) *European Immigration Policy: A Comparative Study*. Cambridge: Cambridge University Press.

Hoffman-Nowotny, H.-J. and Killias, M. (1979) Switzerland. In R. E. Krane (ed.) *International Labour Migration in Europe*. New York: Praeger.

Holton, R. J. (1985) *The Transition from Feudalism to Capitalism*. London: Macmillan.

Hönekopp, E. and Ullman, H. (1982) The Status of Immigrant Workers in the Federal Republic of Germany. In E.-J. Thomas (ed.) *Immigrant Workers in Europe: Their Legal Status*. Paris: UNESCO.

Horn, P. (1975) *The Rise and Fall of the Victorian Servant*. Dublin: Gill and Macmillan.

Horwitz, R. (1967) *The Political Economy of South Africa*. London: Weidenfeld & Nicolson.

Howe, D. (1984) Black Workers Break the French Mould. *Race Today* April/May: 9–15.

Hume, I. (1973) Migrant Workers in Europe. *Finance and Development* 10: 2–6.

Hunt, V. F. (1978) The Rise of Feudalism in Eastern Europe: A Critical Appraisal of the Wallerstein 'World-System Thesis'. *Science and Society* XLII: 43–61.

Hussain, A. and Tribe, K. (1981) *Marxism and the Agrarian Question I: German Social Democracy and the Peasantry 1890–1907*. London: Macmillan.

Huttenback, R. A. (1976) *Racism and Empire: White Settlers and Coloured Immigrants in the British Self-Governing Colonies 1830–1910*. Ithaca: Cornell University Press.

Janowitz, M. (1977) A Sociological Perspective on Wallerstein. *American Journal of Sociology* 82: 1090–7.

Jeeves, A. H. (1975) The Control of Migratory Labour on the South African Gold mines in the Era of Kruger and Milner. *Journal of South African Studies* 2(1): 3–29.

—— (1985) *Migrant Labour in South Africa's Mining Economy: The Struggle for the Gold Mines' Labour Supply 1890–1920*. Kingston and Montreal: McGill Queens University Press.

Jenks, L. H. (1963) *The Migration of British Capital to 1875*. London: Nelson.

Jernegan, M. W. (1931) *Labouring and Dependent Classes in Colonial America, 1607–1783*. Chicago: Chicago University Press.

Johnson, S. C. (1966) *A History of Emigration from the United Kingdom to North America, 1763–1912*. London: Frank Cass.

Johnston, H. J. M. (1972) *British Emigration Policy 1815–1830*. Oxford: Clarendon Press.

Johnstone, F. A. (1976) *Class, Race and Gold*. London: Routledge & Kegan Paul.

Jordan, W. (1968) *White Over Black: American Attitudes Towards the Negro, 1550–1812*. Chapel Hill: University of North Carolina Press.

Kay, G. (1975) *Development and Underdevelopment: A Marxist Analysis*. London: Macmillan.

Kayser, B. (1971) *Manpower Movements and Labour Markets*. Paris: OECD.

—— (1972) *Cyclically Determined Homeward Flows of Migrant Workers*. Paris: OECD.

—— (1977) European Migrations: The New Patterns. *International Migration Review* 11(2): 232–40.

Keles, R. (1985) The Effects of External Migration on Regional Development in Turkey. In R. Hudson and J. Lewis (eds) *Uneven Development in Southern Europe: Studies of Accumulation, Class, Migration and the State*. London: Methuen.

Kellenbenz, H. (1976) The Modern World-System: Capitalist Agriculture and the Origins of the European World Economy in the Sixteenth Century. *Journal of Modern History* 48: 685–92.

Kennedy-Brenner, C. (1979) *Foreign Workers and Immigration Policy: The Case of France*. Paris: OECD.

Kindelberger, C. P. (1967) *Europe's Postwar Growth: The Role of Labour Supply*. Cambridge, Mass.: Harvard University Press.

King, R. (1984) Population Mobility: Emigration, Return Migration and Internal Migration. In A. Williams (ed.) *Southern Europe Transformed: Political Change in Greece, Italy, Portugal and Spain*. London: Harper & Row.

Klima, A. (1985) Agrarian Class Structure and Economic Development in Pre-Industrial Bohemia. In T. H. Aston and C. H. E. Philpin (eds) *The Brenner Debate: Agrarian Class Structure and Economic Development in Pre-Industrial Europe*. Cambridge: Cambridge University Press.

Kloosterboer, W. (1960) *Involuntary Labour Since the Abolition of Slavery*. Leiden: E. J. Brill.

Kubat, D. (ed.) (1979a) *The Politics of Migration Policies: The First World in the 1970s*. New York: Centre for Migration Studies.

—— (1979b) Turkey. In D. Kubat (ed.) *The Politics of Migration Policies: The First World in the 1970s*. New York: Centre for Migration Studies.

—— (1984) *The Politics of Return: International Return Migration in Europe*. Roma: Centro Studi Emigrazione.

Kubicek, R. V. (1979) *Economic Imperialism in Theory and Practice: The Case of South African Gold Mining Finance, 1886–1914*. Durham, NC: Duke University Press.

Kuper, H. (1960) *Indian People in Natal*. Natal: Natal University Press.

Lacey, M. (1981) *Working for Boroko: The Origins of a Coercive Labour System in South Africa*. Johannesburg: Ravan Press.

Laclau, E. (1979) Feudalism and Capitalism in Latin America. In E. Laclau *Politics and Ideology in Marxist Theory*. London: Verso.

Lal, B. V. (1984) Labouring Men and Nothing More: Some Problems of Indian Indenture in Fiji. In K. Saunders (ed.) *Indentured Labour in the British Empire 1834–1920*. London: Croom Helm.

Laurence, K. O. (1965) The Evolution of Long-term Labour Contracts in Trinidad and British Guiana, 1834–1863. *Jamaican Historical Review* 5(1): 9–27.

Layton-Henry, Z. (1984) *The Politics of Race in Britain*. London: Allen & Unwin.

Lazonick, W. (1974) Karl Marx and Enclosures in England. *Review of Radical Political Economics* 6: 1–59.

Legassick, M. (1974a) South Africa: Capital Accumulation and Violence. *Economy and Society* 3(3): 253–91.

—— (1974b) Legislation, Ideology and Economy in Post-1948 South Africa. *Journal of South African Studies* 1(1): 5–35.

—— (1975) South Africa: Forced Labour, Industrialisation and Racial Differentiation. In R. Harris (ed.) *The Political Economy of Africa*. Cambridge, Mass.: Schenkman Publishing Co.

—— (1977) Gold, Agriculture and Secondary Industry in South Africa, 1885–1970: From Periphery to Sub-Metropole as a Forced Labour System. In R. Palmer and N. Parsons (eds) *The Roots of Rural Poverty in Central and Southern Africa*. London: Heinemann.

Legassick, M. and De Clerq, F. (1984) Capitalism and Migrant Labour in Southern Africa: The Origins and Nature of the System. In S. Marks and P. Richardson (eds) *International Labour Migration: Historical Perspectives*. London: Temple Smith.

Lenin, V. I. (1970) Imperialism, the Highest State of Capitalism. In V. I. Lenin *Selected Works* (vol. I). Moscow: Progress Publishers.

Lever-Tracy, C. (1983) Immigrant Workers and Post-War Capitalism: In Reserve or Core Troops in the Front Line. *Politics and Society* 12(2): 127–57.

Levy, N. (1982) *The Foundations of the South African Cheap Labour System.* London: Routledge & Kegan Paul.

Long, N. (ed.) (1984) *Family and Work in Rural Societies: Perspectives on Non-wage Labour.* London: Tavistock.

Loos, N. (1982) *Invasion and Resistance: Aboriginal-European Relations on the North Queensland Frontier 1861–1897.* Canberra: Australian National University Press.

Luxemburg, R. (1951) *The Accumulation of Capital.* London: Routledge & Kegan Paul.

Luxemburg, R. and Bukharin, N. (1972) *Imperialism and the Accumulation of Capital.* London: Allen Lane.

McBride, T. M. (1976) *The Domestic Revolution.* London: Croom Helm.

McDonald, J. R. (1969) Labour Immigration in France, 1946–1965. *Annals of the Assocation of American Geographers* 59(1): 116–34.

McDonald, J. S. and McDonald, L. D. (1964) Chain Migration, Ethnic Neighbourhood Formation and Social Networks. *Milbank Memorial Fund Quarterly* 42: 82–97.

McDonald, R. A. (1979) The Williams Thesis: A Comment on the State of Scholarship. *Caribbean Quarterly* 25(3): 63–8.

McMichael, P. (1984) *Settlers and the Agrarian Question: Foundations of Capitalism in Colonial Australia.* Cambridge: Cambridge University Press.

Macmillan, D. S. (1967) *Scotland and Australia 1788–1850: Emigration, Commerce and Investment.* Oxford: Clarendon Press.

Madwick, R. B. (1937) *Immigration into Eastern Australia, 1788–1851.* London: Longmans Green and Co.

Magubane, B. (1979) *The Political Economy of Race and Class in South Africa.* New York: Monthly Review Press.

Mandel, E. (1975) *Late Capitalism.* London: New Left Books.

Mandle, J. R. (1972) The Plantation Economy: An Essay in Definition. *Science and Society* 36: 49–62.

Mantoux, P. (1961) *The Industrial Revolution in the Eighteenth century: An Outline of the Beginnings of the Modern Factory System in England.* London: Jonathan Cape.

Marais, J. S. (1957) *The Cape Coloured People, 1652–1937.* Johannesburg: Witwatersrand University Press.

Marshall, A. (1973) *The Import of Labour: The Case of the Netherlands.* Rotterdam: Rotterdam University Press.

Marx, K. (1968a) Wage Labour and Capital. In K. Marx and F. Engels *Selected Works.* London: Lawrence & Wishart.

—— (1968b) Theses on Feuerbach. In K. Marx and F. Engels *Selected Works.* London: Lawrence & Wishart.

—— (1968c) The Eighteenth Brumaire of Louis Bonaparte. In K. Marx and F. Engels *Selected Works.* London: Lawrence & Wishart.

—— (1969) *Theories of Surplus Value, Part 2.* London: Lawrence & Wishart.

—— (1970) *Capital* (vol. 2). London: Lawrence & Wishart.

—— (1971) *A Contribution to the Critique of Political Economy.* London: Lawrence & Wishart.

—— (1972) *Capital* (vol. 3);. London: Lawrence & Wishart.

—— (1973) *Grundrisse*. Harmondsworth: Penguin.

—— (1976) *Capital* (vol. 1). Harmondsworth: Penguin.

Marx, K. and Engels, F. (1965) *Selected Correspondence*. Moscow: Progress Publishers.

—— (1968a) *On Colonialism*. Moscow: Progress Publishers.

—— (1968b) *The German Ideology*. Moscow: Progress Publishers.

—— (1968c) Manifesto of the Communist Party. In K. Marx and F. Engels *Selected Works*. London: Lawrence & Wishart.

—— (1971) *Ireland and the Irish Question*. London: Lawrence & Wishart.

—— (1974) *The Civil War in the US*. New York: International Publishers.

Mayer, K. B. (1965) Post-War Immigration in Switzerland. *International Migration* 3(3): 122–32.

Mazier, J. (1982) Growth and Crisis – A Marxist Interpretation. In A. Boltho (ed.) *The European Economy: Growth and Crisis*. London: Oxford University Press.

Medick, H. (1981) The Transition From Feudalism to Capitalism: Renewal of the Debate. In R. Samuel (ed.) *People's History and Socialist Theory*. London: Routledge & Kegan Paul.

Mehrländer, U. (1979) Federal Republic of Germany. In D. Kubat (ed.) *The Politics of Migration Policies: The First World in the 1970s*. New York: Praeger.

Meillassoux, C. (1980) From Reproduction to Production: A Marxist Approach to Economic Anthropology. In H. Wolpe (ed.) *The Articulation of Modes of Production*. London: Routledge & Kegan Paul.

—— (1981) *Maidens, Meal and Money: Capitalism and the Domestic Community*. Cambridge: Cambridge University Press.

Merivale, H. (1928) *Lectures on Colonisation and Colonies*. Oxford: Oxford University Press.

Miles, R. (1980) Class, Race and Ethnicity: A Critique of Cox's Theory. *Ethnic and Racial Studies* 3(2): 169–87.

—— (1982) *Racism and Migrant Labour: A Critical Text*. London: Routledge & Kegan Paul.

—— (1984a) Marxism versus the 'Sociology of Race Relations'? *Ethnic and Racial Studies* 7(2): 217–37.

—— (1984b) Summoned By Capital. In P. Spoonley *et al. Tauiwi: Racism and Ethnicity in New Zealand*. Palmerston North: Dunmore Press.

—— (1986a) Labour Migration, Racism and Capital Accumulation in Western Europe Since 1945: An Overview. *Capital and Class* 28: 49–86.

—— (1986b) Staat, Racisme en Migratie: De Recente Europese Ervarigen. *Vlaams Marxistisch Tijdschrift*.

—— (1987) Recent Marxist Theories of Nationalism and the Issue of Racism. *British Journal of Sociology* 38(1): 24–43.

—— (1988) *Racism*. London: Tavistock.

Miles, R. and Phizacklea, A. (1984) *White Man's Country: Racism in British Politics*. London: Pluto Press.

Miles, R. and Spoonley, P. (1985) The Political Economy of Labour Migration: An Alternative to the Sociology of 'Race' and 'Ethnic Relations' in New Zealand. *Australia and New Zealand Journal of Sociology* 21(1): 3–26.

Miller, M. J. (1981) *Foreign Workers in Western Europe: An Emerging Political Force*. New York: Praeger.

Miller, M. J. and Martin, P. L. (1982) *Administering Foreign-Worker Programs: Lessons for Europe*. Lexington: D.C. Heath.

Minet, G. (1978) Spectators or Participants? Immigrants and Industrial Relations in Western Europe. *International Labour Review* 117(1): 21–35.

Mintz, S. W. (1969) Slavery and Emergent Capitalisms. In L. Foner and E. D. Genovese (eds) *Slavery in the New World*. Englewood Cliffs: Prentice Hall.

—— (1974) *Caribbean Transformations*. Chicago: Aldine Publishing Co.

—— (1977) The So-Called World System: Local Initiative and Local Response. *Dialectical Anthropology* 11: 253–70.

—— (1978) Was The Plantation Slave a Proletarian? *Review* 2(1): 81–98.

—— (1985) *Sweetness and Power: the Place of Sugar in Modern History*. New York: Elisabeth Sifton Books.

Mitter, S. (1986) Industrial Restructuring and Manufacturing Homework: Immigrant Women in the UK Clothing Industry. *Capital and Class* 27: 37–80.

Molyneux, M. (1979) Beyond the Domestic Labour Debate. *New Left Review* 116: 3–28.

Morokvasic, M. (1983) Women in Migration: Beyond the Reductionist Outlook. In A. Phizacklea (ed.) *One-Way Ticket*. London: Routledge & Kegan Paul.

—— (1984) Birds of Passage are also Women. . . . *International Migration Review* 18(4): 886–907.

Morrell, W. P. (1960) *Britain in the Pacific Islands*. Oxford: Clarendon Press.

Morris, M. (1980) The Development of Capitalism in South African Agriculture: Class Struggle in the Countryside. In H. Wolpe (ed.) *The Articulation of Modes of Production*. London: Routledge & Kegan Paul.

Moulier Boutan, Y., Garcon, J.-P., and Silberman, R. (1986) *Économie Politique des Migrations Clandestines de Main-d'Oeuvre*. Paris: Publisud.

Naidu, V. (1980) *The Violence of Indenture in Fiji*. Suva: World University Service/University of the South Pacific.

Nairn, N. B. (1956) A Survey of the History of the White Australia Policy in the Nineteenth Century. *Australian Quarterly* 28: 16–31.

Nairn, T. (1981) *The Break-Up of Britain*. London: Verso.

Nieboer, H. J. (1971) *Slavery as an Industrial System: Ethnological Researches*. New York: Franklin.

Newbury, C. (1980) The Melanesian Labor Reserve: Some Reflections on Pacific Labour Markets in the Nineteenth Century. *Pacific Studies* 4(1): 1–25.

—— (1984) The Imperial Workplace: Competitive and Coerced Labour Systems in New Zealand, Northern Nigeria and Australian New Guinea. In S. Marks and P. Richardson (eds) *International Labour Migration: Historical Perspectives*. London: Temple Smith.

Nichols, T. (ed.) (1980) *Capital and Labour*. London: Fontana.

Nikolinakos, M. (1973a) The Contradictions of Capitalist Development in Greece: Labour Shortages and Emigration. *Studi Emigrazione* 30: 222–35.

—— (1973b) Notes on an Economic Theory of Racism. *Race* 14(4): 365–81.

—— (1975) Notes Towards a General Theory of Migration in Late Capitalism. *Race and Class* 17(1): 5–18.

North-Coombes, M. D. (1984) From Slavery to Indenture: Forced Labour in the Political Economy of Mauritius, 1834–1867. In K. Saunders (ed.) *Indentured Labour in the British Empire, 1834–1920*. London: Croom Helm.

Nowikowski, S. (1984) Snakes and Ladders: Asian Business in Britain., In R. Ward and R. Jenkins (eds) *Ethnic Communities in Business: Strategies for Economic Survival*. Cambridge: Cambridge University Press.

Nzula, N. T., Potekhin, I. I., and Zusmanovich, A. S. (1979) *Forced Labour in Colonial Africa*. London: Zed Press.

O'Brien, P. (1982) European Economic Development: the Contribution of the Periphery. *Economic History Review* 35(1):1–18.

OECD (1979) *Migration, Growth and Development.* Paris:OECD.

Padgug, R. A. (1976) Problems in the Theory of Slavery and Slave Society. *Science and Society* 40(1):3–27.

Paine, S. (1974) *Exporting Workers: The Turkish Case.* Cambridge:Cambridge University Press.

Palfreeman, A. C. (1972) The White Australia Policy. In F. S. Stevens (ed.) *Racism: The Australian Experience.* New York:Taplinger Publishing Co.

Palmer, M. (1977) *A History of the Indians in Natal.* Westport, Conn.:Greenwood Press.

Pares, R. (1937) The Economic Factors in the History of the Empire. *Economic History Review* 7(2):119–44.

Parnaby, O. W. (1964) *Britain and the Labour Trade in the Southwest Pacific.* Durham, NC:Duke University Press.

Patterson, O. (1967) *The Sociology of Slavery.* London:MacGibbon & Kee.

—— (1979) On Slavery and Slave Formations. *New Left Review* 117:31–67.

—— (1982) *Slavery and Social Death: A Comparative Study.* Cambridge, Mass.: Harvard University Press.

Peach, C. (1968) *West Indian Migration to Britain.* London:Oxford University Press.

Penninx, R. (1984a) *Immigrant Populations and Demographic Development in the Member States of the Council of Europe; Part 1: Analysis of General Trends and Possible Future Developments.* Strasbourg:Council of Europe.

—— (1984b) *Migration, Minorities and Policy in the Netherlands: Recent Trends and Developments.* Rijswijk:Ministry of Welfare.

Pentland, H. C. (1981) *Labour and Capital in Canada, 1650–1860.* Toronto:James Lorimer and Co.

Petras, E. M. (1981) The Global Labour Market in the Modern World Economy. In M. M. Kritz *et al.* (eds) *Global Trends in Migration.* New York:Center for Migration Studies.

Phillips, W. D. (1985) *Slavery from Roman Times to the Early Transatlantic Trade.* Manchester:Manchester University Press.

Phizacklea, A. (ed.) (1983a) *One-Way Ticket: Migration and Female Labour.* London:Routledge & Kegan Paul.

—— (1983b) In the Front Line. In A. Phizacklea (ed.) *One-Way Ticket: Migration and Female Labour.* London:Routledge & Kegan Paul.

Phizacklea, A. and Miles, R. (1980) *Labour and Racism.* London:Routledge & Kegan Paul.

Post, K. (1978) *Arise Ye Starvelings.* The Hague:Martinus Nijhoff.

Poulantzas, N. (1978) *Classes in Contemporary Capitalism.* London:Verso.

Ragatz, L. J. (1971) *The Fall of the Planter Class in the British Caribbean, 1763–1833.* New York:Octagon Books.

Ragin, C. and Chirot, D. (1984) The World System of Immanuel Wallerstein: Sociology and Politics as History. In T. Skocpol (ed.) *Vision and Method in Historical Sociology.* Cambridge:Cambridge University Press.

Ramesar, M. D. (1984) Indentured Labour in Trinidad, 1880–1917. In K. Saunders (ed.) *Indentured Labour in the British Empire, 1834–1920.* London Croom Helm.

Redford, A. (1964) *Labour Migration in England, 1800–1850.* Manchester:Manchester University Press.

Reeves, F. and Ward, R. (1984) West Indian Business in Britain. In R. Ward and R. Jenkins (eds) *Ethnic Communities in Business: Strategies for Economic Survival.* Cambridge: Cambridge University Press.

Reimann, H. and Reimann, H. (1979) Federal Republic of Germany. In R. K. Krane (ed.) *International Labour Migration in Europe.* New York: Praeger.

Rex, J. (1970) *Race Relations in Sociological Theory.* London: Weidenfeld & Nicolson.

—— (1973) *Race, Colonialism and the City.* London: Routledge & Kegan Paul.

—— (1980) The Theory of Race Relations: a Weberian Approach. In UNESCO *Sociological Theories: Race and Colonialism.* Paris: UNESCO.

—— (1986) *Race and Ethnicity.* Milton Keynes: Open University Press.

Reynolds, H. (1972) *Aborigines and Settlers: the Australian Experience.* Melbourne: Cassell Australia Ltd.

—— (1982) *The Other Side of the Frontier: Aboriginal Resistance to the European Invasion of Australia.* Victoria: Penguin.

Rhoades, R. E. (1978a) Foreign Labour and German Industrial Capitalism 1871–1978: The Evolution of a Migratory System. *American Ethnologist* 5(3): 553–73.

—— (1978b) Intra-European Return Migration and Rural Development: Lessons from the Spanish Case. *Human Migration* 37: 136–47.

—— (1979) From Caves to Main Street: Return Migration and the Transformation of a Spanish Village. *Papers in Anthropology* 20: 57–74.

Rice, C. D. (1975) *The Rise and Fall of Black Slavery.* London: Macmillan.

Richards, E. (1982) *A History of the Highland Clearances: Agrarian Transformation and the Evictions, 1746–1886.* London: Croom Helm.

—— (1985) *A History of the Highland Clearances: Emigration, Protest, Reasons.* London: Croom Helm.

Richardson, P. (1968) *Empire and Slavery.* London: Longman.

—— (1977) The Recruiting of Chinese Indentured Labour for the South African Gold-Mines, 1903–1908. *Journal of African History* 18(1): 85–108.

—— (1982) *Chinese Mine Labour in the Transvaal.* London: Macmillan.

—— (1984a) Chinese Indentured Labour in the Transvaal Gold Mining Industry, 1904–1910. In K. Saunders (ed.) *Indentured Labour in the British Empire 1834–1920.* London: Croom Helm.

—— (1984b) Coolies, Peasants and Proletarians: The Origins of Chinese Indentured Labour in South Africa, 1904–1907. In S. Marks and P. Richardson (eds) *International Labour Migration: Historical Perspectives.* London: Temple Smith.

Rist, R. (1978) *Guestworkers in Germany: The Prospects for Pluralism.* New York: Praeger.

Riviere, W. E. (1972) Labour Shortage in the British West Indies After Emancipation. *Journal of Caribbean History* 4: 1–30.

Robinson, C. J. (1983) *Black Marxism.* London: Zed Press.

Robinson, K. W. (1969) Land. In G. J. Abbott and N. B. Nairn (eds) *Economic Growth of Australia 1788–1821.* Melbourne: Melbourne University Press.

Robson, L. L. (1965) *The Convict Settlers of Australia.* Melbourne: Melbourne University Press.

Rowley, C. D. (1970) *The Destruction of Aboriginal Society.* Canberra: Australian National University Press.

Rudé, G. (1978) *Protest and Punishment: The Story of Social and Political Protestors Transported to Australia, 1788–1868.* Oxford: Clarendon Press.

Rusche, G. and Kirchheimer, O. (1968) *Punishment and Social Structure*. New York: Russell and Russell.

Saha, P. (1970) *Emigration of Indian Labour, 1834–1900*. Delhi: People's Publishing House.

Salt, J. (1981) International Labour Migration in Western Europe: a Geographical Review. In M. M. Kritz *et al.* (eds) *Global Trends in Migration*. New York: Center for Migration Studies.

Salt, J. and Clout, H. (eds) (1976) *Migration in Post-War Europe*. London: Oxford University Press.

Sassen-Koob, S. (1978) The International Circulation of Resources and Development: The Case of Migrant Labour. *Development and Change* 9: 509–45.

—— (1980) The Internationalisation of the Labour Force. *Studies in Comparative International Development* 15: 3–25.

—— (1981) Towards a Conceptualisation of Immigrant Labour. *Social Problems* 29(1): 65–85.

—— (1985) Capital Mobility and Labour Migration. In S. E. Sanderson (ed.) *The Americas in the New International Division of Labour*. New York: Holmes and Meier.

Saunders, K. (1982) *Workers in Bondage: The Origins and Bases of Unfree Labour in Queensland, 1824–1916*. St Lucia: University of Queensland Press.

—— (ed.) (1984a) *Indentured Labour in the British Empire, 1834–1920*. London: Croom Helm.

—— (1984b) The Workers' Paradox: Indentured Labour in the Queensland Sugar Industry to 1820. In K. Saunders (ed.) *Indentured Labour in the British Empire, 1834–1920*. London: Croom Helm.

Scammell, G. V. (1981) *The World Encompassed: The First European Maritime Empires, c.800–1650*. London: Methuen.

Schechtman, J. B. (1962) *Post-War Population Transfers in Europe 1945–1955*. Philadelphia: University of Pennsylvania Press.

Schmitter, B. (1980) Immigrants and Associations: Their Role in the Socio-Political Process of Immigrant Worker Integration in West Germany and Switzerland. *International Migration Review* 14(2): 179–92.

—— (1983) Immigrant Minorities in West Germany: Some Theoretical Concerns. *Ethnic and Racial Studies* 6(3): 308–19.

Schneider, J. (1977) Was There A Pre-capitalist World-System? *Peasant Studies* 6(1): 20–9.

Schuler, M. (1980) *'Alas, Alas, Kongo.' A Social History of Indentured African Immigration Into Jamaica, 1841–1865*. Baltimore: Johns Hopkins University Press.

Schutte, G. (1979) Company and Colonists at the Cape. In R. Elphick and H. Giliomee (eds) *The Shaping of South African Society, 1652–1820*. Cape Town: Longman.

Seddon, D. (ed.) (1978) *Relations of Production: Marxist Approaches to Economic Anthropology*. London: Frank Cass.

Sellin, J. Thorsten (1976) *Slavery and the Penal System*. New York: Elsevier.

Sérageldin, I., Socknat, J. A., Birks, S., Li, B., and Sinclair, C. A. (1983) *Manpower and International Labor Migration in the Middle East and North Africa*. New York: Oxford University Press.

Shanin, T. (1984) *Late Marx and the Russian Road: Marx and the 'Peripheries of Capitalism'*. London: Routledge & Kegan Paul.

Shann, E. (1948) *An Economic History of Australia*. Cambridge: Cambridge University Press.

Shaw, A. G. L. (1966) *Convicts and the Colonies: A Study of Penal Transportation from Great Britain and Ireland to Australia and Other Parts of the British Empire.* London: Faber & Faber.

—— (1969) Labour. In G. J. Abbott and N. B. Nairn (eds) *Economic Growth of Australia, 1788–1821.* Melbourne: Melbourne University Press.

Sheridan, R. B. (1969) The Plantation Revolution and the Industrial Revolution. *Caribbean studies* 9(3): 5–25.

—— (1970) The Development of the Plantations to 1750. *Chapters in Caribbean History* I.

—— (1974) *Sugar and Slavery: An Economic History of the British West Indies, 1623–1775.* Barbados: Caribbean Universities Press.

—— (1977) The Role of the Scots in the Economy and Society of the West Indies. *Annals of the New York Academy of Sciences* 292: 94–106.

Sherrington, G. (1980) *Australia's Immigrants, 1788–1978.* Sydney: Allen & Unwin.

Simons, H. J. and Simons, R. E. (1969) *Class and Colour in South Africa, 1850–1950.* Harmondsworth: Penguin.

Singer-Kerel, J. (1980) Foreign Labour and the Economic Crisis: The Case of France. Paper presented to European Science Foundation Workshop on Cultural Identity and Structural Marginalisation of Migrant Workers.

—— (1983) *Delivery of Permits for Illegal Immigrants: Special French Programme 1981–1982.* Paris: Group de Récherche et d'Analyse Des Migrations Internationales.

—— (1986) La Population étrangère dans les recensements de 1891 à 1936. Paper presented to Colloque de l'Association Francaise des Anthropologues.

Sirageldin, I. A., Sherbiny, N. A., and Serageldin, I. (1984) *Saudis in Transition: The Challenges of a Changing Labour Market.* New York: Oxford University Press.

Sivanandan, A. (1976) Race, Class and the State: The Black Experience in Britain. *Race and Class* 17(4): 347–68.

Skocpol, T. (1977) Wallerstein's World Capitalist System: A Theoretical and Historical Critique. *American Journal of Sociology* 82: 1075–90.

—— (1984a) Sociology's Historical Imagination. In T. Skocpol (ed.) *Vision and Method in Historical Sociology.* Cambridge: Cambridge University Press.

—— (1984b) Emerging Agendas and Recurrent Strategies in Historical Sociology. In T. Skocpol (ed.) *Vision and Method in Historical Sociology.* Cambridge: Cambridge University Press.

Slater, M. (1979) Migrant Employment, Recessions and Return Migration: Some Consequences for Migration Policy and Development. *Studies in Comparative International Development* 14: 3–22.

Smith, A. E. (1947) *Colonists in Bondage: White Servitude and Convict Labour in America, 1607–1776.* Chapel Hill: University of North Carolina Press.

Smith, D. (1977) *Racial Disadvantage in Britain.* Harmondsworth: Penguin.

Smolders, C. (1982) The Status of Immigrant Workers in the Netherlands. In E.-J. Thomas (ed.) *Immigrant Workers in Europe: Their Legal Status.* Paris: UNESCO.

Sommerville, J. (1982) Women: A Reserve Army of Labour. *M/F* 7: 35–60.

Souden, D. (1978) 'Rogues, Whores and Vagabonds'? Indentured Emigrants to North America, and the Case of Mid-Seventeenth Century Bristol. *Social History* 3(1): 23–41.

—— (1984) English Indentured Servants and the Transatlantic Colonial Economy. In S. Marks and P. Richardson (eds), *International Labour Migration: Historical Perspectives.* London: Temple Smith.

Standing, G. (1981) Migration and Modes of Exploitation: Social Origins of Immobility and Mobility. *Journal of Peasant Studies* 8:173–211.

Stasiulis, D. K. (1980) Pluralist and Marxist Perspectives on Racial Discrimination in South Africa. *British Journal of Sociology* 31(4):463–90.

Steven, M. J. E. (1969) Enterprise. In G. J. Abbott and N. B. Nairn (eds) *Economic Growth of Australia, 1788–1821*. Melbourne: Melbourne University Press.

Stevens, F. (1974) *Aborigines in the Northern Territory Cattle Industry*. Canberra: Australian National University Press.

Stinchcombe, A. (1982) The Growth of the World System. *American Journal of Sociology* 87:1389–395.

Stone, K. (1983) Motherhood and Waged Work: West Indian, Asian and White Mothers Compared. In A. Phizacklea (ed.) *One-Way Ticket: Migration and Female Labour*. London: Routledge & Kegan Paul.

Stuckey, B. and Fay, M. A. (1981) Rural Subsistence, Migration and Urbanisation: The Production, Destruction and Reproduction of Cheap Labour in the World Market. *Antipode* 13(2):1–14.

Tannahill, J. A. (1968) *European Volunteer Workers in Britain*. Manchester: Manchester University Press.

Tayal, M. (1977) Indian Indentured Labour in Natal, 1890–1911. *Indian Economic and Social History Review* 14(4):519–47.

Taylor, J. G. (1979) *From Modernisation to Modes of Production: A Critique of the Sociologies of Development and Underdevelopment*. London: Macmillan.

Temperley, H. (1977) Capitalism, Slavery and Ideology. *Past and Present* 75:94–118.

Thomas, E.-J. (ed.) (1982a) *Immigrant Workers in Europe: Their Legal Status*. Paris: UNESCO.

—— (1982b) Immigrant Workers in France. In E.-J. Thomas (ed.) *Immigrant Workers in France: Their Legal Status*. Paris: UNESCO.

Thomas, R. P. and Bean, R. N. (1974) The Fishers of Men: The Profits of the Slave Trade. *Journal of Economic History* 34:885–914.

Thomson, L. M. (1952) Indian Immigration Into Natal (1860–1872). *Archives Yearbook for South African History* II:1–76.

Tinker, H. (1974) *A New System of Slavery: The Export of Indian Labour Overseas, 1830–1920*. London: Oxford University Press.

Toepfer, H. (1985) The Economic Impact of Returned Migrants in Trabzon, Turkey. In R. Hudson and J. Lewis (eds) *Uneven Development in Southern Europe: Studies of Accumulation, Class, Migration and the State*. London: Methuen.

Tribe, K. (1981) *Genealogies of Capitalism*. London: Macmillan.

—— (1983) Prussian Agriculture – German Politics: Max Weber 1892–7. *Economy and Society* 12(2):181–226.

Trindade, M. B. R. (1979) The Iberian Peninsular. In D. Kubat (ed.) *The Politics of Migration Policies: The First World in the 1970s*. New York: Centre for Migration Studies.

Tuppen, J. N. (1978) A Geographical Appraisal of Trans-Frontier Commuting in Western Europe: The Example of Alsace. *International Migration Review* 12:385–405.

United Nations (1979a) *Labour Supply and Migration in Europe: Demographic Dimensions 1950–1975 and Prospects*. New York: United Nations.

—— (1979b) *Trends and Characteristics of International Migration Since 1950*. New York: United Nations.

Van Amersfoort, H. (1982) *Immigration and the Formation of Minority Groups: The Dutch Experience*. Cambridge: Cambridge University Press.

Van Amersfoort, H., Muus, P., and Penninx, R. (1984) International Migration, the Economic Crisis and the State: An Analysis of Mediterranean Migration to Western Europe. *Ethnic and Racial Studies* 7(2): 238–68.

Van Binsbergen, W. and Geschiere, P. (1985) *Old Modes of Production and Capitalist Encroachment: Anthropological Explorations in Africa*. London: Kegan Paul International.

Van den Berghe, P. (1970) *South Africa: A Study in Conflict*. Berkeley: University of California Press.

Van der Horst, S. T. (1971) *Native Labour in South Africa*. London: Frank Cass.

Van Gendt, R. (1977) *Return Migration and Reintegration Services*. Paris: OECD.

Van Onselen, C. (1976) *Chibaro: African Mine Labour in Southern Rhodesia, 1900–1933*. London: Pluto Press.

—— (1982a) *Studies in the Social and Economic History of the Witwatersrand 1886–1914, Volume 1, New Babylon*. London: Longman.

—— (1982b) *Studies in the Social and Economic History of the Witwatersrand 1886–1914. Volume 2. New Nineveh*. London: Longman.

Verbunt, G. (1985) France. In T. Hammar (ed.) *European Immigration Policy: A Comparative Study*. Cambridge: Cambridge University Press.

Wakefield, E. G. (1869) *A View of the Art of Colonisation*. London: John Parker.

Wallerstein, I. (1974) *The Modern World System I: Capitalist Agriculture and the Origins of the European World Economy in the Sixteenth Century*. New York: Academic Press.

—— (1979) *The Capitalist World-Economy*. Cambridge: Cambridge University Press.

—— (1980) *The Modern World System II: Mercantilism and the Consolidation of the European World Economy, 1600–1750*. New York: Academic Press.

—— (1983) *Historical Capitalism*. London: Verso.

Ward, J. R. (1978) The Profitability of Sugar Planting in the British West Indies, 1650–1834. *Economic History Review* 31: 197–213.

Warren, B. (1980) *Imperialism: Pioneer of Capitalism*. London: Verso.

Watson, J. (ed.) (1977) *Between Two Cultures*. Oxford: Blackwell.

Weber, M. (1976) *The Agrarian Sociology of Ancient Civilisations*. London: New Left Books.

—— (1978) *Economy and Society: An Outline of Interpretive Sociology*. Berkeley: University of California Press.

—— (1979) Developmental Tendencies in the Situation of East Elbian Rural Labourers. *Economy and Society* 8(2): 177–205.

—— (1980) The National State and Economic Policy (Frieburg Address). *Economy and Society* 9(4): 428–49.

—— (1981) *General Economic History*. New Brunswick: Transaction Books.

Weisser, M. R. (1979) *Crime and Punishment in Early Modern Europe*. Hassocks: Harvester Press.

Weller, J. A. (1968) *The East Indian Indenture in Trinidad*. Puerto Rico: Institute of Caribbean Studies.

Welsh, D. (1971) *The Roots of Segregation: Native Policy in Colonial Natal, 1845–1910*. Cape Town: Oxford University Press.

Willard, M. (1967) *History of the White Australia Policy to 1920*. Melbourne: Melbourne University Press.

Williams, E. (1964) *Capitalism and Slavery*. London: Deutsch.

—— (1970) *From Columbus to Castro: The History of the Caribbean 1492–1969*. London: Deutsch.

Wilpert, C. (1983) From Guestworkers to Immigrants (Migrant Workers and Their Families in the FRG). *New Community* 11(1/2): 137–42.

Wilson, F. (1972a) *Labour in the South African Gold Mines, 1911–1969*. Cambridge: Cambridge University Press.

—— (1972b) *Migrant Labour*. Johannesburg: South African Council of Churches/ SPRO-CAS.

Wilson, M. and Thompson, L. (1969) *The Oxford History of South Africa, Volume 1: South Africa to 1870*. Oxford: Clarendon Press.

—— (1971) *The Oxford History of South Africa. Volume II: South Africa 1870–1966*. Oxford: Clarendon Press.

Winson, A. (1982) The 'Prussian Road' of Agrarian Development: A Reconsideration. *Economy and Society* 11(4): 381–408.

Wolf, E. (1982) *Europe and the People Without History*. Berkeley: University of California Press.

Wolpe, H. (1972) Capitalism and Cheap Labour Power in South Africa: From Segregation to Apartheid. *Economy and Society* 1(4): 425–56.

—— (1975) The Theory of Internal Colonialism: The South African Case. In I. Oxaal *et al.* (eds) *Beyond the Sociology of Development*. London: Routledge & Kegan Paul.

—— (ed.) (1980) *The Articulation of Modes of Production*. London: Routledge & Kegan Paul.

Wood, C. H. (1982) Equilibrium and Historical-Structural Perspectives on Migration. *International Migration Review* 16(2): 298–319.

Wood, D. (1968) *Trinidad in Transition: The Years After Slavery*. London: Oxford University Press.

Wright, P. (1985) *On Living in an Old Country*. London: Verso.

WRR (1979) *Ethnic Minorities*. The Hague: WRR.

Yarwood, A. T. (1962) The 'White Australia' Policy: A Reinterpretation of its Development in the Late Colonial Period. *Historical Studies* 10: 257–69.

—— (1964) *Asian Migration to Australia: The Background to Exclusion 1896–1923*. Melbourne: Melbourne University Press.

Yudelman, D. (1983) *The Emergence of Modern South Africa: State, Capital and the Incorporation of Organised Labour on the South African Gold Fields, 1902–1939*. Westport, Conn.: Greenwood Press.

Zolberg, A. R. (1978) International Migration Policies in a Changing World System. In W. H. McNeill and R. S. Adams (eds) *Human Migration: Patterns and Policies*. Bloomington: Indiana University Press.

—— (1981a) International Migrations in Political Perspective. In M. M. Kritz *et al.* (eds) *Global Trends in Migration*. New York: Center for Migration Studies.

—— (1981b) Origins of the Modern World System: a Missing Link. *World Politics* 33: 253–81.

Index

Acts: Pearl Shell Fishing Regulation Act (1837), 112; Sugar Duties Act (1846), 87, 88; Masters and Servants Act (1856), 122, 217; Masters and Servants Act (1861), 114; Polynesian Labourers' Act (1863), 114; Aborigines Protection Act (1866), 109; Pacific Island Labourers' Act (1880), 115; Glen Gray Act (1894), 131; Aborigines Protection and Restriction of Sale of Opium Act (1897), 110; Pacific Island Labourers' Act (1901), 116; Aborigines Act (1905), 109; Mines and Works Act (1911), 139; Native Labour Regulation Act (1911), 139; Natives Land Act (1913), 136–8, 200, 202; Native (Urban Areas) Act (1923), 141; Industrial Conciliation Act (1924), 140; Native Service Contract Act (1932), 138; Aliens Act (1965), 161, 162; Labour Promotion Act (1969), 162, Employment of Foreign Workers Act (1978), 161
Africa, migration from, 5, 74, 79, 85, 89, 90, 120
apprenticeship, 78, 87, 88, 121–2, 123, 173
Australia, 12–13, 52, 94–117, 172, 173, 174, 188–92, 200–1, 202, 205–6, 208–9, 218–19, 220; migration to, 95–6, 100–3, 113–14

Barbados, 74, 76, 78–80
Belgium, 145, 147, 148–9, 150
Britain, 52, 95, 120, 145, 147, 154, 156, 158–9, 180, 205–6; migration from, 75–6, 80, 95–6, 100–3, 121, 129, 132, 139, 209; migration to, 147–8

capital, 22–3, 38, 39, 44, 210–11, 219
capital accumulation, 5, 22, 56, 62, 144–6, 167, 198, 210–13, 215, 221
capitalism, 1–4, 4–7, 57–60, 95, 103, 143, 179–80, 212, 221–2; emergence of, 12, 26, 35–49, 59–60, 76, 94, 198–9, 201, 204–6; as a mode of production, 17–34, 42, 48, 54, 57–69, 196–7, 222; as a system of exchange, 54, 56, 57; and unfree labour, 2–3, 31–4, 50–70, 171–222
Caribbean, 12–13, 48, 73–93, 126, 171–2, 175, 178, 180, 192–3, 203–6, 209, 214–15; migration from, 147–8; migration to, 75–6, 79–81, 85, 89–91
China, emigration from, 5, 90, 99, 202, 209
class (struggle), 10, 20, 37, 59, 69, 77, 158–9, 179, 195, 206–7, 208, 216, 217, 218, 222, 223–4
colonial system, 13, 37–8, 40–2, 45, 47, 50–1, 53, 60, 64, 70
colonization, 73–6, 94–5, 99, 118–24, 142, 182–4, 188–94, 199–210, 221;

consequences for indigenous population, 78, 105–12, 119–24
commodification, 32–3, 36, 39, 44, 63, 89, 98–99, 103, 126, 138, 164, 171, 172, 173–4, 177–81, 198–9, 208, 221, 222; formal, 91, 115, 160, 175, 176, 178–9, 213; partial, 138, 142, 217–18
commodity production, 3, 12, 20, 38, 41–2, 51, 79, 93, 95, 103–4, 114, 117, 118–19, 120, 124, 126, 127, 128, 130, 180, 201, 203, 206, 208–9, 214–15, 216
compound system, 129, 131, 134
contract labour, 32, 52, 109–12, 121, 129, 131, 134, 138, 141, 153, 159–67, 173, 176–7, 177–81, 184–5, 212–13, 217–20
convict labour, 95–100, 108, 122, 172–3, 177–81, 182–4, 200–1, 202
convicts, 77, 80, 95–100; assignment of, 97–8, 100, 104, 172; ticket-of-leave, 98–100, 108
cotton, 43, 48, 51, 90, 112–13

Dobb, M., 51, 53–4
domestic production, 52–3

economic system, 65–6
England, 35–6, 39–41, 42, 43, 46, 48–9, 200

feudalism, 26, 37, 39, 41, 53–6, 60, 73, 76, 197, 200
France, 89, 145, 147, 149–50, 153–4, 155, 158, 166
Frank, A. G., 53–7, 58, 64, 65, 67
free labour, 1–4, 9, 24–6, 36, 40, 42, 58, 70, 86, 142, 177, 217; defined, 31–4, 171

Germany, 2–3, 45, 89, 99, 145, 147, 149, 150, 153, 155, 156, 157–8, 161–3, 164, 166
Guiana, 74, 87–92, 205, 209

historical sociology, 11–12
Horton, W., 102

imperialism, 50–1
indentured labour, 32, 51, 74, 76–81, 90–3, 104–5, 112–16, 121, 126–8,

133–4, 174–5, 177–81, 182–4, 200–2, 204, 206–7, 218
India, 44, 46–7; migration from, 5, 90–2, 104–5, 126–7, 147–8, 158, 202, 209

Jamaica, 74, 79, 85, 87–9, 90, 205, 209

labour power, 20, 33, 36, 39, 44, 63, 126, 142, 171, 174–5, 177–81, 198–9, 212
labour tenancy, 123, 125, 135, 136, 138, 173, 174, 179, 182–4, 200, 216

Marx, K., 12, 17–33, 35–49, 50–3, 56, 60–6, 67–9, 145, 179, 196, 200, 210–13, 222
means of production, 18
merchant capital, 27, 37–9, 48, 66, 75, 80–1, 82–5, 87, 93, 180, 197, 205, 214
migrant labour, 8, 131–2, 136–8, 141, 153, 154, 159–67, 173, 176–7, 177–81, 184–5, 212–13, 219–20
migration, 4–7, 14, 42, 134, 144–55, 210–13, 219, 223–4
mining, 52, 128–34, 137, 139–42, 220
mode(s) of production, 6, 17–24, 39–55, 61, 65, 105–6, 119, 173, 216, 217; articulation of, 35, 40–9, 65–70, 199, 213–21, 222
Mozambique, 132, 134, 202, 209

Natal, 123, 124–8, 135, 202
nationalism, 192, 194–5
nation-state, 10, 66, 184–5, 209–10, 212
Netherlands, 73–5, 119, 145, 147, 150, 153, 155, 158, 160–1, 163, 164, 166
Nieboer, H. J., 204–8

pass system, 91, 97, 121, 127, 129, 131, 133, 138, 183, 186, 220
peasantry, 87, 130, 136
piracy, 74
plantations, 2, 79, 82–5, 88, 114–16, 126–8
primitive (primary) accumulation, 35–40, 48–9, 56, 64, 150, 198, 199–203, 207, 209, 210, 216–17, 222
proletarianization, 36, 59, 61–3, 138, 217

'race relations' problematic, 7–11, 13, 14, 223–4

racialization, 7–9, 10, 14, 190, 192, 208,
216
racism, 7, 10, 107, 116, 186–95, 208,
210, 214, 220
relations of production, 6, 18–19, 33,
39–40, 57–8, 61, 68–9, 77–8, 82–5,
96–7, 109–12, 114–16, 121–3, 131,
133, 135, 171–95, 204–5
repatriation, 165–6
reserve army of labour, 33, 93, 113–14,
158–9, 185, 212
reserves, 109–11, 124–5, 136–8, 183,
217, 218–19, 220
Russia, 47–8, 51

serfdom, 1, 24, 32, 33, 44, 52, 58, 63, 78,
173, 179, 204
servitude (contractual), 52, 78, 121–2,
173–4, 177–81, 182–4, 200, 201–2
sharecropping, 51, 135, 136
slave labour, 1–3, 24, 27–31, 33, 42–5,
51, 58, 73, 79–81, 86, 120–1, 171–2,
175, 177–81, 182–4, 204, 205, 214–15,
216
slave mode of production, 43–4, 45, 48,
180, 214–15
slave trade, 74, 80–1, 85, 86, 121, 215
social formation, 65–6
South Africa, 12–13, 118–42, 171–2,
173, 174, 176–7, 178, 186, 193–4, 201–
3, 205–9, 215–20; migration to, 120,
121, 126–9, 132–4, 139
south Pacific, migration from, 5, 104–
5, 113–16, 192
state, 19, 23, 33–4, 37, 42, 66, 69, 85, 87,
91, 96–8, 100, 101–4, 107, 114, 126–7,
130–3, 137, 139–41, 147–50, 160–6,
172, 175, 176–7, 181–6, 207, 208,
212–13, 217, 221

sugar, 41, 51, 73, 75, 79, 81, 86–8, 110,
112–13, 126–7, 128, 203, 215;
organization of production, 82–5
Sweezy, P., 53–7, 67
Switzerland, 145, 147, 153, 155–6, 163,
164

taxation, 86–7, 125, 131, 138, 184, 216
tobacco, 41, 78, 79, 203
trade, 38–9, 41–2, 48, 54, 63, 74, 197
transition debate, 53–6, 59–60
transportation, 77, 80, 95–6, 100, 113
Trinidad, 74, 87–92, 205, 209

Underdevelopment, 4, 51, 53–6, 61
unfree labour, 1–4, 9, 40–1, 51–3, 58,
60, 67–8, 70, 171–86, 196–221;
defined, 31–4, 171; explained, 196–
9, 222; unfree wage labour, 32–4, 70,
138, 142, 159–67, 178, 217
United States, 2, 5, 13, 43–4, 45, 48, 89,
180

wage labour, 1–4, 6, 9, 22–3, 36, 40, 42,
51, 55–6, 58, 68–9, 78, 88–9, 92–3, 98,
103, 104–5, 108–9, 159–63, 180, 197,
207, 217; as free labour, 24–6; and
slave labour, 27–31, 86
Wakefield, E. G., 102, 207
Wallerstein, I., 5, 53, 56–65, 67, 179,
197, 222
Weber, M., 1–4
Western Europe, 12–13, 41–2, 47, 52,
143–67, 176–7, 184–6, 194–5, 212–13,
219; migration to, 143–4, 147–55
wool, 103–5, 120, 124, 128
world economy/system, 5–6, 37, 51,
55–65, 69, 180, 197, 199, 222